The Maphumulo uprising

Place names in Natal 1906.

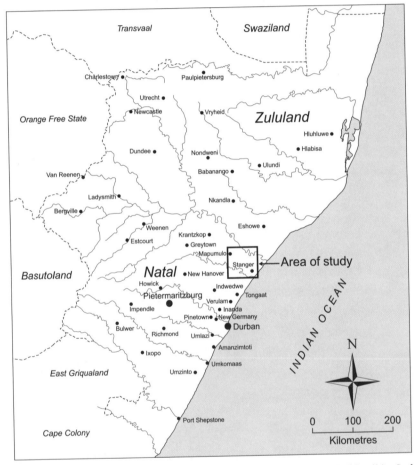

Adapted from map in *Enterprise and Exploitation in a Victorian Colony*, edited by Bill Guest and John M. Sellers, University of Natal Press, 1985.

The Maphumulo uprising

War, law and ritual in the Zulu rebellion

All the people at the Izinsimba were armed. The Chief Mashwili gave it out that Dinuzulu was expected to help them. Their plans were to sweep off Stanger – it was said Mqhawe had swept off Verulam, and that Greytown had also been swept off and it was intended the impi should go as far as Durban. The Chief said the white people were oppressing the Native. He said the Natives had to pay Rents and Taxes for land which belonged to Shaka. The rebels replied 'Yes – we are thankful for the words – the land is ours'.

(Durban Archives Repository: 1/SGR, Martial law
notebook, 1/4/2/1, 51/06)

Jeff Guy

UNIVERSITY OF KWAZULU-NATAL PRESS

Published in 2005 by University of KwaZulu-Natal Press
Private Bag X01
Scottsville 3209
South Africa
Email: books@ukzn.ac.za
www.ukznpress.co.za

ISBN 1-86914-048-6

Editor: Sally Hines
Cover designer: Sebastien Quevauvilliers, Flying Ant Designs
Cover photograph: Pietermaritzburg Archives Repository,
Photograph Collection, C690

Typeset by Trish Comrie
Printed and bound by Interpak Books, Pietermaritzburg

Contents

Acknowledgements

I would like to acknowledge the support of the National Research Foundation; Tessa Marcus for her commitment to historical understandings of the present; the Fellows of Corpus Christi College, Oxford, for the award of a Visiting Fellowship; Makhosini Wellington Qwabe, Thulani Mthethwa, Muziwakhe Simamane, Muzikaye Biyela for their assistance at eMthandeni, and Sicebi Khuzwayo at Ezintandaneni. Thanks also to Bobby Mills for encouragement, hard work, and good advice, generously given; Vukile Khumalo for answering my many questions with such patience; and the help and company of Muzi Hadebe, Vukile Khumalo and Steve Kotze on our visits to the places where the events recounted in this book took place.

Abbreviations

AGO	Attorney-General's Office
BPP	British Parliamentary Papers
CO	Colonial Office
CSO	Colonial Secretary's Office
CNC	Chief Native Commissioner
DAR	Durban Archives Repository
DBN	Durban
GH	Government House
MJPW	Minister of Justice and Public Works
MPO	Maphumulo
PAR	Pietermaritzburg Archives Repository
PM	Prime Minister
PRO	Public Record Office
RH	Rhodes House
RSC	Registrar Supreme Court
SGR	Stanger
SNA	Secretary for Native Affairs
Stuart, *Archive 3*	*The James Stuart Archive of Recorded Oral Evidence Relating to the History of the Zulu and Neighbouring Peoples*, Volume 3, edited and translated by C. de B. Webb and J.B. Wright, Pietermaritzburg and Durban: University of Natal Press and Killie Campbell Africana Library, 1982
Stuart, *Archive 4*	*The James Stuart Archive . . .* Volume 4, 1986
Stuart, *Archive 5*	*The James Stuart Archive . . .* Volume 5, 2001

Glossary

The problems raised when using Zulu words in an English text are immense. To avoid a confusing multiplicity of variants and the perpetuation of colonial forms I have regularised the spelling of places and proper names. It is nonetheless impossible to be entirely consistent. When the context demands it – as in the case of certain citations or when modernising the orthography is inimical to the historical tone of the document – I have retained the original form. I have also edited quotations lightly if this elucidates the meaning. The carelessness and handwriting of the original scribes at times make it impossible, and misleading, to even guess the spelling of some names.

For a useful discussion on problems that arise when using Zulu words in an English text, particularly difficult questions around the initial vowel, inflected forms and capitals, see Adrian Koopman, *Zulu Names*, Pietermaritzburg: University of Natal Press, 2002, Chapter 7. I admit to sympathising with doing what 'somehow feels right' until a standard form is set – an event, however, to which one can only look forward with trepidation.

ukuChela: to sprinkle (thus to use an example from Doke and Vilakazi, *Zulu-English Dictionary*, 'ukuchela impi ngentelezi' – to sprinkle an army with protective medicine)
uDengezi: a potsherd used to heat medicine
amaDlozi: ancestral spirits
inDuna (*izinDuna*): an officer or official

iHubo: the clan anthem

inKatha (izinKatha): a coil of grass incorporating materials that give the owner strength over hostile forces

iKholwa (amaKholwa): believers, Christians

umKhumbi: the arc or circle formed by the participants in a meeting or ceremony

inKosi (amaKhosi): a hereditary ruler

ukuLobola: bridewealth

ukuMisa: to make strong, firm

iMpi: army, battle

iMpi yamakhanda: the war of the heads, the poll tax rebellion of 1906

ukuNcinda: to lick medicine from the fingers

iNtelezi: medicine, a potion, see *ukuchela*

iNtelezi yempi: medicine to give strength in violent conflict

umNyama: foreboding, darkness in a spiritual sense

iNyamazane emhlope: the white buck, euphemism for pursuing a white human being as prey

iNyanga (iziNyanga): a skilled person, a doctor

ubuShokobezi: the white cow tail worn to indicate support for the Zulu royal house

umThakathi: someone in possession of evil powers

Illustrations

List of maps

List of photographs

Prologue

The eNkanini ritual

Introduction

Late in 1905, on a wet Friday, some five hundred men made their way towards their chief's[1] homestead, eNkanini, on the Nonoti river in the Lower Thukela division of the Colony of Natal.[2] They had been called to participate in a cleansing and strengthening ceremony to fortify their ruling lineage in a time of increasing social stress and rumours of coming conflict between Natal's Africans and their colonial rulers. As many participants in the ceremony feared, or hoped, violence did break out and between February and July 1906 spread to different parts of the colony. It was provoked by the imposition of a poll tax and became known by different names: *impi yamakhanda* (the war of the heads), the Zulu rebellion of 1906, or the Bhambatha rebellion, after the most prominent rebel leader.

Just over a year later, in 1907, in one of many attempts to make examples of those who fomented rebellion, three men said to have organised and celebrated this ritual at eNkanini were arrested on the grounds that they had indulged in 'war-doctoring'. They were brought before the Native High Court in the capital Pietermaritzburg on a charge of sedition, found guilty and sentenced to terms of imprisonment. It was a severe punishment for they were old and Natal's gaols were harsh and unhealthy. We can get an idea of the effects of detention from a photograph of one of them, Mbombo

1

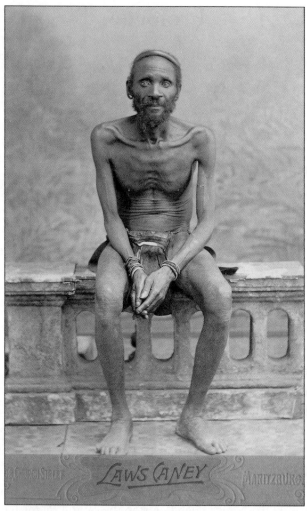

Mbombo kaSibindi Nxumalo, Pietermaritzburg, November 1907.
(PAR: C690)

kaSibindi Nxumalo, the *inyanga* or doctor who had led the ritual. From the lock-up at Stanger he had managed to get a message to an old acquaintance, Harriette Colenso. She bailed him out, and when he arrived in Pietermaritzburg had his photograph taken as a record of what detention had done to an alert, intelligent, widely respected man. It is one of the most tragic images of the rebellion.[3]

It was to discover more about this man that I began the research upon which this book is based. This drew me into a study of the rebellion of 1906 and of the final stage in particular in the magisterial divisions of Lower Thukela and neighbouring Maphumulo. It was the record of the trials of those accused of participating in the rebellion that proved to be the richest source: and not just for the horror of these events – that can be read off directly from the casualty figures – but the nature of the conflict as it affected those directly involved. This conflict was not just between colonisers and colonised, but amongst the colonised themselves, and in the personal predicaments of men and women forced to choose amongst options all of which, in the end, offered only different paths to catastrophe.

I have concentrated on telling the stories of two of the dominant figures in this final episode of the 1906 rebellion: Meseni kaMusi, *inkosi* to the Qwabe, a chief in the Natal colonial system; and Ndlovu kaThimuni, *inkosi* of the Nodunga section of the Zulu. Like the picture of Mbombo, the photographs of these men were also taken after the rebellion, in this case after the two chiefs had just escaped from the guns of the military and were now preparing to defend their lives before a court set up under martial law. These grim images in time of defeat should not be allowed to obscure the longer historical view. Meseni and Ndlovu were strong men in a tough situation, having to control their people while retaining their loyalty, even as their authority was undermined by the colonial government. They had for years used their political skills to defend, not just their own positions, but also Zulu custom, rights and traditions even as the jaws of colonial rule closed on them.

Meseni kaMusi Qwabe, Maphumulo
gaol, July 1906.   (PAR: C727)

Ndlovu kaThimuni Zulu, Maphumulo
gaol, July 1906.   (PAR: C727)

And around their stories of co-operation and resistance, deference and rebellion, ruthlessness and accommodation, swirl those of many others: of *izinyanga* – African doctors, the settlers' witch-doctors, real and imagined; *izinduna* – officials, counsellors responsible for crucial interventions in moments of crisis on the battlefields and in the courts; other *amakhosi* – Natal's chiefs; and rebels and prisoners, allies and enemies, police and informers, witnesses for the crown and for the accused. They gave their accounts in the context of legal struggle – they are adversarial, made to contradict other stories – and as a consequence the narrative discernible in these sources is often unclear and never straight-forward.

The story told here begins, however, not with Meseni or Ndlovu but with Qwabe neighbours towards the coast and the 1905 ritual they held at the eNkanini homestead under the supervision of Mbombo, the man in the photograph on page 2. Many more such ceremonies, organised by different men, were to be held in the months that followed. They came to be an essential feature of the uprising and despite their specific differences do have common features that help us gain an insight into the beliefs, fears and hopes of the participants – and the profoundly religious character of the rebellion.

The ceremony at eNkanini

In October 1905,[4] acting-chief Ntshingumuzi kaMkwetu Qwabe assembled his section of the Qwabe[5] people at the eNkanini homestead built on the middle reaches of the Nonoti river on crown lands in the Lower Thukela division on the right or eastern side of the Stanger-Maphumulo road. In the cattle kraal the men, about five-hundred-strong, carrying dancing shields and sticks, formed themselves into an *umkhumbi* (the semi-circle drawn up by those preparing for organised social activity, a dance, religious ceremony or perhaps a fight). Once assembled, the doctor (*inyanga*), Mbombo kaSibindi Nxumalo, came out of a hut carrying a smoking brand, and moved back and forth with it amongst the gathering. He then picked up a broom in each hand, dipped them into a basket (*iqoma*) containing medicine (*intelezi*) to ward off danger, and sprinkled (*ukuchela*) the assembly with it. He then withdrew to a hut and his assistant carried the basket to the river where the men drank water from it or from water that had flowed through it. This served as an emetic and they moved downstream to cleanse themselves, internally by vomiting (*ukuphalaza*) and externally by washing themselves in the river. When the process of purification was complete they reassembled and, standing still, their shields raised, sang their clan anthem (*ihubo*),[6] a powerful and emotional evocation of past glory which drew the shades of their ancestors especially close. They returned to the cattle kraal where medicine to make them firm and strong (*ukumisa*) had been placed on a fire and heated on potsherds (*udengezi*) into which they dipped their fingers before licking them clean (*ukuncinda*). After a final invocation by the *inyanga* the ritual was brought to an end, there was a collection of cash for his services, and the Qwabe were ordered by Ntshingumuzi to return to their homes.

Figure 1: The Qwabe chiefly lineage.

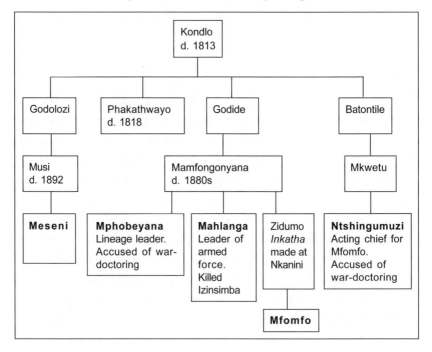

This particular ceremony is typical in its form and general structure of a wide range of cleansing/fortifying ceremonies. The sprinkling of the medicine, purification by purging and washing, and then strengthening by licking from the fingers medicine placed on potsherds and heated on a fire, were common features of various rituals performed in Zulu society – although, of course, they differed in detail and scale, depending on the rank of the organisers and the objectives for which they were held.[7] On this occasion it was believed that 'darkness' (*umnyama*) had fallen over the Qwabe – darkness that this ritual sought to lift by strengthening the people and their chief by appealing to the shades for their intervention.

There had been a number of indications that the ancestors were not at ease. The most apparent was the physical weakness of the chiefs of the ruling lineage. Its founder in Natal had died in 1880; his son and successor, Zidumo, had died in the 1890s; his heir,

Mfomfo, still too young to rule, was sickly. The most obvious reason for this, in the opinion of Ntshingumuzi, acting-chief and regent, was that they were no longer communicating effectively with the shades.

White observers had a different explanation for the increase in ill health in the Lower Thukela division: malarial fever, spreading up the rivers and streams, was one consequence of the new railway line that linked the division with the fever districts of Zululand and just one aspect of the greater mobility of the population as a whole. For the Zulu, however, sickness of this kind suggested that the *amadlozi*, the shades of their ancestors, had turned their backs on the living. These ancestors did not inhabit a remote world of the dead: they were a presence demanding deference and ritual propitiation from their live descendants; the withdrawal of their favour exposed the living to harmful influences. It was clear to Ntshingumuzi and his counsellors that, in these opening years of the twentieth century, the protective presence of the ancestors had for some reason been lost.

Ntshingumuzi obtained the services of an *inyanga* to remedy this. He was Mbombo kaSibindi Nxumalo from the Usuthu district of northern Zululand, a doctor with a considerable reputation. He gave his diagnosis: the Qwabe no longer possessed an *inkatha* – the sacred coil of tightly bound roots and fibres that symbolised the strength of the *inkosi* and facilitated the unity of the lineage by incorporating protective medicines mixed with physical traces of those whose power threatened the Qwabe well-being.[8] Its proper place was the sacred space in the back of the *inkosi*'s own hut. To stand over or sit on the *inkatha* was to proclaim and reinforce the power of the *inkosi*, the unity of his people, and their dominance over their enemies.

But the Qwabe had been careless with this sacred embodiment of their power and strength. When Zidumo died his *inkatha* had been destroyed with the ritual burning of his hut. Moreover no *inkatha* had been made for the young Mfomfo. These oversights had to be repaired. It was necessary, the *inyanga* advised, to carry out a ritual of propitiation and invoke the assistance of the ancestors to restore their descendants' strength by making new *izinkatha*, one for the dead Zidumo, and another for Mfomfo, his son and eventual successor. The men of their lineage of the Qwabe should be gathered together, cleansed of the impurities that had settled upon the chiefdom, and an appeal would then be made to their ancestors to lift the darkness and enable them to see a way out of the troubles that so beset them.

While the men of Ntshingumuzi's section of the Qwabe were down at the river, Mbombo was secluded with the young heir Mfomfo in one of his grandmother's huts, together with the two new *izinkatha* Mbombo had made – one for Mfomfo himself and a larger one for his father. Mfomfo was placed on the *izinkatha* while Mbombo made incisions on the boy's body into which he rubbed medicine. The men then returned and the *ihubo* was sung, fulfilling in song the same function as the *inkatha*, binding the Qwabe lineage together in the solemn invocation of the ancestors. Mbombo came out of the hut and ended the ceremony with the formulaic order to 'close up' – against harmful influences emanating from the world outside.

And the world outside was threatening: a depressed economy, increased rents, evictions, and now the announcement of a new tax, a poll tax that threatened not just the homestead's economy but proper order amongst those who lived within it. Ntshingumuzi's people shared with all Natal the deprivations and tensions of these years, but with a particular intensity. While a handful had their own plots on mission land, most Africans were tenants on private farms or company and crown lands on the rich, rolling country between the Mvoti and the Thukela rivers and the sea, and they had to pay more and more for this privilege. Increasing agricultural investment on the part of white and Indian farmers, large and small-scale, and the development of tea and sugar production, had created growing pressure on land and forced up rents and escalated evictions. Recourse to the law was expensive, even when it succeeded.

It was in this atmosphere of physical, social and material distress that the ritual at eNkanini was held. It had been organised by the lineage-head and carried out by a man with the ability to diagnose the causes of distress and disease, and work a cure. Its immediate object was to ameliorate illness and misfortune, and strengthen its participants against coming hardship by invoking the assistance of the shades. But the wider context was significant. The singing of the *ihubo* not only reinforced clan loyalty but mourned the passing of independence, for it was, according to a sentimental but significant description published in the same year the ceremony was held at eNkanini,

> to the Native patriot the 'dear old song' reminiscent of those good old times – upon which all of us love to look back – when the clan was still free and unfettered by a foreign subjection, when only peacefulness and plenty reigned in the land – days gone never to return! The *ihubo* is, therefore, nowadays only sung on certain solemn occasions, when the feeling of the hour would seem to befit the pathos of the song.[9]

It was a ritual of general purification and fortification that sought to fulfil different specific objectives for those who participated in it. It strengthened and made them firm: for some against the consequences of disease, poverty and exploitation; for some against the threatened violence between the colonial state and its people; for others for the means and the strength to drive out the white man, to revive those good old times, and to reclaim the land of Shaka kaSenzangakhona, founder of the Zulu kingdom. Whatever specific intentions lay in the hearts of the five hundred men who gathered at eNkanini, they returned home, the shades propitiated, and their power consolidated, by the binding of their new *izinkatha*, their lineage fortified not only against physical disease but against the effects of social deprivation, and strengthened for what many believed was a coming confrontation with those in authority over them. The ceremony at eNkanini relieved for the moment the profound sense of distress and alienation caused by poverty and proletarianisation. And in the newly made Qwabe *izinkatha* the African past was restored and re-integrated with the present, endowing the participants with the hope that they would find the strength to confront those who held power over them and exercised it with such callous irresponsibility.

Notes

1. *Inkosi* (plural *amakhosi*) is usually translated as chief. But increasingly 'chief' is objected to because of its colonial associations. To deny the word does not of course deny the historical reality it refers to and I try to move between these terms, using *inkosi* when the context reflects an autonomous African situation and chief the colonial. But it is impossible to be consistent – as in this case where there would be a clash of grammatical constructions if the Zulu word were used.
2. In 1898 the Colony of Natal had incorporated the remnants of the old Zulu kingdom, a territory north of the Thukela and east of the Mzinyathi rivers, which, following popular usage, I generally refer to as Zululand. In 1906 this territory was administered by a Commissioner for Native Affairs, Charles Saunders. The permanent official in Natal was the under-Secretary for Native Affairs (S.O. Samuelson) who reported to the Minister for Native Affairs.
3. The print reproduced here is from the PAR photographic collection, C690. The print in Rhodes House, Oxford, is identified as 'Mbombo, a Zulu Doctor, as bailed out (see back) by Miss Colenso . . .' 'uMbombo as bailed out, 9 11 1907'.
4. The date of the ritual was contested. October 1905 is my guess – but an informed one.
5. When I refer to the Qwabe here I mean this particular section – unless the context indicates otherwise. That is the section over which Ntshingumuzi was appointed as regent, headed by the Mamfongonyana-Zidumo-Mfomfo lineage, which was distinct from, although closely related to, the dominant lineage of the Qwabe represented by Meseni kaMusi. See Figure 1.
6. To better reflect the communal, social elements I have used 'anthem' rather than the more usual 'song' or 'hymn'.
7. For some examples see A.T. Bryant, *The Zulu People*, Pietermaritzburg: Shuter & Shooter, 1967, 468-477, 501-504; Stuart, *Archive 3*, Evidence of Mmemi

kaNguluzawe, 244, Evidence of Mpathshana kaSodondo, 296–301, 304–306, 323–328; *Archive* 5, Evidence of Nsuze kaMfekafuti, 171–174.

8. For the *inkatha* see Bryant, *The Zulu People*, 469 and 476–478; L.H. Samuelson, *Zululand: Its Traditions, Legends, Customs and Folk-lore*, Natal: Mariannhill Mission Press, n.d., 138ff; R.C.A. Samuelson, *Long, Long Ago*, Durban: Knox, 1929, 399–402.

9. A.T. Bryant, *A Zulu-English Dictionary*, Pinetown: Mariannhill Mission Press, 1905.

Part One
WAR

1

Conquering Natal

Bhambatha's head, 14 June 1906

On the 14 June 1906, some seventy kilometres to the north-east of eNkanini on the other side of the Thukela valley, a small party of mounted men left their camp in the Nkandla forest on the northern walls of the mid-Thukela valley, to pick its way down the steep grass-covered ridges between the streams which have cut their way through the valley's sides to the bedrock. One of these streams is the Mome, and the party was heading for the place where it leaves the confines of gorge and begins to meander across the valley floor. From here the men moved upstream, into the gorge, walled in by the ridges and cliffs rising towards the forest margins. It stank of death. Four days before, at dawn, one thousand men had been trapped here. Their remains were everywhere, ripped up by Maxims, blown apart by artillery, corpses bundled in heaps by the devastating fire from the surrounding high ground. The injured and those who had found a cave or crevice in which to hide, had then been finished off by the colonial militia and the African levies that had moved in with small arms, bayonets and assegais.

The mounted party was searching for a particular corpse. It was found a few metres away from the Mome stream on the right bank. There were signs of a fierce hand-to-hand struggle. The dead man had been stabbed with an assegai with such force that the blade had bent and was still in his body. He had been stabbed again and grabbed hold of the shaft but his struggle had been ended by a shot from behind in the head. Now Sergeant Willie Calverley of the Zululand Mounted Rifles dealt a final blow. He cut off the head, rammed it into a saddle bag and carried it out of the Mome gorge, back to military headquarters. Here it was identified, to the satisfaction of the authorities, as that of Bhambatha kaMancinza, once chief of the Zondi, of the Mvoti division of the Colony of Natal, the most prominent figure in the Zulu rebellion of 1906 that came to bear his name. Early the next morning the head was taken back into the valley and buried, with the body.

So the official reports say. But they were only doing what the official reports had to do: to assert that there was evidence to prove that the rebel leader had been killed. For Bhambatha had to die, and die publicly. Of all the chiefs in the Colony of Natal, he was the one who had openly, unequivocally, defied the authorities and then physically attacked them. On 5 April 1906 he had ambushed a police column and fallen back on the Nkandla forest to continue his resistance. It was to terminate this rebellion that the Natal militia and their allies had killed Bhambatha and thousands of those said to be his followers. Now his death had to be confirmed publicly to the people of Natal as a warning to anyone tempted to follow his example.[1]

But this could not be done. The military authorities were unable to kill him. Although Bhambatha kaMancinza's head was positively identified at military headquarters by some of the men closest to him, we are told to this day, often in the conspiratorial tones of a shared secret, how his escape from the massacre at Mome was hidden from the authorities by concocted stories and deliberate misidentifications.

And this is not just retrospective myth-making. From the moment of the first reports of the massacre at Mome there were stories of Bhambatha's escape.[2] Official confirmation of his death, on the evidence of a shattered, decomposing head, only gave more credence to the popular conviction that he was alive. For truly popular leaders are not easily killed – not when so many want in their hearts to have done what their hero had done, even as they deny this with their mouths. For vast numbers of people in Natal wished they had found a way to follow Bhambatha's example, and they invested in him the feelings which now, in the face of massive repression, they had to hide.

The conquest of Natal

For there was anger in Natal, anger rooted in popular grievance. It sprang from the deepening realisation of what they, as the original inhabitants, the natives, the indigenous people, the *uhlanga*, had lost during sixty years of colonial rule, and of the impossibility that their lives could be improved within the existing system. There was a widespread feeling that, in spite of their own and their parents' experiences as a colonised people, they had the right to better, fairer treatment and a voice in affairs.

For there had never been a colonial war of conquest of the people or the territory that became the Colony of Natal in the mid-nineteenth century. Instead a system of shared authority had been negotiated between settler and native. The colonial official responsible for setting up the system of native administration soon after the founding the Colony of Natal in the 1840s was Theophilus Shepstone. He had been confronted with an immense problem rooted in demographic disparity: the settlers numbered some five thousand, the African population a hundred thousand. Without imperial assistance the termination of African power by force was clearly impossible, and Natal had been annexed to forestall, not expedite, British military involvement. As a result, Shepstone instituted a policy of accommodation by which the authority of selected *amakhosi* (chiefs in colonial terminology) was recognised over the Africans of the colony, with communal rights being granted in Native Reserves which made up some two million acres or one twelfth of the colony's land.

Although never sufficient for African needs, it was enough to provide a body of African rulers with sufficient land to reconcile themselves and their people to colonial overrule. But as the nineteenth century progressed so the colonial presence became more invasive. The closely related, historically-intertwined, neighbouring kingdom of the Zulu was attacked by the British and lost its independence in 1879. It was incorporated into Natal in 1898 and similar chiefly administrative structures were instituted, but only after coercion and civil war had brought resistance to an end.[3] Meanwhile in the southern African interior, exploitable deposits of, first, diamonds and then gold were discovered, attracting an increasingly aggressive settler population whose demand for African land and taxes intensified. In the decades bracketing the turn of the century, the amount of land under agricultural production in Natal increased more than five times, and the settler population more than doubled.[4] This had an impact on the lives of all classes of Africans. It was felt keenly by the chiefs, who found themselves being treated as instruments of, rather than participants in, local government, and who were trapped by the dual and contradictory demands of their people and those of the colonial state. The *isibalo* system, whereby labour was demanded for road-making, was deeply resented by those forced to work and by the chiefs responsible for supplying the workers. This was intensified in the closing decades of the nineteenth century as the new mining industry gained confidence and the imperatives of the South African industrial revolution demanded a larger and more controlled labour force. The men directly below the chiefs – the *abanumzana*, husbands and fathers, patriarchal homestead-heads in the rural areas – found their authority and autonomy steadily undermined in the process of rapid social change and increasing exploitation. This was shared by their sons, working on the docks, the mines and in settler homes, and their hopes of succeeding to the patriarchy receded as more external demands were made on their wages and their fathers' land and property. The women, the aged and the children felt this directly as more labour in the fields did nothing to still the hunger in their bellies, and a significant proportion, to the great consternation of the men who controlled them, sought alternative, and what were seen as dissolute, ways of life by moving to the towns.

The deep dissatisfaction created by such changes was shared by those who had broken with the traditional patriarchal system and lived as converts, ministers, teachers, farmers and traders on crown, private or mission land. The market's promise of profit on earth, like the Christian promise of glory for eternity, had a profound effect on African people in Natal but, for those who chose to follow these precepts, the changed ways of life they entailed proved difficult to sustain. Discrimination in the missionary churches so blatantly contradicted the message of equality and compassion that some African pastors broke with their parent institutions and set up congregations of their own – African churches, preaching a message better suited to African ambitions and sensibilities.

By the opening years of the twentieth century a wide range of dangerous influences seemed to be working against the African people of Natal. The region had just experienced the effects of the war between the British and the Boers. This had meant boom times for those who sold their crops, livestock and labour to the British military – but war also meant disruption and the chaos of conflict. And it was followed by economic depression. The social and psychological consequences of economic failure, drought, plagues and epidemics, the drop in wages and prices, increased exploitation and legislative control, and the overbearing attitudes and racist brutality of the settlers were intensified by persistent rumours of coming catastrophe and conflict as Africans prepared for confrontation with the whites.

Africans in Natal, regardless of their economic status or social position, were angry: angry at the daily insult of wage labour; at the humiliations they suffered in a racialised system of authority; at the changes that had been forced upon their lives by the sale of land upon which they lived; at the fetters placed on their autonomy by the demands of a money economy; at the irresponsible appropriation of the products of their labour. Protests, like the following, were made against a failure in government: the failure of the state to ensure that its subjects were able to lead productive lives. It is a protest not just against colonial exploitation but capitalist individualism:

> We cut away the wild forests for sugar plantations and towns; we dig your roads. When will this digging of roads cease? We are made to live on farms and pay rent, and are imprisoned if we cannot pay. You chase our wives out of our homes by facilitating divorce. How is it you come to treat us thus, seeing we are your people? Where is that government or king that owns no land? Why are individuals able to oust government subjects from the soil? Why are we put to trouble in respect to farms, with the numerous regulations in connection therewith? We have, in fact, finished all the roads. We have to go out leaving no one in charge of our homes and children behind. Where shall we run to? . . .
>
> We are in trouble. Our children *lose contact with their homes*, and we lose that wealth which according to ancient custom is vested in them. Let that land which is government land appear, and let us black people build and dwell thereon, and enjoy some security and rest. *The natives belong to one ruler*; they may not be owned just by everyone and anyone.[5]

Any hope Africans had that the defeat of the Boers by the British in 1902 would lead to reform from London had by now disappeared: if anything the local officials were more arrogant, the police more violent, the settlers determined to show racial solidarity as victors who could demonstrate again if need be the killing power of modern military technology – when the time came to put blacks in their place and rid South Africa finally of the fear of black autonomy. Rumours abounded on both sides of the racial divide. Africans killed white pigs and chickens and destroyed industrially manufactured goods; they spoke of the coming conflict, to be heralded by unnatural disturbances, immense floods, lightning, supernatural portents, Dinuzulu, son of Cetshwayo, of Shaka the kingdom's founder, leading the way. Settlers spoke of the coming black uprising that threatened white South Africa and civilisation. Amongst African Christians – the *amakholwa* or believers – there were indications of the most severe social and psychic distress in the growing belief in the coming millennium

> when another wind will blow and a state of affairs different to what is now existing will be brought about. God will bring about this difference and in some way cause this change. When such day comes an end will be put to present modes of government

and

> God will destroy the world with a flood when a new race will appear in the land.[6]

It was in these tense times that the Natal authorities sought to remedy fiscal shortfall by adding another burden – a poll tax, a tax on heads – on all men who did not already pay the hut tax. The new tax was not only an added material burden, but a social provocation because it taxed young men, or, more accurately, men who had yet to marry, build homesteads of their own, and become liable for hut tax. It was therefore a direct challenge to the customary rights of fathers over their families. Responsibility for payment of this poll tax lay with the young men on whom it was levied – not on their fathers who, in the Natal system of patriarchal authority, held that it was their right to redistribute their sons' earnings. Taxing sons independently hastened the breaking up of the patriarchal rural homestead, the rupture of kinship links, and the further fragmentation of African communal life. More than this, it disrupted the spiritual forces that linked sons to their fathers and their fathers' fathers whose shades watched over the homestead. Materially and spiritually the poll tax threatened the well-being of the communities in which Africans had always lived. They already had to pay a tax on huts, a tax on dogs, a tax to marry, but a tax on heads! – it was simply preposterous: '*Insumansuman' imali yamakhanda* – It is incomprehensible, it is the poll tax.'[7]

African protests were met with the announcement that the implementation of the tax was not open to discussion: the cash could be raised by a greater commitment to working for wages on the mines and in Natal's growing urban centres, especially Durban. African anger intensified, for objections to the tax were not just narrowly material. While wage labour brought some cash to the homestead, it had to be earned in a distant, violent, dangerous, demeaning, alien, racialised, working environment. To add to this, the manner in which the imposition of the poll tax was announced was an insult and a provocation. It ignored the proper relations between the governed and those who governed, failing to respect the conventions of consultation and discussion that, it was felt, those in authority were obliged to honour in their relations with those whom they ruled. And when chiefs objected, as was not only their right but their duty, they were met with contempt; and if their people protested they were treated with ferocity.

For the times had changed, irrevocably. By terminating the independence of the Boer republics, Britain, as the imperial power, had begun to remove what it saw as major obstructions on the path of South African progress. The centre of power in South Africa was now in the interior, and the forces generated on the Witwatersrand mines were increasingly influencing the colonial peripheries. For the settler population in Natal the benefits were mixed: economic development generally worked to the advantage of those with extensive investments in commerce and banking, but the wages offered on the mines threatened the farmers, who saw cheap African labour as essential to their economic well-being and all settlers who felt that Africans, as domestic servants especially, were essential not just to their economic but their physical comfort and their social status.

Natal had been granted responsible government in 1893. It was, of course, a settler government, without African representation, in a colony in which there were nearly one million Africans, a hundred thousand whites and roughly the same number of Indians. The Legislative Assembly was dominated by farmers who, while they pursued their particular objectives, were as united as other members of the Assembly in the pursuit of white interests. While there were different opinions on the role and future of Africans in settler society, these were fundamentally about the best means to ensure white power, not qualify it, just as the differences between English chauvinism and Afrikaner nationalism disputed but did not challenge racial attitudes. But racial arrogance, the jingoistic 'Englishness' of Natal, mixed with insecurity, felt especially keenly in the aftermath of the South African war, made Natal's settlers particularly sensitive to criticism and stridently assertive. There was also a racial antagonism that created tension and at times violence against Africans, often with sadistic overtones. Although punishment under the law was usually sufficient to satisfy such attitudes, it meant that there were on occasion incidents that approached judicial lynching. But it was economic insecurity that fuelled the racism and political policy in Natal. The war against the Boers was supposed to leave Britons dominant in South Africa. Now, in that most British of colonies, many settlers were out of work, threatened with retrenchment, marginalised.

Since the onset of the post-war depression Natal ministries had sought to find some way to increase revenue. The poll tax was a means to this end. It would not only raise revenue from a portion of its population that was taking advantage of the demand for African labour, but would also ensure that a greater proportion of these earnings would be retained in the colony. The onset of severe economic recession in 1904 only made the case for a poll tax more urgent. It was promulgated in August 1905 for implementation in the following year. Natal's legislature was convinced that it had the political and military strength and the local knowledge to control any resistance.

The now anachronistic system of rule based on the shared interests of white and black patriarchs had to end. The time had come to rein in the remaining pretensions of the chiefs to be co-rulers of the African population: to move from a policy that sought domination through accommodation, towards one of domination by compulsion. By the beginning of the twentieth century it was time for the colonial authorities to carry out the act that it had been unable to perform half a century previously: the subordination – if necessary, the violent subordination, the conquest – of the people of Natal.

Bhambatha's rebellion

Early in February 1906, to the south of the colonial capital, Pietermaritzburg, a small party of police, attending to a report of a protest against the poll tax, got caught up in a skirmish with a party of men, members of an independent church congregation, already in conflict with their chief. Two white policemen were killed.

The Commandant of the Militia, Colonel H.T. Bru-de-Wold, a Norwegian who had jumped ship as a boy, was convinced that 'an open rupture between the white and the black races would occur in the near future'.[8] Martial law was declared in the colony. It would not be lifted for nine months. Seventeen men accused of being amongst those who killed the policemen were to die as a consequence of this initial clash, some publicly by firing squad, others on the gallows. Colonel Duncan McKenzie was appointed over a force that swept through the southern districts of Natal, flogging, fining and torching homesteads, convinced, he said, that the killing of the policemen had prematurely disclosed plans for a general uprising.

To the north, on the southern side of the Thukela valley, there were a number of protests against the tax which the magistrate interpreted as disloyal and disrespectful. Bhambatha kaMancinza was a chief in the area and most of his people lived as tenants on settler farms. His reputation amongst the authorities was that of a difficult man. Crop failures and increased rents had been pressing on him and his people for years, and when the poll tax was added to their burdens the demands made on them became intolerable and were resisted. Bhambatha was deposed early in March. He disappeared into the bush from where he abducted the man chosen to replace him. Mobilising his supporters, he announced his decision to defy authorities by firing on the magistrate, and looting a rural hotel and homestead. A police column was ambushed at Mpanza on 5 April 1906. Three of the police were killed and parts of the body of one of them were cut away to be added to ritual medicines. This gave the rebels protection against their enemies – *intelezi*, which stopped the bullets.

Gathering more men, the rebels then moved to the east, across the Thukela river into what had been the Zulu kingdom, making for the cliffs, caves and forest of the Nkandla as a secure base. There were many people, including numbers of chiefs, who felt as angry as Bhambatha, and some of them, particularly to the north and west of the Nkandla, close to the deep valleys of the Thukela and Mzinyathi, moved towards the Nkandla in support. But these southern parts of the old Zulu kingdom had since conquest been subjected to intense political manipulation by Natal officials seeking to establish local African allies. In the end most of the chiefs equivocated, publicly at least – and not necessarily for cowardly or selfish reasons. They were men of rank, and as leaders they were responsible for their people and their well-being. They were very aware of the disparities between themselves and those by whom they were ruled: disparities that could be fatal in a violent situation. For they lived in homesteads scattered across open grassland, on the crests of ridges, amongst which they planted their crops and grazed their cattle. If conflict broke out, the younger men might be able to fight and then escape the consequences by taking cover in the forest or the thornveld, or disappearing into the compounds or slums now growing round the towns. But this still left most of the people, the women and children, and the grain stores and stock on which they depended, vulnerable to the forces upon which the authorities could draw. And these consisted of mobile, mounted men with high-power rifles, automatic weapons and artillery, and experience as mounted infantry in the recent South African war, and rapacious armed African levies, pressed into service but ready for loot and pillage. Armed confrontation, open rebellion, like Bhambatha's, meant not only sacrificing yourself, but also exposing your people, risking their lives, their homes, property and means of livelihood. It was dangerous, but still safer, to prevaricate: to go through the motions of deference, and hide what was in your heart.

But those in authority were blind to such niceties. Racial arrogance, the drive for dominance, ignorance compounded with fear, cast their world in rigid categories. Anything but deference was suspect: expressions of dissatisfaction meant incipient rebellion; signs of disobedience meant insurrection. The colonial authorities mobilised the militia and there were a number of clashes. One in particular, at Bhobe ridge, saw heavy casualties amongst the rebels, and their reputation as men whose medicine protected them from enemy fire-power. And the bullets of the Natal militia had their own particular non-medicinal properties. They were .303 calibre, but the Mark V, the soft-nosed 'dum dum' that fragmented on impact, caused terrible injuries. Their use was prohibited under the Hague convention, but Britain had not signed this clause and agreed in 1904 that Natal should be supplied with two million rounds. According to Natal's Governor the dum dum was

> introduced for the purposes of warfare against uncivilized races, and has been used for such purposes since then. Members of savage and semi-savage tribes, – it must be remembered, are not

creatures of nerves, and the solid drawn bullet would only in exceptional cases stop a rush.[9]

For much of May the Nkandla and its environs witnessed skirmishes, ambushes, raids, cattle-looting and homestead-burning as the Natal militia searched for Bhambatha and those who had joined him. On 1 June Duncan McKenzie, Natal-born and vicious, was made supreme commander of the militias and he began to plan a co-ordinated final confrontation. The opportunity came on the night of 9 and 10 June when Bhambatha, his allies, and their men were found camped in the Mome valley. The guns were set up on the high, flanking ground waiting for the dawn.

For the Governor, Sir Henry McCallum, the annihilation of the rebels in Mome and the decapitation of their leader were the inevitable and justifiable end of the violent rebellion that had so exercised him for most of the year. '. . . there is no longer any chance of a concerted rising taking place' he wrote on 16 June.[10]

Three days later, fifty kilometres to the south of the Nkandla, five hundred armed men mobilised for an attack on local stores and militia. It initiated another phase of the rebellion that was to last for three weeks, to be followed first by retribution on the part of the militia then by months, and in some cases years, of retribution in the courts. This final stage of the rebellion took place first in the Maphumulo division, large, densely populated, occupying the deep valleys of the Thukela and Mvoti rivers and the highland that separated them. It then spread eastwards towards the sea into the settler farmlands of the Lower Thukela division, and to the south, through the canefields, towards the port city of Durban.

It is this final stage of the rebellion that is the subject of this book.

Notes

1. For an official account see BPP: C.3247, No. 37, McCallum to Elgin, 26 July 1906, Enc. 7, John Howard Alexander, Sworn statement, PMB, 26 July 1906; J. Stuart, *A History of the Zulu Rebellion 1906 and of Dinizulu's Arrest, Trial and Expatriation*, London: Macmillan, 1913, 310–311 and 336–338. To sample subsequent rumours, mystifications and misidentifications see C.T. Binns, *Dinuzulu: The Death of the House of Shaka*, London: Longman, 1968, Appendix IX; H.C. Lugg, *Historic Natal and Zululand*, Pietermaritzburg: Shuter & Shooter, 1949, 72–74; *The Reader's Digest Illustrated History of South Africa*, third edition, 1995, compare photographs on p. 287 and 190. Rumours that photographs were taken but destroyed were current at the time and there was a botched attempt to sell such a print to an English periodical.
2. RH: Mss. African s. 1286/1, H.E. Colenso to F.E. Colenso, 16 June 1906.
3. Jeff Guy, *The Destruction of the Zulu Kingdom: The Civil War in Zululand 1879–1884*, London: Longman, 1979; and 'The destruction and reconstruction of Zulu society' in *Industrialisation and Social Change in South Africa* (eds. Shula Marks and Richard Rathbone), London: Longman, 1982.
4. Very rough estimates taken from Shula Marks' work on economic change in this period in 'Class, ideology and the Bambata rebellion' in *Banditry, Rebellion and Social Protest in Africa* (ed. Donald Crumney), London: James Currey, 1986, 354.
5. Stuart, *Archive 3*, Mkando kaDhlova, 29 July 1902, 155.
6. Stuart, *Archive 3*, Jantshi and Ndukwana, 10 February 1903, 24.
7. C.L. Sibusiso Nyembezi, *Zulu Proverbs*, Johannesburg: Witwatersrand University Press, 1963, 208. *Insumansumane* was used in 1906 by rebels as a password. See PAR: AGO, I/1/317, Statement by Sambana, 14 March 1907.
8. Stuart, *Zulu Rebellion*, 46.
9. PRO: CO 179/237 30630, McCallum to Elgin, 26 July 1906, confidential.
10. BPP: C.3027, No. 88, Governor to Secretary of State, 16 June 1906.

2

19 June 1906

The road to Maphumulo, 17–18 June 1906

Essential to an understanding of the 1906 rebellion at a local level is a knowledge of local geography – the topography, vegetation, landscape and patterns of settlement did much to determine the patterns of conflict. The immediate objectives and strategies, and the predicaments, of leaders like Meseni and Ndlovu, and of the colonial troops, were profoundly affected by the topographical context in which they had to operate.

For much of the nineteenth century the border between the Colony of Natal and the Zulu kingdom was the Thukela river. The Lower Thukela and the Maphumulo divisions lay on the southern side of the Thukela as it ran through the formidable, wide, deep, hot valley it had cut on its way from the Drakensberg to the sea. The southern flanks of the valley rose abruptly to a great ridge of high ground along which ran the road that connected the centres of colonial authority (Stanger and Maphumulo) before falling away again into the valley of the Mvoti river.

On Sunday 17 June, a convoy of five wagons loaded with military stores left Stanger, the administrative centre of the Lower Thukela division. It made its way inland along this road towards the garrison at the Maphumulo magistracy, forty kilometres away. It is a steep climb out of Stanger and the wagons moved slowly along the road on to the high land separating the wide valleys of the Thukela and the Mvoti rivers. For the first half of the journey the road was in the Lower Thukela division, passing through the well-established

Lower Thukela and Maphumulo divisions, c.1905.

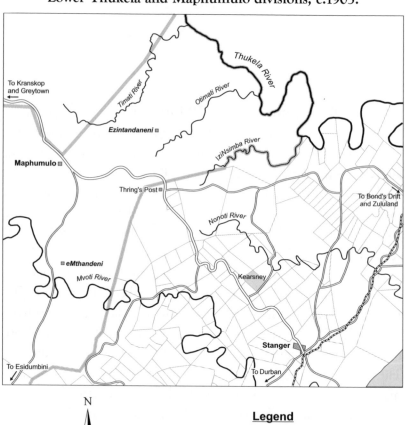

settler farms and sugar estates near the coast. Then, as it gained altitude, it reached the tea plantations and ostentatious country residences of Sir James Liege Hulett whose private railway line now linked his estate at Kearsney with the Natal government railway at Stanger. Africans living here did so under the administrative authority of their chiefs, but they were scattered throughout the division as tenants on private or company farms and crown land. On the right, in the middle distance, was the upper Nonoti river on the banks of which was the eNkanini homestead where in the previous year the cleansing and strengthening ritual had been held by Mbombo, the *inyanga*.

Sergeant Leonard Knox and Trooper Albert Powell were the two men in charge of the wagons, their drivers and *voorloopers*. They were unaware of any tension or danger in the countryside through which they travelled, and took no special precautions. By Monday afternoon the high ground had been gained, near the store at Thring's Post, where the road passed out of the Lower Thukela and entered the Maphumulo division. Here the landscape changed, for this was Native Reserve, administered by chiefs exercising customary law, under the supervision of colonial magistrates and their police. On either side of the road the ground fell away steeply, and the streams feeding the Thukela and Mvoti passed through deep bush-covered gorges and across valleys of dry thornveld, divided by grass-covered ridges, in places capped with sandstone cliffs. At intervals along the steeply undulating winding track there were scattered, still tentative, signs of change – stores, police posts, mission stations, and then the courthouse and the gaol of the Maphumulo magistracy itself. Colonial and commercial influence kept close to the road, occupying the strategically important high ground and leaving most of the African homesteads at some distance, beyond direct surveillance and with considerable local autonomy. While men left the division in their thousands to work in the cities and on the mines of Natal and the Transvaal, women living in the division told the local stock inspector in 1906 that they had not

Lower Thukela and Maphumulo divisions topography.

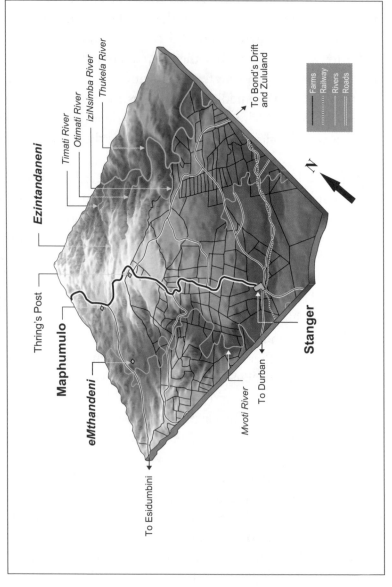

seen a white man on horseback near their homes since the 1879 war with the Zulu.[1] Official oversight was attempted by increasing the administrative tasks and legislative demands on the chiefs, mounting more frequent police patrols, and recruiting more informers. But in the valleys and the thornveld beyond the road, out of sight of the magistracy and police posts, patriarchal rule continued, with women working daily in the fields and the homesteads, boys herding cattle and goats, the systems of deference and authority linking the colonial present uneasily with the pre-colonial past.

There were about twenty chiefs in each division. Most were responsible for a few dozen homesteads, but some were responsible for hundreds. And there were some *amakhosi* who, regardless of the number of people under their control, were men of status, linked closely to great figures and events in Zulu history.

Mashwili kaMngoye

Mashwili kaMngoye was such an *inkosi*. He lived to the right of the road as it crossed the boundary between the Lower Thukela and the Maphumulo divisions. Mashwili was responsible for over one hundred homesteads in each division. He was now old and barely mobile. His father had come into Natal in 1849, and he was the grandson of one of the great figures in Zulu history – Dingiswayo kaJobe of the Mthethwa, protector and mentor of Shaka kaSenzangakhona, founder of the Zulu kingdom. Mashwili's homestead was built at the head of the valley formed by the upper reaches of the Izinsimba river as it fell into a narrow bush-covered gorge on its way to the Thukela. On the northern horizon, across the Thukela valley, lay the southern reaches of the old Zulu kingdom. To the south-east from Mashwili's homestead, on the edge of the Izinsimba valley, the boundaries of the white-owned farmland of the Lower Thukela division were just visible. The Izinsimba gorge was soon to become a rebel mobilising centre and stronghold.

Chiefdoms.

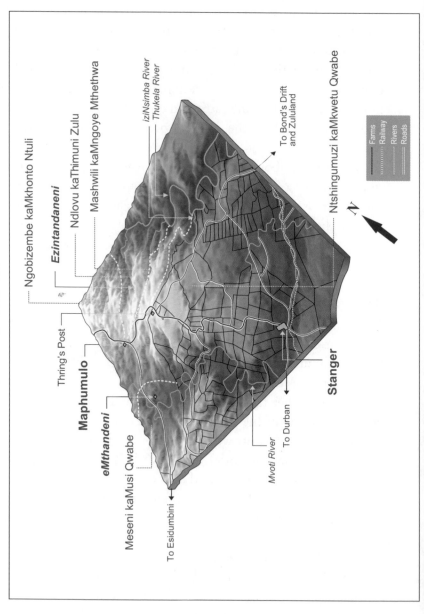

Ngobizembe kaMkhonto Ntuli

Ezintandaneni

Ndlovu kaThimuni Zulu

Mashwili kaMngoye Mthethwa

iziNsimba River
Thukela River

To Bond's Drift
and Zululand

Ntshingumuzi kaMkwetu Qwabe

Thring's Post

Maphumulo

eMthandeni

Meseni kaMusi Qwabe

To Esidumbini

Mvoti River
To Durban

Stanger

Farms
Railway
Rivers
Roads

N

Meseni kaMusi

As the wagons continued to move towards Maphumulo, the ground on the left fell away precipitously towards the large chiefdom of the Qwabe under chief Meseni kaMusi that dominated the Mvoti valley. From his eMthandeni homestead Meseni exercised authority over two hundred and fifty homesteads in this division alone. Meseni was one of the most powerful and best-known chiefs in Natal, and the story of the establishment of the Qwabe in the nineteenth century, in the sweep of country between the port of Durban and the Thukela river, is an extraordinary one. It illustrates vividly all the contradictions and complexities implicit in the system devised by the men who ruled colonial Natal in the nineteenth century: the African patriarchs moving into the future to assert their past; and Theophilus Shepstone, the colonial patriarch, evoking the African past to secure the colonial future.

The Qwabe and the Zulu originated from a single lineage, which had divided two-and-a-half centuries previously. One hundred years and fifty years later, in the conflicts associated with the rise of Shaka kaSenzangakhona, most of the *amakhosi* of the huge Qwabe chiefdom were killed and their people broken up and dispersed. After a series of epic conflicts and journeys, small groups of Qwabe settled south of the kingdom, just at the time when first the Boers and then the British were taking steps to establish themselves in the territory between the Indian ocean and the Drakensberg mountains, which in the 1840s became the British Colony of Natal.

Once they had settled in related but scattered groups, Africans like the Qwabe sought to establish themselves by setting in motion conventional productive processes organised within the homestead.[2] These were premised on access to arable land on which women could produce the staple cereals, on sufficient grazing to support livestock, and on the principle that the fertility and productive capacity of women had value in terms of cattle. The process was initiated by the passage of what is called (inadequately) bridewealth, and consolidated by what is called (also inadequately) marriage into the male-dominated, polygamous homestead where wives from different houses worked in the fields, and produced children: boys who would in time head homesteads themselves from which they would control the reproductive and productive capacity of the women they exchanged for cattle; and girls who would in time be exchanged for the cattle of males from other lineages. Thus, beyond being a vital source of sustenance, cattle were also the means by which houses within homesteads were founded and their occupants mobilised to drive the processes of material production and surplus accumulation.

Although the principles upon which they were founded were the same, there were great differences between the size of the commoner's homestead, containing the houses of two or three wives, and that of the *inkosi* with perhaps a score of wives. Wealth and power depended on the resources under the authority of the *inkosi* and were indicated by the number of people under his direct control in his homesteads, the cattle he possessed, was owed, and could mobilise in exchange for labour power in the form of wives and their reproductive and productive capacity, together with the number of people who gave him their military support and political loyalty and for whom he was responsible. But, with all their variations and differences, the principle at the heart of these societies was the value placed on productive human beings and the accumulation of such human beings or their equivalents, the most obvious being cattle. The necessary tension between African societies organised on such principles – in which people were the goal of production – and the intrusive colonial one in which production was their goal[3] – drove the conflicts of these times.

Political contestation within the ruling house tended to take the form of quarrels between different homesteads over questions of rank and succession, and was often manifested in disputes over the payment of bridewealth, tracked down over generations and carried out by the inkosi's sons, their mothers, supported by factions of commoners that coalesced around them. Much of the history of the great chiefdoms, including the Zulu kingdom, can be written in terms of these disputes within the ruling lineages.

We can see them at work in the history of Musi and his son Meseni in Natal.[4] At the time when the first white settlers arrived, there were small concentrations of Qwabe north and south of what became Durban. News reached them that there was a male descendant of the Qwabe chiefly line still alive in the Zulu kingdom, a boy called Musi, the son of Gondolozi, the brother of the late inkosi Phakathwayo.[5] If the Qwabe were to re-establish themselves as a power in the land, it would greatly assist them if they could revive their historically famous ruling lineage. Emissaries were sent to bring the boy south to live with the Qwabe. He came with no property, but the people who had arranged for him to be moved to live amongst them provided him with cattle. These were used for his support and were supplemented when his cousin, the only surviving child of their inkosi Phakathwayo, married, and her bridewealth was given to Musi to perpetuate her father's lineage. Musi kaGondolozi began to take wives – that is, establish the homesteads upon which his power in Natal was to be based – and he moved north into a Native Reserve just established by the colonial authorities where he founded another larger Qwabe settlement.

It was from here that Musi built one of the most powerful chieftainships in colonial Natal – and one whose very nature was contradictory. He was established by his people, using African systems of law and succession, and recognised by Theophilus Shepstone of the new colonial authority. When another cousin came from the Zulu kingdom and claimed the Qwabe chieftainship in the late 1840s it was Shepstone who decided in Musi's favour. (The new claimant and his followers were relegated to a district on the northern margins of the Lower Thukela division, largely as tenants on still undeveloped private, mission and crown land – to become half a century later the people of Ntshingumuzi, the man who organised the ritual at eNkanini with which this book began.)

In this test case Shepstone laid down the legal precedent that it was the government of Natal that appointed chiefs. In so doing he established *de jure* Musi's authority as colonial chief; but Musi's power *de facto* was as a living representative of the Qwabe ruling lineage. It was measured in the number of people who recognised his authority – as reflected in his wives, children and cattle, organised in different homesteads throughout his chiefdom, and in the homesteads built by the people who came to live under his authority in the land he came to dominate between Durban and the Thukela river.

The colonial authority exploited this pre-colonial feature: like all African homestead-heads in Natal, Musi was taxed according to the number of houses under his direct control – that is, by the productive capacity of his own homesteads and the wives living in them. As a recognised chief in the Natal system, responsible for the payment of the hut tax of the people who considered him their chief, Musi was an official of the colonial administration as well as an African *inkosi*; but he was also the living representative of one of the great chiefdoms of the region. Amongst his wives was the daughter of one of the best-known historical figures of south-east Africa, Matiwane of the Ngwane, and two daughters of the Swazi king. Plans (unsuccessful) were made for him to marry one of the Zulu king Mpande's daughters, Bathonyile. Such links with the famous chiefly houses of south-east Africa indicate the continuing vitality of the pre-colonial past, laying down a network of African connections and structures while simultaneously working with and sustained by the new world of magistrates and missionaries, taxation and litigation, and the ever-increasing financial obligations as settler agriculture, sugar and tea estates, and land-speculating companies established their influence in and around the homesteads of the Qwabe. This had the effect of reducing their options, forcing change as their young men began to move in larger numbers away from their homes, to return with wages to assist their fathers meet their fiscal obligations – and in time to attempt to establish homesteads

of their own, but in increasingly changed and constrained conditions.

A recurring theme in the history of African chiefdoms in the
region was the rivalry between different sons of the *inkosi* over
succession – an obvious enough site of conflict given that power in
these societies lay with the male homestead-heads and the most
powerful of these patriarchs were to be found in the chiefly lineage.
The *amakhosi* also tended to secure their own positions by selecting
their successors as late as they could from amongst their younger
sons, frequently encouraging differences among them. *Divide et
impera* was not just a colonial device.

Whether deliberately created by Musi or not, it was this sort of
situation that developed amongst the Qwabe. As a young *inkosi*
building his power base in the reserves north of Durban, he had
established a number of homesteads at different places. There were
conflicting assessments over which was of higher status, or to make
the same point from a different perspective, who was to be Musi's
chief wife and the mother of his successor. Musi's failure to formally
announce his successor created confusion amongst his people and
rivalry amongst his sons. But it was understandable: to settle the
future succession might well have encouraged the creation of a
faction within the chiefdom which could in time threaten the ruler
himself.

But failure to announce his successor did not stop the growth
of rival political powers. Two houses and two of Musi's sons came
to the fore, and their rivalry came to dominate Qwabe politics.
Meseni was born in the 1850s and associated with the eMthandeni
homestead; Miso was younger and associated with the Nkwenkwezi
homestead. It was hoped that Musi would name his chief wife at
the Qwabe *umkhosi* in 1869. Some believed he did, others that he
did not, others that he tried but failed to do so decisively or effectively.
The historical and legal implications of this confusion were to
become notorious – and insoluble – in the decades to come.

It was around Meseni and those associated with the eMthandeni
homestead that the predictable tension between father and son

began to develop. In 1879 Meseni left the chiefdom for two years. His return was marked by increasing conflict with Musi, who complained that his son was unilaterally assuming his father's chiefly duties and interfering in his jurisdiction. Factions began to coalesce around Meseni's eMthandeni and Miso's Nkwenkwezi, each threatening and, on occasion, fighting with the other. A large number of the young men involved were now also wage labourers, who brought back to their rural homes an urban unruliness and a truculence exacerbated by rural insecurity, as land resources were reduced, and overcrowding and disputes over boundaries increased. In 1890 Musi hired a lawyer to make a formal complaint to the authorities over Meseni's attempts to assume authority over the Qwabe, and in the following year Meseni was brought before the local magistrate to answer charges of interfering in his father's administration.

Meseni had by now acquired the reputation of being an outspoken, ambitious and aggressive man determined to overcome his rival, his father's favourite Miso. At the same time his chiefly status and his capacity to defend it impressed some of those with influence and, although he was censured for his behaviour towards his father, he was not punished.

Then in 1892 Miso died. At his burial Musi publicly announced the successor to the Qwabe chieftainship. Miso's young son, Siziba, was made to stand next to his father's grave holding the Qwabe inkosi's ritual assegai. But he was much too young to take office – this would be assumed by an older brother – so the immediate succession dispute was solved by the creation of a new set of unpredictable unknowns.

Meseni did not attend the funeral. It was impossible for him to do so in safety. It was believed by the Nkwenkwezi that he had been in some way responsible for his brother's death – a suspicion confirmed when his father Musi died shortly afterwards. The authorities now had to intervene – and an enquiry was held into who should succeed the Qwabe chieftainship. The evidence taken was vast and included statements from some of the old people who had been involved in Qwabe history from the time of their dispersal by Shaka. It makes fascinating reading for historians, but proved to be impossibly contradictory for those who had to make quick legal assessments and administrative decisions. It was left to Theophilus Shepstone, from his death bed, to make the final intervention: as the most prominent son of Musi, the man whom Shepstone had formally recognised as chief forty years earlier, Meseni should succeed his father.[6]

The Nkwenkwezi, of course, objected and hired lawyers to make their case. The battles in the Native High Court and the Supreme Court over the powers of the Supreme Chief will not be followed here. It is enough to say that it was decided that while Meseni should retain his position as his father's successor, his father's property would devolve on the Nkwenkwezi. It was a decision that did nothing to reduce the tension between the two parties. The under-Secretary for Native Affairs carried out an on-site investigation and reported that the eMthandeni and Nkwenkwezi homesteads were roughly equal in numbers and so inextricably intermingled that he saw no way of separating the rival claimants. But in 1898 James Hulett, the new Minister for Native Affairs, who lived and prospered in the Lower Thukela division, was determined to act. He divided the Qwabe: those living in the Lower Thukela division would come under the regent of Miso's young son, Siziba; those in the Maphumulo division would come under Meseni. Anyone unwilling to recognise Meseni's authority should move out of the Maphumulo divisions and establish themselves amongst the Nkwenkwezi.

For Meseni it was an outrageous decision that usurped his historical inheritance and tore his people from him. But it is possible to go beyond his predictable personal protests at this substantial reduction in his power and to see in these decisions radical shifts away from the pre-colonial foundations upon which Qwabe power had been built in colonial Natal. In the pre-colonial system, political power was built on property in the form of people:

to separate the one from the other – as had been done by the decision that Meseni inherit his father's office and Miso his property – was to deny the very essence of chiefly power. Furthermore, integral to political power were the people who gave their allegiance to the chief: to define political loyalty in terms of territory again denied the essential fact of chiefly authority.

At the turn of the century Meseni, now chief of the eMthandeni section of the Qwabe, was a very angry man. His mood was not improved when the Nkwenkwezi regent died and the Lower Thukela magistrate Frank Shuter was ordered to replace him. The alienation of his father's property, the removal of his people, and the appointment of a white official over them were an unacceptable slight to the man who believed that 'the Qwabe tribe is really of higher rank than the Zulu' and that he himself 'holds the highest rank among all the natives of Natal'.[7] The authorities were wary of this proud and vociferous man and his capacity to make trouble, as he employed lawyers to defend his rights as one of Natal's most prestigious and powerful chiefs, and took action on his own initiative when he felt it would escape the attention of magistrates and the office of the Secretary for Native Affairs. By the beginning of the century, with the Qwabe involved in often murderous conflict not only amongst themselves but also with their Nyuswa neighbours, the colonial officials were determined to gain control over these fractious people and punish those directly responsible for the violence and their chief as well. To Meseni's complaints about loss of land, the alienation of his people, their poverty, and the imposition of the poll tax, he now added the charge of deliberate provocation. His sense of personal grievance against the authorities was a significant factor in what happened in June and July 1906 in the Maphumulo division.

Ndlovu kaThimuni

Further along the Stanger-Maphumulo road, on the northern side, in the valleys of the Otimati and the Timati streams, was the Nodunga chiefdom of Ndlovu kaThimuni Zulu with just over one hundred homesteads. Although his chiefdom was much smaller than that of the sprawling Qwabe chiefdom, Ndlovu was a man of status, stature and authority. In 1902 he visited James Stuart in Durban, who recorded his conversation with this 'bright young man of about 45, medium height, light-coloured, talkative, agreeable, intelligent, with a keen interest in larger questions'.[8]

Ndlovu was also descended from a significant figure in the history of the Zulu kingdom, and his grandfather had been intimately involved in the history of the young Shaka kaSenzangakhona when he laid the foundations of the Zulu kingdom at the beginning of the nineteenth century. Ndlovu's father, Thimuni, had fallen out with Shaka's successor, Dingane, over the decision to use violence against the first Boer intruders into the region in 1838. Thimuni established himself to the south of the Thukela river where Shepstone recognised him as a colonial chief. When the painter and traveller Angas visited Natal in 1848, it was Thimuni who provided his model for a Zulu warrior in the well-known portrait.

The Secretary for Native Affairs, Theophilus Shepstone, was extraordinarily skilful at exploiting not only divisions amongst chiefs, but also their conservatism and desire for authority, while holding out promises of more land and better things to come. At first Thimuni believed him. But as settler power became more entrenched, so the authority of the chiefs declined. When Thimuni took his complaints to the authorities, Shepstone urged patience. By the time Thimuni died, he had lost faith. As his son Ndlovu said, 'Timuni considered Sir T[heophilus] S[hepstone] had on the whole *deceived* the people, for he told them it would all come right and the times would come when they would *laugh*.'[9]

The time for laughter never came. Shepstone wheeled and dealed, promised and prevaricated, using all his insights into custom and local politics to deflect African anger with promises or silence

Thimuni, father of Ndlovu.   (G.F. Angas, *Kaffirs Illustrated*, London, 1849, Plate XIII)

it by persuading the Governor to exercise the unlimited power under customary law of the Supreme Chief. But, as the settler economy developed and the demands on African land and labour became greater, so the traditional order which the chiefs had tried to preserve was undermined by settler rule and the capitalist market.

Ndlovu kaThimuni experienced the consequences of these changes directly. Like Meseni, he had been in conflict with a brother over his succession to their father, and his inheritance had been divided. Ndlovu had a great interest in history and politics, and was well aware of what subsequent historians failed to comprehend: that the single, most important fact of Natal's colonial history was that the colony had been founded on a compromise between the colonial and African authorities; it had not been conquered by force, but acquired by negotiation – or as Ndlovu saw it in retrospect, by stealth.

> The white man (Englishman) entered the country very quietly and unostentatiously; now, however, having a firm foothold, they are *immoveable* (*qiyeme*).[10]

Ndlovu tried to discover how this had happened, and what Africans had lost in the process. He had made a particular effort to get his father and other older men to give accounts of the Zulu past and the role of his lineage in Zulu history. But histories of loss, for those who experienced it directly and were left without hope of regaining the past or changing the present, were painful. As one man said:

> Why do you stir up these old graves? When the tribe is still standing and flourishing it is something, but now we are broken and scattered. *War* is *talked about* when the heart is light and cheerful, when the future is in some way assured; but to talk over things dead and gone appears painful and unnecessary. We rejoice greatly that England has brought about a state of peace, but owing to non-recognition of tribes and the members

composing them, their ranks and distinctions, hereditary and due to personal effort, we feel that we are becoming dead indeed.[11]

When Ndlovu tried to get an old man to tell him about the origins of the Zulu

he refused on the ground that he no longer had any heart in anything. Formerly he was a man of position and treated with respect. Now he was a dog, and had been reduced to living on mere sweet potatoes (*batata*).[12]

By the beginning of the twentieth century Ndlovu viewed the situation with a concern that approached despair. It was not just the poverty and the increasing demands made on his people: it was that he, a man of authority and the descendant of men of authority, was not allowed to govern his people effectively. The colonial authorities had destroyed the patriarchal hierarchy necessary for the effective exercise of authority and with it the principles and means of good governance: as a result African society was in the process of disintegration.

In a proper system of government all had a right to be heard, but in Natal the authorities refused to listen. Africans had been silenced and reduced to mere empty shells (*izigubu*). The colonial authorities had failed in their responsibilities. By now they should all have been taught to read and write. Instead the young disobeyed their parents and left the homesteads to work for wages. Women were selling themselves in the towns. Africans should be consulted on the crises they faced. The authority of the chiefs had been broken down, and their people now wandered about, unable to find the way – the word Ndlvou used was *ukweduka* – they were lost, had gone astray. Africans had a voice and it should be heard. They needed their own parliament and the right to manage their own affairs.

Ndlovu had, as a young man, personally experienced the absence of governance and the resultant confusion. He had never forgotten it. In the mid-1880s he had gone with a party of Zulu men to work at the diamond mines at Kimberley. Many of them had become ill before they reached their place of employment. Once there, others succumbed to the easy availability of liquor. They were set upon by Basotho gangs. Very few of the party returned, and those who did brought little money with them. Ndlovu's direct experience of the opening years of South Africa's industrial revolution was significant in the development of his thinking – he saw the white man's much-vaunted civilisation as violence and anarchy. A way had to be found of gaining the advantages of what the white man had brought to Africa without abandoning the all-important African notions of justice, order and authority. He felt that to do this, the people as a whole should be gathered together, listened to, and a plan worked out for the future. He compiled a list of grievances and took them to the authorities in Pietermaritzburg, only to be fobbed off.

And then, in this moment of crisis, of disintegration, the Natal government had, without consultation, imposed a further tax, this time on the heads of all men not paying the hut tax. The magistrates were instructed to warn the chiefs that they were responsible for the collection of the tax and that any signs of 'neglect' would jeopardise their formal status as chiefs. Furthermore, 'No discussion in connection with the matter should be entered into . . .'[13] By Ndlovu's standards this was not government but subordination, and confirmed his charges of maladministration in the present and his fears for the future.

Taxing Maphumulo, January 1906

In January 1906 the magistrates ordered the chiefs of Natal to come to their offices with the men liable for the poll tax to make payment. Some, like Dinuzulu, a local chief in the eyes of the colonial government, the Zulu *inkosi* in the eyes of most Africans, paid without public protest. Whatever they felt personally, the political consequences of refusal persuaded them to go through the motions of compliance. Others paid with reluctance, and in a few cases there were outward signs of dissatisfaction, and in some protest and refusal. For the authorities anything but unquestioning obedience to authority was defiance, and the death on 8 February of two policemen, in search of alleged tax-protesters, in a confused skirmish in the mist and the dark near Richmond, was evidence of plans for a colony-wide rebellion.

Some magistrates managed to absorb the antagonism created by the imposition of the tax, but this was not the case in Maphumulo. The magistrate, R.E. Dunn, called a number of meetings in January and February 1906 where chiefs were ordered to attend together with the young men liable for the poll tax. The chiefs, standing between their angry men, and the magistrate and his receipt books, tried to turn the meetings into demonstrations of their people's incapacity to pay. This was, of course, not accepted and the chiefs were held responsible for their followers' protests.

The largest chiefdom in the Maphumulo district was that under Ngobizembe kaMkhonto Ntuli, occupying the area to the north east of the magistracy and, like all the chiefdoms in this region to the right of the main road, characterised by steep valleys and gorges and, towards the Thukela, dense thornveld. On 22 January, at Allan's store, the magistrate and his police were approached by three hundred of Ngobizembe's men who, the magistrate asserted, threatened him. Ngobizembe was instructed to bring them to order but failed. When Dunn's report reached his superiors in Pietermaritzburg, it was decided that Ngobizembe's men were rebellious and that an example should be made of them and their chief.

On the 24 January Dunn was at the store at Thring's Post, and the three most important chiefs – Ndlovu, Mashwili and Ngqokwane (Mbedu) – attended with their men. Dunn was informed that they did not have the money to pay. The magistrate moved on, into the Mvoti valley to Butler's store. Again he was confronted by men who said they could not pay and threatened the magistrate – but on this occasion their chief Swayimana (Nyuswa) drove them back with a sjambok. The magistrate was no more successful in collecting the tax here than elsewhere – but the chief successfully persuaded the authorities that he had attempted to force his men to pay and he not only escaped punishment but persuaded them of his loyalty.

The next meeting was in the Mvoti valley, at Gaillard's store, just across the river from Meseni's eMthandeni homestead. Meseni was not there but was attending the court at Stanger. Amongst the four hundred assembled at Gaillard's store the officials noted that some were wearing the white cow tail insignia of the Zulu royal house, the *shokobezi*. They behaved in a threatening manner and told the officials that the Qwabe could not pay the tax.

Attempts to persuade the authorities that the chiefs were unable to control their people's opposition to the tax, were not successful. Furthermore, the argument of poverty was ignored, as was the seemingly incontrovertible one that the refusal of the authorities to grant men passes to leave the district until the poll tax was paid made it impossible for those who wished to pay to earn the money to do so. Dunn wrote his reports of defiance and resistance, drank himself into a stupor, was removed from the district and replaced by Thomas Maxwell, the very man who twenty years earlier had recruited the party of Zulu, of which Ndlovu was a member, to work on the diamond mines.

It was decided to make an example of Ngobizembe kaMkhonto. Lieutenant-Colonel George Leuchars, a local farmer, politician and prominent military officer was ordered to take troops to Maphumulo. On the way he consulted John Wesley Shepstone, brother of Theophilus, whose career as a native administrator had been marked by violence and duplicity. He told Leuchars what he wanted to hear: the protests over the poll tax were the first signs of black uprising whose aim was to drive whites out of South Africa.[14]

The price of chieftainship: Meseni, Ngobizembe and Ndlovu photographed at Maphumulo.
(*The Natal Mercury Pictorial*, 18 April 1906)

The chiefs were ordered to attend a meeting at the magistracy on 27 February and, with great ceremony in the presence of troops, Maxwell gave Ngobizembe six days to hand over the men who had 'defied' Dunn. If he failed, the order would be enforced by the soldiers. Ngobizembe made an attempt to carry out the instruction, but it was an impossible demand. On 5 March police and military 'swept' the chiefdom, arrested Ngobizembe, seized hundreds of head of livestock, then surrounded the chief's homestead and destroyed it with shell fire.

It was an action provoked by frustration. From the other side of the Thukela, Zulu had surprised the Commissioner for Native Affairs by refusing to volunteer to advance across the river and into the thick bush into which Ngobizembe's people had retreated. As a consequence Leuchars was unwilling to 'drive' the inhospitable terrain from his side. But publicly the Natal militia and its leaders had to present themselves as victors and in control[15] and they covered this example of Zulu solidarity and their own inability to remove the people from the Thukela bush with the destruction of the chief's homestead at a distance with artillery – a brilliant stroke, according to Governor Sir Henry McCallum, which changed at an instant the attitude of Africans throughout Natal from 'studied insolence' to 'thorough submission'. Leuchars'

> idea of destroying the kraal by artillery fire instead of by the match, although perhaps somewhat theatrical, has had splendid effect, and it is only those who know the natives as well as Colonel Leuchars who would probably have undertaken the work in this way.[16]

Further raids and arrests followed, the chiefdom was divided, and Ngobizembe deposed. He died the next year in Pietermaritzburg gaol. His brother, Sambela, however, took control of his people in the thick bush and broken country towards the Thukela, which became a safe retreat and centre of resistance.

His neighbour, Ndlovu kaThimuni Zulu, tried to put the case of his people to the new magistrate, Thomas Maxwell. But any expectations Ndlovu had that his prospects would improve with the appointment of his old employer as the magistrate, soon disappeared. The chief's request that he be allowed to go to Pietermaritzburg to argue his case, was refused. When he pointed out that his chiefdom was arid, rocky and unproductive, and particularly vulnerable to the economic vicissitudes of recent years, Ndlovu was instructed to obey orders.

The magistracy at Maphumulo was turned into a base for the militia. The troops moved up and down the main road that bisected the division, terrorising the people it came across and thrashing those who did not show respect. Ndlovu was, he said

> surprised to find the troops being poured into the country. We were told that the troops were . . . an enemy to us because we

refused to pay the Poll tax, instead of it being put in the right way and saying 'we had not the money to pay.' We were startled by hearing the firing of canon. Our children were frightened.[17]

Maxwell ordered Ndlovu to report to the magistrate in Stanger. The chief, attempting to please, did not question why he should attend the magistrate of a neighbouring division and hired a cart to take him the forty kilometres. But there had been a mistake, the order should have gone to another chief of the same name. Ndlovu was ordered to report to Maphumulo – as he asked the man who gave him the instruction 'am I a bird that I am expected to fly to Maphumulo on the same day?'. But the Stanger magistrate,

> Mr Shuter took me into a room and shut the door and said 'What have you done that we have to arrest you'. I said 'I do not know. I came here because I was called. I do not know what crime I have committed against the Authorities.' I remained 3 days in the jail at Stanger and was then brought to Maphumulo and put in jail here. I was 29 days in jail.

Meseni was also in trouble. Although he wasn't at the poll tax meeting he was ordered to hand over those who had protested there. He was berated and humiliated by Leuchars, and ordered to turn over one hundred of the men within three days or pay a fine of two hundred head of cattle. He was detained, and released only when he hired a lawyer to intervene on his behalf. It was then decided to curtail radically the extent of his authority by restricting his jurisdiction to his followers living in the Maphumulo and Ndwedwe divisions. This reduced the number of his people by half. He was outraged:

> I was imprisoned, but my case was not heard. I was imprisoned for nothing at all. I was told that the reason was that my people had made disturbances when the tax was being collected. It was

not true. I was imprisoned for eleven days, and when I was released I was told that I had been imprisoned not for what I have just said, but for a faction fight that took place some time ago between my tribe and another. The case was tried at Stanger Court. I was then told that I was deprived of all the private lands on which my people were living and that they were to be confined to the Location only. The case was never gone into as to why I was imprisoned. I was simply imprisoned without cause, and no further notice was taken of it.[18]

In the opinion of both Meseni and Ndlovu, the government had decided to destroy them. The behaviour of the militia garrisoned in their divisions did nothing to disabuse them of this. The main line of communication on which the men depended for supplies was the road between the garrison at the Maphumulo magistracy and Stanger near the coast. The movement of soldiers and wagons up and down this road placed great strain on the people in its proximity. Martial law gave the troopers free rein to harass and punish any African they came across: respect 'for the uniform' was enforced by the lash; and cattle were removed from homesteads that could not account for the whereabouts of their young men. Captain W.A. Campbell caused great consternation amongst Meseni's people when he burnt down a Qwabe homestead. A Natal Mounted Rifles patrol under Lieutenant Cornelius Landsberg shot dead a brother of Ndlovu for failing to respond to a call to halt. He was a deaf mute.

Even the historian continually exposed to the racial violence of the South African past has to be surprised by the degree of racial hostility and cruelty in the actions of the colonial militia in 1906 – at the uncompromising severity with which authority was enforced, and at the arbitrary punishments inflicted on those who crossed the militia's path. This was felt amongst some of Natal's ruling elite at the time. Sir James Hulett, local plantation owner, ex-Minister for Native Affairs, and enormously successful businessman, was no liberal in native affairs. And yet even he protested at the actions of the military on the road from Stanger to Maphumulo. Indiscipline and alcohol seemed to be an important factor, and Hulett feared it would provoke, not inhibit, an African revolt. He telegraphed the Prime Minister from his estate, Kearsney, urging him to

> stop the lawless conduct of the parties in charge of Mapumulo. Unless you desire having the whole of this peaceable District in flame with Consequent Ruin. Added to other outrages a poor deaf & dumb kafir shot in the road by militia men Friday evening able to drag himself to a friend's kraal on Kearsney then died having five revolver wounds in him . . . This is probably reported as an attack upon patrol. Funk on the part of those in charge of Mapumulo & Irresponsible conduct of some officers & troopers . . . If you fail and natives are driven into rebellion here then the responsibility will be on the head of the Government.[19]

Ndlovu, already harassed and gaoled for, as he chose to depict it, doing his duty by bringing his people's poverty to the attention of the officials, watched with increasing distress at what was happening.

> It made my heart sore that, though I was willing to pay the tax my near relative should be shot and that these things should take place unless it was true, what had been told me about the authorities and I was then their enemy.[20]

His followers were putting him under pressure. Responding to rumour and to messages from their elders and their chiefs about the coming crisis, men were arriving in increasing numbers from the farms and towns where they had been working. They gathered round their chiefs, discussing the rumours of coming conflict, which seemed to be confirmed by the arrival of the troops in the division and by their aggressive treatment of the local population. There were reports passing along the depths of the Thukela valley of the success of Bhambatha in the Nkandla, of the way he had attacked and killed the police, and of his powerful *intelezi*, which protected his force from bullets. Even the mid-June reports that the rebels in the Nkandla had finally been trapped and Bhambatha and his followers killed in Mome gorge came with a message of hope. Regardless of what the officials said, Bhambatha's medicine had allowed him to escape. Then there were the messages that Dinuzulu was sending a force to support those in armed resistance. These were followed by the threats: the Zulu when they arrived would attack not only the whites but those who sided with them. There was a special warning for Ndlovu: the Zulu had not forgotten that it was his grandfather who had refused to support his king, Dingane kaSenzangakhona, when he decided to attack the Boers on their arrival in Zululand.

The Zulu past, its powerful beliefs and history, could be invoked against these settler newcomers who had inveigled their way into the lives of the African people of the region only sixty years before. When Shaka had proved to be tyrannical, his people had overthrown him. They were now being tyrannised again, this time by foreign conquerors, and it was time to send them back and reclaim their African past. It was dangerous, this idea that African beliefs and rituals could be used to restore the African past, and it was controversial. Many believed that such dreams of a just, African future should be dismissed as just that – dangerous dreams of restoring what had gone forever. But for many others such dreams had a reality – and even gained credibility when reports were received of men and women who would mobilise spiritual forces to assist those claiming their heritage, with the help of medicines which would negate the destructive power of the enemy's weaponry.

Many of the men debating these ideas were of a generation that had experienced directly the impact of increasing poverty and exploitation at their homes, and insult and injury at their places of work. Already overtaxed, it now seemed all too clear that what they had left – their rural homes, their families, their fields and their cattle – were under threat. The troops ignored the authority of the chiefs, rode their horses where they liked, flogged, insulted and threatened. What, his people asked Ndlovu, not only as their *inkosi* but also as the white man's chief, was he going to do about it? 'You pay your taxes by us and these white people kill us.'[21] If he continued to do nothing, they might act without him.

On the evening of 18 June Ndlovu called his men to Ezintandaneni to be strengthened by ritual.[22] Present was a newcomer to Ndlovu's, an *inyanga* with the skills needed to organise the ceremony. He was known by a number of names, but the one with which he became associated, and under which someone was eventually tried and hanged, was Mabalengwe – 'the leopard's spots'. And just as he was known by different names, he also had different histories. It was said that he came from Ndlovu's neighbour, Sambela, who had replaced the gaoled Ngobizembe and had gathered his people and cattle in the thornbush near the Thukela. But before that he had been with Bhambatha. Others believed that he came from Dinuzulu himself. He carried with him powerful medicine, especially effective because it included parts of the body of a white policeman, killed in the opening stages of the rebellion.

Nearby, on the main road, the convoy of wagons that had left Stanger the day before, had crossed the Otimati stream at the drift and begun the climb out of the valley, with Oglesbys' store and the track to the Norwegian mission station on the right. It was late when it reached the nineteen-mile post, and, with another ten kilometres to go to Maphumulo, Knox and Powell decided that they should outspan. They were still oblivious to the anger in the valleys around them and took no special precautions for their own safety. The Nkandla forest was on the other side of the Thukela valley fifty kilometres away, Bhambatha had been dead for a week, his followers dispersed, and the people of Natal cowed, their lesson learnt. The troops said that the natives they came across were suitably deferent. The police informers reported that whatever was happening elsewhere in the country, and in the depths of the ravines towards the Thukela, the main road was secure.

As the men with the wagons prepared for the night, in the next valley, beyond the Norwegian mission station at Ndlovu's homestead, Ezintandaneni, ritual preparations were being made for an armed expedition. For a month now the troops had been seizing their cattle and plundering their homesteads. They now had had enough. They were going to raid cattle from the store at Thring's Post to compensate for the losses they had suffered over the months at the hands of the troops, and over the years at the hands of the civil authorities.

19 June 1906

The party sleeping with the wagons did not hear the five hundred armed men move out of the valley before dawn on the morning of 19 June, making their way to the cattle kraaled at the store at Thring's Post about ten kilometres down the road towards Stanger. The force was joined by people from the Mbedu chiefdom under Ngqokwane. There were two white men sleeping at the house a few hundred metres from the store. William C. Robbins was a stock inspector, doubling as a spy for the Stanger militia. The previous day Africans had warned him of coming trouble, and he had given up his intention of making a reconnaissance through Ndlovu's area. He had returned to Thring's Post on the main road, where the young Norwegian storekeeper, Adolf Sangereid, had persuaded him to spend the night. Robbins was woken at five in the morning by a noise. Thinking it was his African servant getting ready for their early departure, he got out of bed and opened the door onto the veranda.

As he did so he was stabbed in the right side. It was just light enough for him to see the glinting of the assegais of the crowd of Zulu in what he believed to be war-dress outside. As the blade penetrated, their silence was broken with 'Usuthu' of the Zulu royal

The road to Maphumulo: 17–19 June 1906.

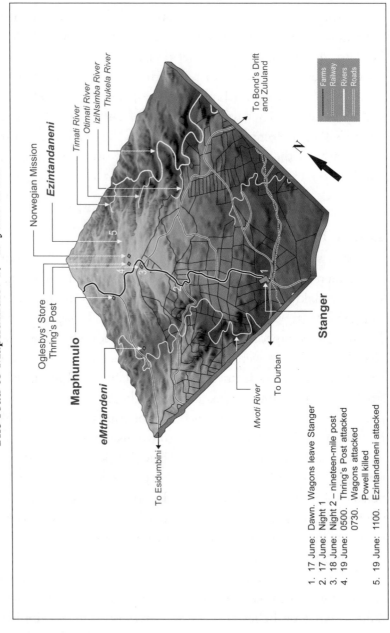

1. 17 June: Dawn. Wagons leave Stanger
2. 17 June: Night 1
3. 18 June: Night 2 – nineteen-mile post
4. 19 June: 0500.   Thring's Post attacked
              0730.   Wagons attacked
                      Powell killed
5. 19 June: 1100.   Ezintandaneni attacked

house, followed by the celebratory 'Ji!', 'it is done'. But Robbins was not finished: he grabbed hold of the assegai and was pulled out of the room onto the veranda, the weapon lacerating his hand as he tried to wrestle it away from his attacker. He was stabbed again three times, then stunned by a blow to the head by a knobkerrie, but managed to shout out, 'Why are you killing me?'. At this three men came forward, two driving off his assailants while one protected him with his shield. They got Robbins through the crowd, off the veranda, around to the back of the house. He had terrible abdominal wounds, and the blood pouring down his face obscured his vision, but he did hear Sangereid shout, 'Save me Mr Robbins', as he ran from the house, stumbled, and was stabbed to death. The store was looted, and the cattle and other livestock taken from the kraal.

Robbins never discovered who the men who saved him were, but one of them hid him in the shrubbery in the garden. Here he managed to press some leaves onto his wounds and heard Ndlovu's and the Mbedu men singing as they moved off in different directions. He then passed out. When he came round the sun was up, and he staggered towards the house, where his servant got him onto a bed, dressed his wounds with strips of calico, then went to get help. By mid-morning troops and a doctor had arrived to bury Sangereid and arrange for Robbins to be taken on an agonising cart journey to Stanger.

The main body of the attackers had driven the cattle out of the kraal and back down the road. Just before they got to the Otimati stream, Ndlovu and a party of men turned off left, following a path steeper but more direct than the road. Once they had reached the high ground, just after seven, they saw that the convoy of wagons had started its journey to Maphumulo and was moving out of the Otimati valley. Looking towards the right, they could see another store, this one belonging to the Oglesbys', father and son. A section of Ndlovu's men made for the road along which the wagons were moving, in order to cut them off. Sergeant Knox was in the lead wagon when the attack was made from both sides of the road. The drivers and *voorloopers* made off despite the shouts that no black man would be killed. Taken by surprise Knox was struck on the head, his rifle seized, and he was stabbed. But he gathered all his strength, burst through his attackers, and ran for his life up the road towards Maphumulo. Trooper Powell in the last wagon ran off in the other direction towards the Oglesbys' store a few hundred metres away.

Fred Oglesby was already about. He had been woken by two customers who warned him that there was an *impi* on the road. Fred's father, Thomas Oglesby, was still in bed drinking his morning coffee when his son told him to dress as an *impi* was coming. His reply of 'Nonsense' was contradicted by the arrival of the terrified Powell, who jumped over the store counter pleading for help. Behind the store, over the brow of the steep hill, there was a krans that could serve as a hiding place. Oglesby senior and Powell began to scramble up the hill while Fred stayed behind to secure the store. He then followed his father and the trooper, and was about fifty metres behind them when he heard a shout and an order to stop. It was given by an *induna* of Ndlovu's, Luhoho:

> 'We are Ndhlovu's men and you are not to run away. We have not come to stick you, or to kill you . . .' I asked what chance I had if I came back. 'You have known us long enough. You know Ndhlovu. We never break our word.'[23]

Fred Oglesby halted and shouted to his father to do the same. But Trooper Powell was terrified and pleaded with the older man to show him the way down to the krans. As they moved over the crest of the hill, a number of armed Zulu rushed past them, ignored Thomas Oglesby, but seized the uniformed Powell. One man disarmed him and pulled his tunic aside, feeling for his heart. In terror Powell, the master to the end, shouted, 'No! No! Ikona (don't) boy!'. He was held upright and an assegai was thrust downwards, from the right, into his heart, then twisted. The blood gushed from the wound, his head fell back, and Oglesby heard the deep sigh as his lungs contracted. Just at this moment the now distraught and exhausted seventy-two-year-old Oglesby heard his Zulu name being called.

> I looked round to see what it was, and they said 'Tekwana, Tekwana'. I went towards him; and when I got a few yards, he says 'Pansi pansi,' so I sat down. He came up towards me, about 20 yards off, I should think then, just over the rise, and he says 'Don't be frightened'. He spoke in English. 'Tekwana, I won't hurt you.'[24]

The man was Mbhixa, who, as Charlie, had worked for Oglesby years before in Durban. He grabbed hold of his ex-boss, and, fighting off the men who surrounded him, got him away down the hill to the store.

Fred was already there on the veranda confronting a crowd of armed men who abused and taunted him. One of them, still a boy, made a grab for the revolver hanging round his neck but another of the men who had worked with the Oglesbys in Durban intervened, and a blow to the head sent the boy reeling. Oglesby then handed the revolver over to Luhoho, on condition that he give it to Ndlovu.[25]

The chief was sitting next to the road a few hundred metres away from the store. He knew the Oglesbys well: the store was close to Ndlovu's main homestead, Ezintandaneni, and was a meeting place where not only goods but also information were traded. Ndlovu apologised for what had happened to them, but said it was beyond his control. The people had risen because they had been imprisoned, thrashed, had their cattle taken, and were unjustly taxed. They had had enough and were determined to get some of their money back, by taking the cattle from Thring's Post. Ndlovu knew he could not stop them, but he might control them:

he had insisted that they were not to harm women, children, or those not fighting. The Oglesbys were to go back to the store, get some food and clothing, make the place secure, and they would then be escorted to the mission station where Ndlovu would place a guard to make sure that neither they nor the missionary and his family would be harmed.

This was done. Ndlovu assured the Norwegian missionary and his wife they would be safe if they kept close to the station, and the armed party moved past the mission station on to Ndlovu's homestead. They had just reached it when a small mounted party of militia, alerted by the wounded Knox, arrived from Maphumulo. It hurried past the mission station, and onto the high ground over the valley in which Ezintandaneni was built. Groups of Zulu were hiding in the caves, cliffs and the reeds of the streams. The dozen troopers began to scramble down into the valley and, using their rifles, scattered the Zulu close to the path who tried to stop them. They might have been in trouble, but before the Zulu could organise a defence, a squadron of fifty more mounted men arrived and began to move down into the valley in support. Ndlovu's Zulu fell back looking for protection in the broken country and bushveld downstream. The troopers came after them and 'swept' the valley for an hour-and-a-half. They killed a hundred and fifty Zulu without loss to themselves.

James Stuart's history of the rebellion makes the point that, in terms of the ratio of the number of men involved, Zulu losses were the highest in this 'Action at Otimati'. He writes up the clash as if it had been only the troops' dash and bravery that saved them from the ambush Ndlovu's men had laid for them. This is just one example of the sustained attempt to characterise violent actions on the part of the troops as battles undertaken by courageous troopers against a wily foe, a distortion that has profoundly affected subsequent histories of the rebellion. The evidence in fact shows that most of the Zulu were overtaken by the troops as they sought to get themselves and their cattle out of the way and down towards the broken terrain nearer the Thukela – and that the delay caused by Ndlovu making arrangements for the protection of the Oglesbys and the missionary worked to their disadvantage.

After dispersing Ndlovu's men the militia then moved back to Oglesbys' store and searched for Trooper Powell. They found his mutilated body later in the day, pulled away from the path to the krans, into the longer grass.

The attack on Thring's Post was a cattle raid provoked by military harassment. It is probable that the attack on the wagon train was made primarily to obtain the body of a soldier. In the various skirmishes on 19 June all the civilians were saved by the direct intervention of either armed Zulu or by Ndlovu himself – with the exception of the storekeeper Sangereid, who seems to have been killed in the undisciplined confusion of the raid, although some said it was to stop him telegraphing a warning. His body had not been mutilated. Attempts were made to kill both the troopers with the wagon train: Sergeant Knox's athleticism allowed him to escape; Trooper Powell was caught and killed by a precise assegai thrust to the heart. His abdominal cavity had not been opened by the assailant as was the ritual practice after a violent killing; but pieces of scalp and skull, eyebrow and upper lip, and penis had been removed as ingredients to be used in the ritual strengthening of men for battle.

The use of the body to transfer the strengths and skills from the dead to the living was a feature of African beliefs with precedents deep in Zulu history. It was an extension of the ideas underlying the making of the *inkatha* – the collection and binding of materials associated with the bodies of those over whom one wished to exercise power and control. Its workings were mysterious, as were the *izinyanga* with the reputation for preparing such materials. The Colensos felt that using human body parts as *materia medica* was a 'practice generally reprobated, but which has been supposed to have been resorted to occasionally', and one which colonial medical practice influenced and confirmed:

Various scientific practices, e.g. the preservation in spirits of strange growths extracted from the human body, the dissection of the body, &c., of which they hear by report, have tended to keep up, among the more credulous natives, the belief that such materials are efficacious for healing or injury, and in use among Europeans. The fear of this is one great difficulty with which European practicioners have to contend, until they become known and trusted. Quacks among the native medicine men possibly encourage the belief as tending to increase the prestige of the profession.[26]

Events in Natal in 1906 encouraged it as well. As the Natal militia spread violence and death, so more people had to find ways to protect themselves from the rifles, machine guns and artillery. They had numbers, but did not have the weapons to match the militia's fire-power. There were, however, *izinyanga* who knew how to draw on African beliefs to give protection and strength. And this included supplementing their medicine with parts of the bodies of those ranged against them.

It was not an easy idea to accept. Many of the older men had seen personally the effects of the British fire-power on the Zulu army in 1879. But it was rooted deep in history and belief, and was now given added strength by the increasingly desperate situation of so many Africans. And they would be wrong to ignore any chance of gaining an advantage over an enemy possessed not only with formidable weaponry, but also with powerful medicine themselves. Why else would the troopers have delivered the decomposing head from the Mome gorge to the militia's doctors?

Notes

1. *Native Affairs Commission 1906-7*, Evidence, Evidence of William Clark Robbins, 1 November 1906, 40.
2. For the analysis on which this is based see Jeff Guy, 'Gender oppression in southern Africa's precapitalist societies' in *Women and Gender in Southern Africa to 1945* (ed. Cherryl Walker), Cape Town: David Philip, 1990.
3. Paraphrasing Marx: 'Thus the ancient conception, in which man always appears ... as the aim of production, seems very more exalted than the modern world, in which production is the aim of man and wealth the aim of production', *Karl Marx: Pre-Capitalist Economic Formations* (translated by Jack Cohen and edited by E.J. Hobsbawm), New York: International Publishers, 1965, 84.
4. This history forms a major part of Michael Mahoney, 'Between the Zulu king and the great white chief: political culture in a Natal chiefdom, 1879-1906', PhD, UCLA, 1998. My approach and reading of the sources, however, produces a different interpretation.
5. For the genealogical connections refer to Figure 1.
6. The documentation of this investigation can be found in PAR: SNA, I/1/277, an extraordinarily rich collection of historical sources – from which no definite conclusions were, or can be, drawn. The Stuart *Archive* is replete with references to these disputes – but anyone wishing to sample them through the words of a participant should refer to *Archive* 3, Evidence of Mmemi kaNguluzawe, 267ff.
7. Stuart, *Archive* 3, Meseni kaMusi, 9 August 1904, 100.
8. Stuart, *Archive* 4, Evidence of Ndhlovu kaTimuni, 8 November 1902.
9. Stuart, *Archive* 4, Evidence of Ndhlovu kaTimuni, 8 November 1902.
10. Stuart, *Archive* 4, Evidence of Ndhlovu kaTimuni, 10 November 1902.
11. Stuart, *Archive* 3, Mbovu kaMtshumayeli, 16 September 1904, Note by Mbovu.
12. Stuart, *Archive* 4, Evidence of Ndhlovu kaTimuni, 1 January 1903.
13. PAR: SNA I/1/333, 84/06, Circular 22/12/05, RR172.
14. Stuart, *Archive*, 5, Evidence of J. Shepstone, 310-311.
15. Compare BPP: 2905, No. 29, McCallum to Elgin, 23 February 1906 paragraph 2 with No. 39, 9 March 1906 paragraph 4. See also Stuart, *Archive* 5, C.R. Saunders, 5 December 1906, 265.
16. BPP: C.2905, No. 39, McCallum to Elgin, 9 March 1906.
17. PAR: RSC I/1/96, Rex *v.* Meseni and Ndhlvou ka Timuni, Notes of Evidence and Findings of the Court, Evidence of Ndlovu,17 July 1906.
18. PAR: RSC I/1/96, Rex *v.* Meseni and Ndhlvou ka Timuni, Statement by Meseni, 17 July 1906.
19. PAR: PM 60, Hulett to Smythe, 20 May 1906.
20. PAR: RSC I/1/96, Rex *v.* Meseni and Ndhlvou ka Timuni, Evidence of Ndlovu, 17 July 1906.
21. PAR: RSC I/1/95, Rex *v.* Sifo and Mabalengwe, Evidence of Ndlovu, 30 May 1907.

22. PAR: 1/MPO, 5/4, Statement by Bixa, 2 August 1906.
23. PAR: RSC I/1/96, Rex *v.* Meseni and Ndhlovu ka Timuni, Evidence of Fred Howard Oglesby, 16 July 1906.
24. PAR: RSC I/1/95, Rex *v.* Sifo and Mabalengwe, Evidence of Thomas Davey Oglesby, 28 May 1907.
25. As the time passed, and additional legal investigation further complicated the evidence, so it becomes less clear just who these men who saved the Oglesbys were. But the fact of their being saved on Ndlovu's order, by men who had once worked for them, is clear.
26. Colenso's *Zulu-English Dictionary* entry for *Cwata (U)*. This entry is not in the 1861 edition of the dictionary but can be found in the 4th revised edition of 1905 and seems to have been added by Harriette Colenso. This is the only reference I have come across in the contemporary records to the word – literally 'hairless' – and used in this context as a euphemism.

3

Confrontation

19–29 June 1906

Mutual mobilisation

The same morning, 19 June 1906, *The Natal Mercury* informed its readers that the 'Rebellion Ceases To Exist'. Within hours the telegraph announced its resurgence, this time in the densely populated Maphumulo division on the borders of the vulnerable farms and sugar estates of the Lower Thukela division, only a day's journey from Durban itself. The scares began immediately. Ndlovu's people were in rebellion. White civilians had been attacked. A trooper had been killed and his body hideously mutilated. Meseni was planning to attack Hulett's Kearsney estate and then move on Stanger. The cane fields would be burnt, the railway line sabotaged, Durban was to be attacked. The houses on the sugar and tea estates were barricaded, a laager was constructed at Stanger and women and children were sent out of the district. The militia commanders, still mopping up higher in the Thukela river valley, began to prepare to move troops, supplies and artillery towards Maphumulo, and call in more reinforcements. In the days that followed, squadrons of troops began to converge on Maphumulo. Some came from Zululand, crossing the Thukela at Middle drift and moving up to Kranskop and then on to Greytown; others crossed the river further down at Bond's drift, reaching the Stanger-Maphumulo road at Thring's Post. They were supplemented by the volunteer militia from the Durban area, and by the end of the week the Durban militia (with Sergeant-Major Gandhi's stretcher-bearers in attendance) were marching from Stanger along the main road, past the Hulett tea estates at Kearsney, to Maphumulo to join the troops gathering there.

Every action on one side caused a counter-reaction on the other. In response to the mobilisation of the militia, Africans did what they could to move their non-combatants and livestock nearer to the centres of authority like Stanger where they might be less vulnerable to opportunistic violence from either side. Some armed and mobilised, and began to search for a place to gather in safety away from the eyes of the scouts and spies of the militia; others, at different times, did both.

The movement of squadrons of troops in the direction of the Native Reserves provoked a further movement of Africans towards their rural homesteads and their chiefs. Many left their places of employment to do so. African workers in Durban were dominated by men whose homesteads were in the Lower Thukela and Maphumulo divisions, just a day or two's journey from their place of work, and many of them were Qwabe. Before the rebellion began, soon after the announcement of the poll tax, James Stuart, then magistrate in Durban, had taken it upon himself to call a meeting to inform Durban workers of what was happening. He was soon brought into line by his administrative superiors, who felt orders and not explanations were called for, and by chiefs who felt that they should be consulted over what messages were conveyed to the men under them. As a result, what Stuart sought to avoid, happened. Rumours about the tax, the manner in which it was being implemented, and resistance to it back at home spread rapidly amongst the Durban workers, while chiefs like Mashwili and Meseni sent messages warning of coming conflict and ordering their people to return to protect their homes and their chiefs. To the waverers the mobilisation of the Durban militia late in June confirmed that the expected trouble had arrived. It was estimated that within ten days some two thousand men left the city – one thousand leaving their jobs at the harbour, seven hundred rickshaw-pullers, nearly half the Africans in the Durban borough police – while the middle-class houses on the Berea went into crisis as their domestic servants deserted, to make their way to their own homes in the Maphumulo and Lower Thukela divisions.[1]

Once they arrived at their homesteads, their next step was determined largely by where they were situated in relation to their chief, the authorities and centres of resistance. Differences in topography and systems of land tenure demanded different tactics. The response of those with homesteads in the Lower Thukela division and therefore living in open country on or amongst privately-owned farms, had to be different from that of those from the depths of the Maphumulo division on communal land and a two-day walk from their chief or the magistrate.

There were three areas of mobilisation in the divisions, all differently structured according to such demands. Meseni's homestead, eMthandeni, in the fairly remote middle reaches of the Mvoti river valley, became a centre of mobilisation for his people and their sympathisers, spread through the four divisions north of Durban. Ngobizembe's Ntuli (now under Sambela) and Ndlovu's Zulu, living between Maphumulo and the Thukela, fell back on the fastnesses in the direction of the river, seeking protection in the thornbush and broken ground through which mounted troops found it difficult to move. Once secure they were able to make contact with Mashwili's Mthethwa, who had gathered downriver, in the bush of the ravine that the Izinsimba stream had cut on its way to the Thukela. There the caves and crevices of Izinsimba gorge provided cover only a few hundred metres from Mashwili's homestead. But they were also within a few kilometres of a police post, stores and farms of the Lower Thukela division.

Lower Thukela: Mashwili at Izinsimba

The Maphumulo division had been split from the Lower Thukela division in 1894. Although geographically adjacent, the two divisions exemplified different extremes of the systems of rural land tenure and administration in Natal. Maphumulo was a Native Reserve, away from the sea, much of the land lying in the hot, deep river valleys, but including the higher, cooler high ground along which ran the main road. Apart from the mission reserves, the land was directly under the authority of chiefs who reported to the division's magistrate. In Maphumulo there were concentrations of homesteads under chiefly rule often remote from the administrative centres and their police.

In the Lower Thukela division the homesteads were under chiefs, but scattered on the privately-owned farms and crown lands of this fertile, rolling strip of territory twenty to thirty kilometres wide, running parallel with the coast. With the Thukela and the Thongati rivers marking its extremes, and divided by another (the Mvoti), the Lower Thukela division was topographically typical of the Natal coastal districts: undulating grassland with extensive tracts of coastal bush on rain-facing slopes and river valleys and their feeder streams, steeper and deeper, away from the coast. Apart from mission reserves and some crown land, the Lower Thukela division had been settled since the early years of the colony as private or company property. By the turn of the century some of the colony's best known families – the Addisons, Huletts, Hindsons, Colenbranders – had built their wealth on tea and sugar estates in the Lower Thukela division. In amongst their plantations were extensive tracts of land belonging to the Natal Land and Colonisation Company occupied by large numbers of rent-paying African families who, with small white farmers, looked with resentment at the Indian families, newly-released from indenture, who used family labour to exploit the produce market in a way they had never been able to. Although the African population was grouped under specific chiefs, this did not necessarily give rise to spatially contiguous social groupings, and people owing their allegiance to individual chiefs were often scattered throughout the division.

In the Lower Thukela division the proximity of the colonial presence forced a different response from that which characterised the rebellion in Maphumulo. For here, in Lower Thukela, living amongst the mission stations, farm houses, tea and sugar plantations and mills, men could not assemble, hunt and march, wearing the *shokobezi* and carrying shields and assegais. They had to make their way to the borders or out of the Lower Thukela division altogether if they were to assemble beyond the reach of the authorities and their spies, in places of safety.

The northern reaches of the Lower Thukela division were dominated by the section of the Qwabe in the charge of Ntshingumuzi, the acting-chief and regent, whose people were settled on private farms, mission lands, company farms and crown lands in these rich, coastal lands between the Mvoti river and the Thukela valley. But they paid for the privilege. Of the one thousand two hundred huts in the possession of Ntshingumuzi's people in 1905, one hundred were situated on mission reserve land and thus had recently become subject to a £3 tax per house, two hundred on crown land taxed at £2 a hut, and nine hundred on private farms and thus subject to increasing rentals for occupation, land and grazing and, when they failed to pay, the expense of uncertain legal protection.

Ntshingumuzi's people experienced all the deprivations arising from the crop failures and epidemics that characterised the opening years of the twentieth century, and the tensions caused by the rumours of coming conflict. Living on white and state-owned land, they were particularly vulnerable economically. Increasing agricultural investment on the part of white and Indian farmers, large and small-scale, and the development of tea and sugar production in the Lower Thukela division especially, had created pressure on land and forced up rents. The answer to this was clear enough, and carried with it a host of painful social problems – wage labour on the mines and in the towns.

As we have seen, in the latter part of 1905 Ntshingumuzi had employed the *inyanga* Mbombo to strengthen his section of the Qwabe and cure the illness that so weakened the chiefs of this lineage. Mbombo's diagnosis was that the problem lay in the inadvertent destruction of the *inkatha*, the grass coil which, through its incorporation of physical traces of the chief's opponents, asserted his power and strength. Two new *izinkatha* were made and a ceremony held where the men of the lineage were cleansed, strengthened, and the shades of the ancestors invoked to attend to the living. But in these difficult times Ntshingumuzi was not content just with ritual strategies. He joined in the protests made by the Lower Thukela division chiefs at the meetings called by the magistrate to proclaim the poll tax. These meetings were not as tumultuous as those held in Maphumulo at the end of January – but they were protests nonetheless – firm statements that this tax could not be added to the financial burdens the people were already carrying.

Ntshingumuzi came with his leading men. His statement was succinct:

> We have come to say the poll tax is oppressive. We find it a burden to pay the rents to our Landlords. We ask why has the Government imposed the Tax upon us.[2]

Two days later another of the division's leading chiefs made his protest: the poll tax was not only oppressive in itself, but it also broke the conventions that determined the proper relations between ruler and subject. It was delivered by Langalibalele, son of Mashwili and the great-grandson of Dingiswayo of the Mthethwa.

> We say that the poll tax will overcome us. It is a burden upon us and is worse than if illness was upon us. We say do we not belong to the Government, if not to whom do we belong? Why has this thing been done? Is there anything which has been hidden by us from the Government? We contribute to the support of the Government. That which we were called upon to pay we

have paid. The payment of Hut Tax is a burden as also is the payment of the Dog tax. We say there is not Government, but that there is a person who has no consideration for us who does not hear us. The Poll Tax has even stirred up the stupid person.[3]

But the Lower Thukela division did not experience serious disruption in the opening months of 1906, when the militia were sweeping southern Natal, and Bhambatha attacked the police and made for the Nkandla. Patrols on the roads used terror to install what they considered to be due respect for the king's uniform, and martial law was used against those believed to be spreading rumours or secreting weapons, but there were no obvious acts of open resistance. This suddenly changed, however, with the news of Ndlovu's 19 June attack on Thring's Post store, and the movement of colonial troops towards the area.

The two hundred and fifty homesteads for which Mashwili was responsible were in both the Lower Thukela and Maphumulo divisions, and straddled the boundary that followed the Izinsimba river, much of its course deeply incised between the precipitous bush-covered cliffs. Mashwili was too old to lead directly, and this role was assumed by his son, Langalibalele. Ntshingumuzi was also old, and his options limited by his proximity to the centre of authority at Stanger. The leadership of the armed Qwabe was taken up by Mahlanga, a son of Mamfongonyana, the founder of this section of the Qwabe lineage. He had been working in Johannesburg for seven years when his wives succeeded in securing his arrest for desertion, and he had been returned to his homestead by the authorities. Mahlanga mobilised the section of the Qwabe who lived on the Thukela side of the Nonoti, adjacent to the people of Mashwili with whom they joined forces.[4] The right bank of the Thukela was now under rebel authority for some thirty kilometres, as the Qwabe and Mthethwa of the Lower Thukela linked with Ndlovu's Zulu and Sambela's Ntuli of the Maphumulo division in their retreats further up the Thukela valley.

Mahlanga's section of Ntshingumuzi's Qwabe, and Mashwili's Mthethwa, made for a point on the Izinsimba about half-way along its length, where it leaves the higher grasslands, and enters the dry riverine bushveld, and where it has cut a deep gorge with extensive patches of bush covering its steep rocky sides. It was a border position in all its aspects: on the one side just a few kilometres away was a police station, a few stores, then the white-owned estates on which the Qwabe lived as tenants; on the other the open fields and communal grazing land of the Mthethwa; and beyond them the people of Ndlovu kaThimuni, who had precipitated this episode with their attack on Thring's Post on 19 June. Between these tracts of privately-owned and communal land, hidden in the Izinsimba gorge which separated them, were the rebel Qwabe and Mthethwa. Here they could protest at increased taxes and rents; share their experiences of wage labour in docks, settler homes and mines; wear military dress, sing songs of defiance, celebrate rituals, out of sight of the spies, the scouts, police patrols, African levies and settler militia. When newcomers arrived at Izinsimba they were kept apart until they had been purified, after which they could participate in the rituals essential for their strength and protection when the time for direct conflict arrived. The common view amongst their enemies was that these rituals were carried out in order to destroy the effectiveness of the bullets used against them. Too many of the men at Izinsimba had experience of colonial fire-power to believe this unreservedly. But it was generally accepted that the strengthening of the soldiers, and its reciprocal effect, the weakening of the enemy, was essential; and perhaps with powerful medicine, like that which Ndlovu was said to have obtained from the body of the trooper, the bullets might be stopped.

We can get an idea of what it is was like in the Izinsimba gorge from the evidence of Mahagawu, a Durban worker whose homestead was situated in the northern parts of the Lower Thukela division.[5] He had previously been contacted at work by messengers from his chief, Mashwili, who instructed him to return home as there was trouble there caused by the white people. He delayed until the news of Ndlovu's attack of 19 June when he joined the hundreds of Durban workers making their way to the Lower Thukela division.

From Stanger he began to walk in the direction of his homestead but found it deserted. On the way the people he met asked him anxiously where the whites were. He broke into a hut and spent a night disturbed by the sound of people running by in the dark. The next day he came across an armed man who responded angrily to his questions: 'I spoke and asked what was the matter? He replied "We are being done to death by the white people." I asked him how? He said "Do you ask, they are oppressing us that we must die." ' He followed the tracks made by large numbers of people, until he came across women carrying provisions for the men[6] who had gathered around his chief, Mashwili, in the Izinsimba gorge.

It was now Monday 25 June. Most of the men were camped on the Ndaka stream, which ran its short length into the Izinsimba gorge from its source just below Mashwili's homestead. When Mahagawu arrived there, he was ordered not to mix with them until he had been purified and strengthened as they had been. Sitting apart he watched the slaughtering of cattle taken from the homesteads of the uncommitted, and listened to the men around their fires in the mid-winter cold. They congratulated him on changing his mind and coming to Izinsimba: 'You are with us today – you deserted us in Durban – and he called the doctor to doctor me.'

While waiting, he saw that preparations were being made for the ritual sprinkling (ukuchela) of soldiers with medicine. Then there was a stir amongst the men. Someone shouted a command – it was in English: 'Fall in!' 'Fall in!' The people around Mahagawu asked who the man was. They were told it was 'Benetu' – 'Bayonet' – better known as Ndlovu kaThimuni. One of the izinyanga present was called Mabalengwe.

Six days had passed since the raid on the Thring's Post store, the killing of trooper Powell, and the attack on Ndlovu's people. Much of 20 June had been spent attending to the wounded, and gathering and regrouping the women and children who had been scattered by the militia's attack. They assembled further down the Timati river, with the assistance of Sambela. Here a number of rituals took place, including a cleansing ceremony for those who had killed in battle.[7] The women, children and livestock had been secured in the broken, precipitous thornbush country towards the Thukela, and they had escaped two attempts by the militia to flush them out on 22 and 23 June. Ndlovu and Mabalengwe, the *inyanga* from Sambela, were then able to move to where the armed Mthethwa and Qwabe had gathered in the Izinsimba gorge under Mashwili.

One purpose of the visit was to instil in the men the conviction that it was possible to confront white troops and survive. It was still believed, or at least hoped, that a Zulu force sent by Dinuzulu would soon reach the Thukela. With these reinforcements they would have sufficient numbers to mobilise, and drive the troops from the Maphumulo heights, cross over into the Mvoti valley, where they could join the thousands of armed men gathered around Meseni at eMthandeni.

But this could only be done if they mobilised enough men to offset the advantages that manoeuvrability and advanced military technology gave the militia. They had to forget the losses inflicted on them by a few dozen colonial troopers on the slopes below Ndlovu's Ezintandaneni. In order to encourage this Mabalengwe brought with him medicine made potent with the flesh of the recently killed Trooper Powell. It was dreadful and strong enough to counter the medicines made by those who had removed the head from the body at Mome gorge, and the terrible killing power that mobility and modern arms gave the force that opposed them.

Ndlovu and Mabalengwe came to the stronghold in the Izinsimba to demonstrate what could be done. Ndlovu carried Trooper Powell's rifle and bayonet and he presented Mashwili with the revolver that had belonged to Fred Oglesby.[8] He also used the enemy's military rituals. 'Fall in!' became an incantation. And he appropriated not just the command – 'Fix bayonets' – but the name of the weapon for himself: 'The people said "Who is that?" Others said "Do you not know it is the voice of Benetu who is Ndhlovu?" '[9] Then the armed men of Mashwili and Ntshingumuzi were 'formed into line and they sang these words "I am thus, what has made me go wrong, It is the Poll Tax that has made me go wrong" – they fell in, and made a noise "qo, qo qo" '.

That evening a party of Mthethwa and Qwabe under the leadership of Mahlanga left the stronghold for a foray into the Lower Thukela division. Their target was one John Boziana, an African Christian and owner of a thousand acres of land in the Nonoti area. His cattle were seized, he was dragged out his house, assaulted, and force-marched the ten kilometres to the Izinsimba.

After a freezing cold night he was brought before Mashwili. The previous day the *inkosi* Ndlovu, alias 'Benetu' – the Bayonet, had appropriated the enemy's military ritual and incorporated it into the Zulu one. Now Mashwili kaMngoye, the old Mthethwa *inkosi*, appropriated the judicial ones.[10] Presiding over a court he charged Boziana with being a 'scout' – that is, a spy, an informer, a traitor to his people – who had sold the inheritance left them by their founder Shaka.

'Scout, you are here today. Where is Mr Shuter? How can you go now to make secret reports. You take letters from Jackson and find out the people. Where is Jackson today? – you are alone – You buy the land which belonged to Shaka, now you worry the Natives. You worry the Natives by chasing them from the land and you put on Indians. You also say the people must pay the Poll Tax.'

Then Mashwili said 'Make reply scout'.

I replied 'My only sin is that I have buried Chiefs who died'. I said 'I had buried Sotondose and Manepu of Nxumalo tribe, and Zidumo of the Qwabe tribe.'

> Then Mashwili called the men to bring up the cattle belonging
> to the scout – and four of my cattle were there and then killed.
> He said the others would be slaughtered the next day. Then the
> order was given that I was to be kept under an armed guard.[11]

The lines were being drawn. Those men not gathering around their
chiefs and rebel leaders were seen to be on the side of the
authorities, those who had taken the land of Shaka. Threats turned
to violence, kidnapping and physical assault. On 28 June, one of
Mamfongonyana's sons killed a man living on the crown lands at
Nonoti, some said because he was not with the rebels at the
Izinsimba, some said because of personal differences for which the
rebellion provided a 'shield' to cover the deed.[12] As June drew to
an end, more and more people began to fear the repercussions of
attempted neutrality, and took up their weapons and made their
way to Izinsimba.

But there were also those who moved in the opposite direction.
Ntshingumuzi, the man who in the previous year had overseen the
ritual that sought to strengthen the unity of his people alive and
dead, himself broke the bonds that united them. On 29 June[13] he
left his homestead and moved his property towards the Mvoti. He
then reported to the magistrate, who placed his ward, Mfomfo, in
the Stanger gaol for safety. Most of his people, however, had already
moved to Izinsimba – or joined the dominant section of the Qwabe
assembled at the chief Meseni's homestead at eMthandeni in the
Mvoti valley.

Maphumulo: Meseni at eMthandeni

On the southern side of the road between Stanger and Maphumulo,
near the middle reaches of the Mvoti river, armed men were
assembling around Meseni at the famous Qwabe homestead,
eMthandeni. Most of the men gathered there were Qwabe with
homes in the Maphumulo and Lower Thukela divisions, but as the

days passed so men from more distant homesteads arrived, including the Ndwedwe and Inanda divisions which shared a boundary with Durban itself. And they were not only Meseni's Qwabe. There were men from his rival Qwabe faction, the Nkwenkwezi, and from chiefdoms like the Nyuswa, who had been in conflict with the Qwabe for years and whose chief had committed himself to the government side. eMthandeni was becoming a focus for all those who had decided that the movement of colonial troops had to be countered. On Friday 22 June, Meseni organised a hunt thus keeping the men present productively occupied and creating a sense of solidarity through shared activity and ritual.

eMthandeni was only some fifteen kilometres south of the Maphumulo magistracy, but it was three hundred metres below it, and the steep sides of the Mvoti valley made access difficult. The militia, now arriving in increasing numbers, were concentrated on the high ground along the main road between Maphumulo and Thring's Post from where they made sorties in a northerly direction down the river valleys, trying to find where Sambela and Ndlovu's people and cattle had taken cover. But, as we have seen, they were unable to locate them in the dense thornbush and precipitous broken country towards the Thukela. The result was that on 27 June Lieutenant-Colonel George Leuchars, commander of the Natal Mounted Rifles, turned his attention to the south towards eMthandeni. He ordered the militia onto a spur of high ground above the Mvoti valley and in sight of eMthandeni about ten kilometres away. The official history calls the move a 'recon-naissance', but it is hard to see what sort of reconnaissance required over five hundred troops supported by Maxims and artillery. It seems more likely that Leuchars hoped to provoke an attack that would expose the assailants to the militia's modern weaponry. As the militia dragged its guns over the steep broken country, it came across Qwabe hiding on the Pheyana hill and guarding the path into the valley. They broke cover and charged, thereby coming under fire from rifles, machine guns and the 15-pounders loaded

Lieutenant-Colonel George Leuchars, the victor
at Pheyana.
(*The Natal Mercury Pictorial*, 4 July 1906)

with shrapnel. Some seventy men were killed. A force estimated at
about four thousand was seen further down the valley towards
eMthandeni, but after firing some rounds of artillery in its direction
the colonial militia withdrew. It left behind a hundred and fifty
dead, most of them Qwabe from the Mhlali district, without loss to
themselves.

The clash was immediately misrepresented. The Governor
telegraphed London: 'two rebel impis . . . attacked Leuchars this
morning, but [were] repulsed without loss to us'.[14] Stuart's history
writes up this 'Action at Peyana' as if the colonial militia successfully
avoided a number of 'ingenious' attempts to draw it into carefully
laid ambushes. But Stuart is again creating the tactically aggressive
enemy he needs to demonstrate the military 'brilliance' of the

Although not taken at Pheyana, this photograph gives an idea of the way the guns were deployed in the rebellion generally.   (*The Natal Mercury Pictorial*, 22 August 1906)

colonial force and its leaders. For there is no evidence to suggest that the Qwabe, lying up on tracks leading down to the eMthandeni homestead, were on the offensive militarily; everything points to an essentially defensive strategy and that they were guarding one of the approaches to Meseni's homestead.

Meseni's men were armed of course. They wore the *shokobezi* and had been ritually treated to give them strength for conflict – but their orders were to defend the *inkosi* and his homestead. Whatever Meseni might wish to have done, or might have done if circumstances had suggested an effective aggressive strategy, there is no evidence that he did more than threaten the destruction of his enemies. Rather than initiate an attack, Meseni, only too aware of the consequences of arming his people, brooded on his predicament, deeply angry at the way he had been treated, indeed trapped, by those in authority.

Meseni was convinced that it been decided in Pietermaritzburg that he must be destroyed. After all, he had not been present in January when his people had shown their dissatisfaction at the poll tax – and yet he was held responsible for their behaviour. He had been gaoled for eleven days before his lawyer persuaded the authorities to release him. Then in spite of having no case against him, those in charge had removed from his authority all his people living on private lands, thereby arbitrarily reducing the power and status of a chief who believed his lineage to be of a higher status than that of the Zulu themselves. To him it was clear: the authorities, having failed in court, had decided to bring him down by force. And it was in response to this that he had called his people to gather around him and defend their *inkosi*, which they did willingly from all parts of the northern coastal districts of Natal. And there they waited, preparing themselves for the unavoidable conflict; some hoping against hope that the rumours of a Zulu army crossing the Thukela would become a reality, but unwilling to initiate an attack on an enemy with vastly superior weapons, thereby enabling the authorities to argue that Meseni was responsible for his own destruction, the despoiling of his lands, and the ruin of his people.

Now that his numerous appeals to the colonial courts had failed and colonial troops had appeared on the high ground to the north of his chiefdom, machine-gunned his sentinels, and lobbed artillery shells into the Mvoti valley amongst the homesteads of his people, Meseni had very few options open to him. The Mvoti valley did not have the deep, broken, thornbush-covered valleys like those into which Ndlovu and Sambela were able to retreat and hide their families and stock. The homesteads of the Qwabe were spread across the steeply rolling hills and up the lower slopes of the Mvoti valley and consequently, although rather remote and difficult of access, eMthandeni was still vulnerable to co-ordinated mounted attack.

But although there seemed no way to make an effective armed counter-attack on the enemy, there were other means that the Qwabe could use to defend themselves. Many of the men gathered round Meseni at eMthandeni believed that the storms, gales and floods which recently struck Natal were portents of change, perhaps even of the coming millennium and a new world. Resistance to the authorities was a necessary contribution to this imminent revelation of the kingdom of God and the creation of new people, free of the evil and greed in which the old world was trapped. A number of Christian preachers from nearby missions made their way to eMthandeni where they joined their prayers for assistance to those being made to the shades of the ancestors. The Qwabe shared in the widely held belief that the Zulu royal house was going to act and the forces from the north would cross the Thukela and join the struggle to repossess the land of Shaka Zulu's kingdom. As widespread, and as deep, was the belief that the rebels possessed powerful medicine that would weaken and bring darkness down upon the authorities, while strengthening and making firm those who resisted them. And while events like the massacre at Mome undermined these beliefs for some, for others despair and desperation made it only more necessary to find in recent events signs and portents upon which to base hope. The white soldiers had announced Bhambatha's death and sought to prove it by decapitating his corpse; but many knew that he was still alive, his medicine strong enough to overcome all the white troops' attempts to kill him. Dinuzulu, it was felt, must soon give substance to the reports that he would lead the uprising and reclaim the African inheritance left by Shaka to his descendants.

Rituals were an essential feature of life amongst the men gathered in the strongholds or around their chiefs' homesteads. Even before the rebellion broke out, Ntshingumuzi at eNkanini sought strength for his people by appeasing the shades, and all men who armed at Ndlovu's Ezintandaneni and joined Mashwili in the Izinsimba gorge were ritually cleansed and fortified. It was the same in the Mvoti valley. Men arriving at the eMthandeni homestead were only allowed to build their shelters and associate with those already there once they had been ritually purified. And as the numbers of the militia arriving in the division grew, so did the need for more potent medicine.

The use of such medicine had played an important role in Qwabe history. For example, it was said that, when Meseni's great-uncle, Phakathwayo, was an independent *inkosi*, the Qwabe had turned away an *inyanga* from the eMthandeni homestead – then built just south of the Mhlatuze river. The *inyanga* moved on to offer his skills to the young, still comparatively insignificant, *inkosi*, Shaka of the Zulu. Together they devised a plan to weaken Phakathwayo and the powerful Qwabe by inviting them to a dance at the Zulu homestead. Afterwards the *inyanga* carefully collected the dust thrown up by the dancers' feet and incorporated it into the Zulu *inkatha*. He gathered the excrement they left behind and mixed it with that of hyenas. From this he made a medicine that he placed in baskets in rivers, and in gourds, near the Qwabe homesteads. The streams spread the *intelezi* into the Qwabe's water supply, and cockroaches ate it then infected the Qwabe's eating utensils. As a result when the Zulu attacked the Qwabe, they were physically weak, suffering from diarrhoea, and could not defend themselves.[15]

Less than a century had passed since this incident which remained, with many other such stories, part of the Qwabe's historical tradition. Meseni had his own doctors: one of the most prominent was Sibhoko. He had come from the north, from Thonga country, half a century before, and was particularly successful in treating women with a tendency to miscarry. In mid-1906 he was at eMthandeni where he extended the range of his activities. After the Pheyana fight he had found an unexploded shell, removed the contents and added them to his *intelezi*. With the assistance of other *izinyanga* he purified the new arrivals by sprinkling them, after which they could associate with those already there. It was later said that the *inyanga* Mabalengwe, after his appearance at Izinsimba with Ndlovu, had moved rapidly over the ridge to eMthandeni arriving the day before the fight at Pheyana, carrying with him the powerful medicine that linked Meseni's men with those of Mashwili, Ndlovu, Sambela, Bhambatha and Dinuzulu. Strengthening took place under an *umGanu* tree near the homestead. Here a fire had been built upon whichs was placed the *udengezi* containing *intelezi*. The men formed up in *amaviyo*, companies, from their different districts. Sibhoko carried with him horns, and from these he produced medicine that he applied to Meseni's face, black on the one side, red on the other. The assembled men had been sprinkled as they walked past the pots, through the smoke and fumes, chanting, 'It is darkness for the whiteman'.

And as they did so, high on the Maphumulo ridge, the white man watched these movements at eMthandeni far below, and moved the troops and guns along the high road, preparing to attack.

Notes

1. *The Natal Mercury*, 29 June 1906, 'The Native Exodus' and BPP: C.3247, No. 13, McCallum to Elgin, 5 July 1906.
2. PAR: SNA I/4/15, 21/06, Shuter to under Secretary for Affairs, 3 January 1906, Statement by Ntshingumuzi and 43 others, 28 December 1906.
3. PAR: SNA I/4/15, 21/06, Shuter to under-Secretary for Affairs, 3 January 1906, Statement by Langalibalele, son of Mashwili and 9 others, 30 December 1906.
4. This information is derived from the report of Friend Addison, Commandant Stanger and District in PAR: CSO 2588, 5 December 1906.
5. Mahagawu became a regular witness before the Stanger Martial Law court when the crown needed to prove the presence of certain accused at Izinsimba. These paragraphs are a compilation of his evidence. While it is possible that he cast himself in a particularly favourable light with the authorities, his evidence is consistent and convincing. DAR: 1/SGR, Martial law note book, 1/4/2/1, 44/06, 30 July 1906 and (more important) 1/4/2/2, 56/06, 3 August 1906, Evidence of Mahagau.
6. The dominance of men in this narrative is obvious: to relegate women to a footnote might be seen as compounding this bias. For the crucial and unrecognised role of women not just in this rebellion but in the history of war in South Africa see Guy, 'Non-combatants and war: the unexplored factor in the conquest of the Zulu kingdom', (forthcoming).
7. From evidence given at subsequent trials it seems to me that rituals that took place after 19 June, in the comparative safety of the valley retreats, were transposed by crown witnesses to create a ritual that took place immediately after the killing but was interrupted by the arrival of the troops.
8. This is very much my reading of the events in the gorge, for evidence on the tactical thinking of the leaders is sparse. At the same time it is suggestive, and it would be an error to ignore it. A possible chronology is: 19 June, Ndlovu's

attack and the death of Powell; 20 June, Ndlovu and Mabalengwe down the Timati regrouping; 22 June and 23 June, avoiding troops near the Isiwasembuzi; 25 June, they are at the Izinsimba.

9. DAR: 1/SGR, Martial law note book, 1/4/2/2, 56/06, Evidence of Mahagau, 3 August 1906.

10. I would suggest that in this mimicking of colonial military and judicial structures there is an echo here, of a widespread feature of rebellious movements – the creation of alternative state hierarchies – be it King John and his court in early eighteenth-century England (Chapter 5, 'King John' in E.P. Thompson, *Whigs and Hunters: The Origin of the Black Act*, New York: Pantheon, 1975), or an African kingdom in industrialising South Africa (as in Chapter 4 'The Regiment of the Hills – Umkosi Wezintaba', of Charles van Onselen's, *New Nineveh*, Johannesburg: Ravan Press, 1982). *Umkhosi* is difficult to translate in this context but 'Kingdom' is a better rendition than 'regiment'.

11. DAR: 1/SGR, Martial law note book, 1/4/2/1, 43/06, 28 July 1906. Boziana gave evidence for the crown in a number of cases and this statement is a representative one.

12. PAR: AGO I/1/318, 52/07 , Rex *v.* Mtwasana, Deposition by Mapakete, 26 April 1907.

13. It was reported in *The Natal Mercury*, 30 June 1906.

14. BPP: C.3027, No. 74, McCallum to Elgin, 27 June 1906.

15. Stuart, *Archive*, 3, Evidence of Mmeni, 11 October 1904.

4

Manoeuvre and massacre

The encircling movement, 29 June – 5 July 1906

By the end of June, just ten days after Ndlovu's attack on the store and the wagon train, the number of soldiers in the Maphumulo division had increased from a few hundred to two-and-a-half thousand. They were from different colonial backgrounds but were united in their conviction that it was time to assert the authority of the white race in South Africa. The military ethos was a powerful force in colonial political and social life. From the short biographies of *The Natal Who's Who* of 1906 it is apparent that 'volunteering' was a popular form of recreation amongst the socially prominent, and an ominous one. Twenty-five-year-old W.A.Campbell wrote breathless with excitement to his sugar-baron father after the attack at Otimati: 'After we drove off the main attack we fixed Bayonets & cleared the bush. Several Natives were bayonetted & shot. I shot one old Buck with my revolver & wounded another. I fired over 50 rounds & of course cannot say whether I happened to have killed more as other men were firing. One I know I killed myself.'[1]

For the less prominent in this time of recession, active service against a vulnerable African enemy seemed an attractive alternative to unemployment. The Chief Constable of Durban was relieved that the 'very large number of unemployed Europeans, capable of bearing arms have joined our volunteers in the field',[2] and there is a photograph of unemployed Transvaal whites queuing for service in Zululand. When the head of the Natal Police left Johannesburg at the start of the rebellion, he had to be escorted through the crowd of men demanding the chance to join the colonial forces. As the train pulled out of the station they ran alongside throwing their business cards into his compartment. For Governor McCallum these were men who 'abandoned the ploughshare for the sword, and placed at our disposal your lives, your heart, and your strong right arm'.[3] For Harriette Colenso they were the 'out of works and Weary Willies'.[4] From the little evidence in their diaries and correspondence, and the enormous evidence of their actions, they were armed racists at the apex of the age of British imperialism, eager to loot and kill.

The Commandant, Colonel Duncan McKenzie, had crossed over the Thukela from Zululand and reached Thring's Post, where he was joined by his Acting-Commandant Major-General Sir John Dartnell – who had experienced the 'Indian Mutiny' half a century before, participated in the 1879 British invasion of Zululand, been Commissioner of Police and Commandant of the Volunteers in Natal, and served in the South African war. He was in retirement in England, and his return to Natal, accompanied by a newly developed light machine gun, had been sponsored by Natal businessmen in London. Other military commanders had also gained their reputations in the South African war. They included Lieutenant-Colonel Leuchars, commander of the Mvoti Rifles, who had destroyed Ngobizembe's homestead with artillery and was the victor in the 'Battle of Peyana'. Lieutenant-Colonel W. Barker of the South African Light Horse was in command of the Transvaal Mounted Rifles, a corps of some four hundred men raised at the Transvaal government's expense, who crossed over the Thukela into Natal 'flushed with their recent and brilliant successes in Zululand'.[5] Lieutenant-Colonel D.W. Mackay led the Natal Carbineers, and the Chief Staff Officer was Lieutenant-Colonel Sir Aubrey Woolls-Sampson who had gained some notoriety commanding irregulars raised by randlords in the South African war. Sir Abe Bailey personally sponsored another corps of

Sir Duncan McKenzie –
knighted for his services
during the rebellion.
(*The Natal Mercury Pictorial*,
12 December 1907)

mercenaries to whose thuggery ironic reference was made in their nickname, the 'rosebuds'. The Castle Beer Company sponsored a machine gun and the men needed to transport and fire it.

The commanders, like many of the men under them, were experienced in fighting in South African conditions, and conducting highly mobile campaigns of a fairly informal character using mounted infantry, supported by automatic weapons and artillery. Kipling's poem on the mounted infantry in the South African war extols their rough methods, contempt for authority, and reputation for thieving and looting. Their adaptation to local conditions is indicated by his use of South African slang – he calls them the 'Ikonas' – taken from the limited vocabulary of 'fanakolo' or 'kitchen kaffir', developed to give orders and derived from Zulu for 'Don't!', or 'Never!'. Although the poem celebrates the way in which English soldiers were brutalised by South African conditions, the sentiments apply just as well to the 'five-bob Colonials' who made up the troops in the 1906 rebellion.[6]

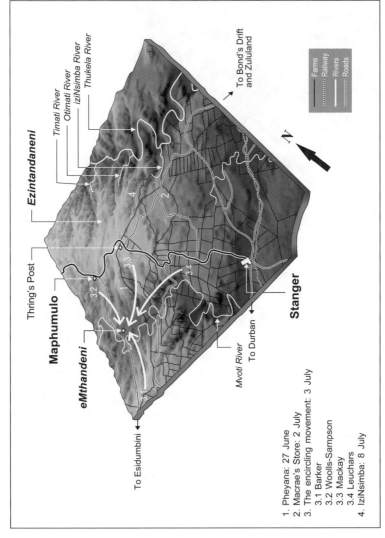

Conflict: 27 June – 8 July 1906.

Ezintandaneni

Timati River
Otimati River
iziNsimba River
Thukela River

To Bond's Drift
and Zululand

Farms
Railway
Rivers
Roads

N

Thring's Post

Maphumulo

eMthandeni

To Esidumbini

Stanger

Mvoti River
To Durban

1. Pheyana: 27 June
2. Macrae's Store: 2 July
3. The encircling movement: 3 July
   3.1 Barker
   3.2 Woolls-Sampson
   3.3 Mackay
   3.4 Leuchars
4. IziNsimba: 8 July

The Zulu rebels, by selecting ground through which it was difficult for horses, guns and heavy transport to move, were able to offset the militia's logistical advantages to a degree. Thus Ndlovu and Sambela retired to their hideouts in the bush and cliffs of their chiefdoms, out of which the militia were unable to drive them, at least without putting African 'loyals' in first, an action which the Zulu on the other side of the Thukela had refused to carry out. Towards the end of the month Leuchars made another attempt to drive the Thukela bush, but again the terrain proved too difficult for the mounted militia, and it was impossible to drag the guns into attacking positions. The tactic was abandoned and the militia once again turned its attention south towards the eMthandeni homestead that lay in the opposite direction in rather more open country. From the Maphumulo heights, thousands of armed men could be seen in the Mvoti valley, with the access routes guarded by smaller detachments – like the ones at Pheyana that had clashed with Leuchars's 'reconnaissance' force on 27 June.

McKenzie's new initiative was devised on a much larger scale. The forces north of the Thukela in Zululand were to be greatly reduced and military efforts would be concentrated south of the river in Natal. Meseni's eMthandeni homestead was selected as the focal point of a combined attack. Four columns would move on eMthandeni from different points, to converge on the homestead early on Tuesday 3 July, trapping the people there by means of this massive encircling movement. Crucial to the plan were the mobile Transvaal Mounted Rifles under Lieutenant-Colonel Barker, with two 15-pounders and two Maxims. They had the furthest to travel: after moving out of the Thukela valley to Kranskop, they were to travel by train from Greytown to Dalton on 29 June, where they were to wait for supplies railed from Pietermaritzburg. They would cross the drift on the Nsuze river, on their way on to the mission station Esidumbini. Here they would join the road that ran northwards to Maphumulo, crossing the drift on the Mvoti a few miles upstream from eMthandeni. The other columns disposed

themselves at different places on the Maphumulo heights, preparing
to rendezvous with Barker's column first thing on 3 July, after night
marches into the Mvoti valley.

On the opposing side meanwhile, the mobilisation of Qwabe
was spreading south. From Ndwedwe and Thongathi it was reported
that men had been seen making their way to eMthandeni, armed
with assegais and wearing the *shokobezi*. Others were gathering in
the more remote valleys or shouting challenges from the tops of
mountains. This alarmed the local colonial volunteers and the New
Hanover Reserves were convinced that they were about to be
attacked. Barker, making his way in from the west in order to get
in a position to move on eMthandeni on 3 July, was persuaded to
spend much of Sunday 1 July attempting to reach these volunteers
and give them protection.

eMthandeni, 1 July 1906: A wager lost

On the same day, on the same road for which Barker's column was
heading, but moving in the opposite direction, a man was making
his way, on a bicycle, down the steep track from Maphumulo, into
the Mvoti valley. He was Oliver Veal, an employee of the Public
Works Department, who on this weekend had taken a bet that he
could leave Pietermaritzburg after work on Friday, visit a friend of
his serving with the militia in Kranskop, and be back in
Pietermaritzburg via Durban by eight on Monday morning. He
was a keen cyclist, and for some of his more adventurous rides
through Natal borrowed an imported Haymarket Special from a
friend in Durban. He had the bicycle railed to Pietermaritzburg
over Friday night, and on Saturday morning transferred it to the
train that he caught to Greytown. He was unable, however, to find
his friend, and by midday on Sunday 1 July Oliver Veal was heading
for Durban. He reached the Maphumulo magistracy and military
post where he spoke with an officer who advised him for safety's
sake to keep to the Maphumulo-Stanger road. But Oliver Veal was
in a hurry. He decided to take a more direct route, turned off to

the right, down the track into the Mvoti valley, heading for the drift on the road that passed just west of eMthandeni on its way to Esidumbini and Thongati, where he hoped to get a train to Durban.

The drift at the Mvoti river was guarded by men from the Nyuswa chiefdom. Their chief, Swayimana, had placed himself under the protection of the authorities but many of his men had joined the Qwabe. Meseni had ordered them to watch the drift but, on that Sunday afternoon, instead of a squadron of mounted infantry, along the steep, rough track from Maphumulo came Oliver Veal, in the cycling gear of the time – hat, heather-brown jacket and knickerbockers. In the leather satchel on the cross bar were his toiletries, a change of underclothing and biscuits. The shout went up that a white man was coming. Veal outdistanced the main group of guards, and the assegais thrown in his direction, but two young Nyuswa men caught up with him further down the road. He dismounted protesting that he was merely passing through the district and had nothing to do with the conflict; but he had little *isiZulu* and, anyway, the men in the crowd that had gathered around were not interested in what he had to say and began to threaten him. *Izinduna* who were drinking beer at homesteads along the road, heard the shouts and ran down to get some control of the situation. Veal had to be taken to the *inkosi*. The metaphor of the hunt was used: Veal was the quarry, the white buck, *inyamazane emhlope*. Singing a song of victory, the party of armed men force-marched Veal along the track to eMthandeni some eight kilometres away.

Meseni was there at the time but he had appointed Macabacaba kaMagceni from the Ndwedwe district to take charge of the *impi*.[7] He was supervising the slaughter of cattle when news came that a white man had been captured. He ordered the Qwabe out of their temporary huts and to form a half circle on the open ground at the back of the homestead. With the arrival of the Nyuswa force escorting Veal, the circle closed. The crowd pressed on to those in the centre, the older men forcing the younger men to the back.

Some of them climbed trees for a better view. Meseni looked on for a while, and then left the homestead and went up the hill behind it to dig for medicinal roots. The path on which he later returned passed close to the assembled crowd. Meseni did not stop.

Macabacaba took charge and called on the young men who had captured the white buck to identify themselves. Veal was exhausted, weeping and hanging desperately onto an induna's arm, many felt for protection. The crowd around him was terrifying. There were a number of *amakholwa*, some dressed in clerical black with the white cow tail insignia of the Zulu royal house attached to their hats. There were *izinyanga* there as well. The Qwabe in the crowd then began to sing 'the great War song of the Qwabe tribe'.[8]

The singing was brought to an end and the circle broken up, and Macabacaba ordered the rank and file to go to their huts where they would be given meat. Some left; others moved some distance but could not tear themselves away completely, in spite of attempts by senior men to drive them off. Veal was moved some twenty metres and his pockets were searched. Amongst their contents was a diary. A *kholwa* read it and said it contained evidence that Veal was paid for his journey. Someone said that he had taken a wager that he would get through. It appeared that he was not a private citizen but a spy. Now under an *umVithi* tree, Veal was told to take off his coat, and as he was doing so he was struck with a knobkerrie. He turned on his assailant making a grab for his throat, only to receive a thrust from his assegai. Veal got a grip on the shaft and struck back weakly, but he was hit on the back of the neck with a cane knife before being killed by another assegai thrust. From the crowd came the shout of 'Ji' as he fell.

The next morning, Monday 2 July, the men at eMthandeni were assembled to have their weapons treated with the newly strengthened *intelezi* so that those who wielded them 'may gain courage and follow the spirits so that you may kill the white people'.[9] A fire was built and an *udengezi* placed on it containing the medicine. The young men who had captured Veal were ordered to step up

Oliver Veal.
(Stuart, *Zulu Rebellion*)

and place their assegais over the pot, in the fumes coming from it, so that they could 'smell' it. The process was then repeated by the assembled Nyuswa, followed by the Qwabe and they were then sprinkled with *intelezi*. But they were interrupted. Just at this moment, across the Mvoti valley, rolled the boom of artillery fire. Barker's column, the one responsible for closing the southern approaches, was moving towards eMthandeni, and had met the men guarding the drift over the Nsuze river. While it was preparing to cross the drift, the column was attacked by two different bodies of Zulu, each about five-hundred-strong. They were driven off by rifle fire, some of them running down the Nsuze valley along which the troops chased them, riding along the ridges on either side while the field guns fired twenty rounds into the fleeing men. The militia spent till early afternoon mopping up – it was estimated that it killed some four hundred men before reaching the Esidumbini mission where it spent the night.

Early the next morning Barker's column moved on towards eMthandeni to meet the other columns and complete the great encircling movement. But it had already destroyed McKenzie's plan to surround Meseni's homestead and annihilate those gathered there. The roar of its guns the day before, which had interrupted the strengthening ritual at eMthandeni, had also warned Meseni that the men guarding the roadways had not been able to hold the militia back. Orders were given to make preparations to abandon the homestead and disperse. Meseni had no intention of being trapped by McKenzie at eMthandeni as Bhambatha had been at Mome.

Macrae's store, 2 July 1906

But Meseni's decision early on Monday morning, 2 July, to disperse his men and abandon eMthandeni was not known to the strategists at Thring's Post, and the plans to encircle eMthandeni by daybreak the next morning continued. Woolls-Sampson had arrived at headquarters early in the morning and sent an order back down the road to Bond's drift on the Thukela for the wagon train with his supplies to move at once to Thring's Post. The Bond's drift-Thring's Post road ran along the north-western border of the Lower Thukela division, on the south-eastern side of the Izinsimba valley and parallel to it, for something over forty-five kilometres. Near Macrae's store, it passed within a few kilometres of the Izinsimba gorge, where the Mthethwa under Mashwili, and the Qwabe under Mahlanga, supplemented by men of Ndlovu and Ngobizembe, were hiding out.

The officer in charge of the wagon train was Major S.G. Campbell, a medical doctor in civilian life, and another member of one of the best-known sugar-planting settler families in Natal. His force numbered about a hundred and twenty, with a 15-pounder, a Maxim and Rexer guns, and it escorted a train of twenty-eight wagons, which on the move stretched for nearly three kilometres along the road. The convoy left at one in the afternoon on 2 July and after a six-hour march, with the sun already set, they had reached the vicinity of Macrae's store. They were looking for a place to camp for the night when they were attacked by the *impi* from the Izinsimba. It had been hiding on both sides of the road, but its presence was exposed by the barking of a dog belonging to a member of the escort's advance guard. The Zulu charged, and the advance guard had to get back to the main body through the attackers and lost a trooper while doing so. But the premature attack gave Campbell the time to pull his men into a defensive position across the road and they drove off the attackers with close range rifle fire and case shot. The *impi* regrouped and charged once more, but again heavy fire kept them away.

There was then a lull of about twenty minutes during which time Campbell reorganised his force. It was therefore ready when a sustained shout of 'Usuthu' gave warning of the third charge. The Zulu were cut down by rifle and automatic weapon fire, while the gun fired case shot into positions where Zulu might be hiding. At this point the rear guard came up and assisted in keeping the attackers away from the wagons. The Zulu then retired to Izinsimba, moving deeper down into the gorge. Campbell's men pulled the wagons into a laager and spent an uneasy night, but no more attacks were made.[10]

It was estimated that the attacking force had numbered five hundred. It was supposed that its plan was to attack the head and rear of the wagon train simultaneously but the element of surprise was lost when the advance guard's barking dog precipitated the charge. Forty bodies were found in the morning before the escort made its way to Thring's Post. But the action at Macrae's store had further terrible consequences for it attracted the attention of the militia at Maphumulo to the men gathered at Izinsimba, singling them out for military action once Meseni had been dealt with by the encircling movement.

eMthandeni, 3 July 1906

As Campbell's wagon train was waiting under arms for the sun to rise and to resume its march to Thring's Post, so three columns were moving to arrive at eMthandeni at dawn. Woolls-Sampson led six hundred men with Maxims down the road from the Maphumulo magistracy towards eMthandeni. A thousand men with artillery under Mackay would come down the track from Thring's Post past where the Pheyana fight had taken place. The day before the planned rendezvous, Leuchars, with five hundred men would move into the Mvoti valley slightly downstream on the Glendale road, bivouac, and then, early in the morning, move further up the valley. Here they would move towards the other columns from Maphumulo, and Barker's coming from the south, hopefully trapping thousands of Qwabe at eMthandeni.

But the encircling movement was a failure. Well warned by the sound of Barker's guns at Nsuze on the morning of the 2nd, Meseni had ordered that the eMthandeni homestead be evacuated.[11] Mackay's column, with which McKenzie travelled, arrived to find the homestead deserted and that none of the other columns had made the rendezvous.

They had all met with resistance; at times in the south from *izimpi* of some size and fighting weight, but more often by small groups whom the militia pursued and attempted to destroy. The most substantial resistance came from Zulu trying to hold up Barker's column as it came along the road from Esidumbini. After marching for five kilometres, the column's scouts found a party of about four hundred men to the right of the road. The advance party fired into it and provoked a charge,[12] which was driven off just as another charge was made from the rear. This was also driven off, the defenders losing about one hundred men. The column reached the rendezvous only at noon.

Woolls-Sampson's column coming down from Maphumulo first lost its way, and then got into a number of skirmishes with small bodies of men, of whom it also killed about one hundred. Leuchars, coming up the Mvoti, first found the road blocked and then, when it ended at the Glendale mill, was held up by the difficulties of travelling through trackless thornbush. He repeated his tactic of keeping his distance and lobbing artillery shells towards his opponents: 'a few Natives were seen running into a densely-wooded valley on the right. Two shells were fired at them.'[13] He made the dawn rendezvous at half-past two in the afternoon.

It was estimated that in their various conflicts the militia had killed four hundred and forty-four men that day. But they failed to find the concentrated body of men whom they had hoped to eradicate with artillery and heavy arms fire. They did, however, find Oliver Veal.

> The body was lying face downwards. The sternum was cut right through, and the back bone was cut down, thus detaching the whole of the right chest. The right hand was gone, was cut off at the wrist. The sole of the right foot had been cut off. The whole of the internal organs were gone complete. The penis and testicles had been cut away and skinned right through to the anus which had also been cut away. The head was missing.[14]

The discovery of Veal's mutilated body, the failure of McKenzie's strategy and the escape of the enemy from the now deserted eMthandeni brought out the worst in the troops. They wanted their actions to be perceived as a brave attempt to put down a determined act of rebellion, not as a skirmish with men who believed they were defending their *inkosi* from attack. Denied their 'front line battle', against the 'enemy', the militia moved up and down the Mvoti valley, seizing cattle, destroying homesteads, driving the bush and forest where people might be hiding. Barker's column returned to Esidumbini 'as wild as Vandals', looting, then burning homesteads and shooting those who tried to escape. Amongst the dead were men who regarded themselves as 'loyal', and women and children. The pillage continued for days, and less intensively for weeks.

1 July 15:00 Veal killed.

2 July 06:30 Strengthening ritual at eMthandeni interrupted by sound of guns from Nsuze drift. Orders given to begin to abandon eMthandeni.
     13:00 Wagons under Campbell leave Bond's drift.
     19:00 Wagons reach Macrae's store and attacked by the force from Izinsimba.

3 July (day of the planned dawn 'rendezvous' at eMthandeni) Mackay reaches eMthandeni at
    ?08:00 to find it deserted.
    12:00 Barker reaches eMthandeni and Woolls-Sampson, Leuchars at **14:30**.

4 July The sweeping of the Mvoti valley begins.

Izinsimba, 8 July 1906

There was one concentration of armed men, however, who still had to be dealt with: those who had attacked the wagon escort at Macrae's store on 2 July, and were gathered under Mashwili in the Izinsimba valley.[15] It seemed from reports that they might be vulnerable to McKenzie's favourite tactic: the night march to gain the high ground for the artillery and clear lines of fire for the Maxims which would soften up the enemy in preparation for the infantry's drives. McKenzie's attacking force now consisted of three columns and after leaving Thring's Post proceeded about twenty kilometres in an easterly direction to surround the men asleep in the Izinsimba gorge. Leuchars's column moved along the north-east side to place its guns on the high ground on the left of the valley. Woolls-Sampson moved down the road which ran on the right side and, after he reached Macrae's store, cut down into the Izinsimba valley to block off any attempt to escape downstream to the Thukela. McKenzie, with Mackay's column, moved directly towards Mashwili's homestead, on the high ground close to the

Izinsimba gorge. A bayonet charge was made, but Mashwili was not there. He was close by, however, hiding in the caves in the deeply-incised valley of the Ndaka stream, which runs its short length into the Izinsimba.

With the sunrise some of the men in the gorge broke cover and tried to escape up the steep sides, but were driven back by rifle fire. Then the artillery began to 'search' the bush with shells loaded with shrapnel. When it was clear that all exits were covered, the militia, moving up- and downstream in close formation, began to search the gorge.

Whether they attempted to rally and defend themselves, or whether they tried to surrender, the rebels were driven out of the rocks and shot. Amongst the dead were the leaders: *inkosi* Mashwili, grandson of Dingiswayo; his son, Langalibalele, who had earlier told the magistrate that the imposition of the poll tax was a breach of the principles of good government; and Mahlanga, brother of Mphobeyana, who had been ordered back from the Witwatersrand to attend to his domestic affairs and had led the Qwabe of Ntshingumuzi into the Izinsimba valley. Many of the dead had been workers. One colonial historian wrote with smug satisfaction of the 'ricksha pullers and domestic servants from Durban, who left town for a day's outing to fight the white man. It was not to be wondered at that the surprise in the morning had the effect of demoralising such an undisciplined rabble'.[16] There was a newspaper report of a man dressed in a frock coat, white shirt and bowler, and carrying a bible, who appealed to the men who killed him not to shoot as he was a Christian.[17] Later before the courts the number of men who referred to fathers and brothers who died at Izinsimba, suggests there could hardly have been a homestead in the northern parts of the Lower Thukela division that was not affected. Stuart gives the number killed as five hundred and forty-seven. The militia suffered no losses.

It is hard to find any details of just what happened. One has to suspect that orders had been given to take no prisoners, and keep quiet about what had happened in the Izinsimba valley on the morning of 8 July 1906. Photographs of some of the men involved, grinning with their loot, disturb their silence, however, and bear an ominous message – a message that was heard clearly enough by Ndlovu and Sambela's people hiding in the valleys and thornbush up river from where the Izinsimba runs into the Thukela. When, in the days that followed, the militia tried to find them, their hideouts were deserted. On 9 and 10 July Woolls-Sampson moved up the Thukela valley, while the columns under Leuchars, Mackay and McKenzie moved down the Otimati and Timati, all to rendezvous where the Timati and Maseli streams meet. They had to force their way through thick thornbush, were without water for much of the time, they lost pack animals over the precipices of Isiwasembuzi, but saw no one. On the 11th, exhausted and angry, they had to retrace their steps. One column came across the homestead of Ndlovu's *induna*, which, according to an official account, they burnt. Oral tradition supplements the historical record. The man's name was Nzoyikane Gumede and he was Ndlovu's *indunankulu*. The militia cut off his head and impaled it on the stockade round the cattle byre.[18]

This was an atrocity committed out of frustration as well as cruelty. Meseni and Ndlovu knew the ground on which they had grown up, and the colonial authorities, too well to risk suffering another such horror. They were found the next day – not in the Maphumulo division but across the Thukela on the road to Eshowe, making their way to surrender to Sir Charles Saunders, Commissioner for Native Affairs of the Zululand province.

Mopping up, July–October 1906

Soon reports of atrocities began to appear in the newspapers – some originated in letters from 'the front', others by troopers sickened by what they had seen. The Natal authorities were asked by London for more details. For example, why homesteads were being burnt,

Looters after the massacre at Izinsimba. Note the bayonet in the centre.   (PAR: C572)

cattle looted, and men not under arms taken prisoner? As is usually the case, the officials and the officers had little difficulty in evading the questions (no homesteads were burnt – except when necessary) or in providing the necessary justificatory explanation (shot while trying to escape).[19]

The Governor tried to convince his superiors that the heavy losses were the result of the rebels' failure to comprehend the effectiveness of modern weaponry, although his argument for using dum dum bullets – needed to stop nerveless, uncivilised opponents – remained confidential. In his public despatch McCallum wrote:

> Without guns or rifles, the natives, with their assegais and shields, could not approach our lines sufficiently closely to inflict any substantial damage on our men. The Kafirs have entirely failed to appreciate the retaining power of the modern rifle, and after one or two unsuccessful efforts to break our line have invariably fled.[20]

But this was nonsense. The rebels understood only too well the power of the modern rifle, and how vulnerable they were to it. It was this fatal disparity in fire-power that limited the numbers participating in the rebellion – and persuaded so many of those who did participate to make use of supernatural powers to narrow the gap and even to destroy the penetrative capacities of the bullets fired against them. But when these powers failed, the rebels did not have the means to defend themselves against a force which sought to provoke armed confrontation, took no prisoners and, once it succeeded in scattering its opponents and occupying their territory, destroyed the means of support of everyone it confronted, combatants and non-combatants alike.

For once large bodies of assembled Zulu, like those at eMthandeni and Izinsimba, had broken up, or been broken up, the people experienced just the situation they had feared – and which had been such an argument against rebellion. The militia rode without opposition through the southern parts of the division, scattering all before them, shooting, seizing livestock, looting then burning homesteads. They were followed by African levies who grabbed what was left, too often maltreating and killing the people they flushed out of their hiding places. The whole district 'wiped out and burnt' was the entry for 5 July in a field diary. 'A Black pall of smoke hanging over the valley for many miles.' It was so dense that it was impossible for the militia to use the heliograph, and the countryside reeked with the stench of corpses, evidence of the damage done by expanding bullets. 'Mark V bullets do not argue with a man.' 'Much loot secured by troops, hidden in caves, holes and rocks. Rebels struck a "snag" when they went for Barker.'[21]

The details of the mopping up that took place in July 1906 and, in certain places, in the months that followed, were suppressed. But the American missionaries who visited their stations at the end of the month obtained some idea of what had happened. Having to travel through these areas still under martial law and occupied by the militia, they went to ask Leuchars permission. Slouched in his tent he met the missionaries' request with a silent, contemptuous stare. They left hurriedly and made their way through

the burned and desolated district, rode along the highways strewn with the unburied, putrefying carcasses of the slain, heard the

Looter, Transvaal Mounted Rifles, Maphumulo 1906.
(W.J. Powell, *The Zulu Rebellion of 1906*, Johannesburg, 1906, 54, 'A successful forager')

tales of over mastering superstition on the part of the natives and of atrocities on the part of some of the white soldiers & tried to comfort the survivors. The latter were living in booths, almost starving for lack of food and shivering from cold at night. They were bitter in spirit. Multitudes were dead, and the living stripped of almost every thing save life itself. We came home sick at heart, and took up the burdens of the year.[22]

They had, in effect, seen in the Maphumulo division the culmination of the rebellion of 1906: the unqualified assertion of colonial authority by violent means; the very response that chiefs like Meseni, Ndlovu and Mashwili had feared and persuaded them to call up their men. But such localised mobilisation, ultimately, only revealed the chiefs' vulnerability. It is true that for a time the forests of the Nkandla and the thornbush of the Thukela offered some protection, but these were isolated geographical features that offered only a temporary safe haven. In the end mobilisation invited occupation and attack by the militia. It was impossible, given the general topographical context of the chiefdoms within Natal and Zululand, to protect herds and homesteads, foodstuffs, possessions and grain stores, the old, the young, women and children, against a militia which, when their mobile, mounted infantry's rifles, backed by machine guns and artillery, had done their work, had no compunction in shooting, looting and burning homes, scattering non-combatants before them, and driving the men who survived in batches to the magistracies to await their punishment.

For this was not just the suppression of a rebellion, at least not in the first instance. It was primarily war – war on those people of Natal who believed that under chiefly rule they retained some recourse to responsible, answerable government. It was the act of conquest that the colonists had been unable to carry out when Natal was established sixty years before.

Notes

1. Campbell Collections: W.A. Campbell to Marshall Campbell, 19 June 1906, File 3, Bantu.
2. DAR: Durban 3/DBN, Chief Constables Report Book, Report for June 1906.
3. BPP: C.3247, No. 37, McCallum to Elgin, 26 July 1906, Enc. 1; *The Natal Witness*, 23 July 1906.
4. RH: Mss. African s. 1286/1, Harriette Colenso to Frank Colenso, 29 April 1906.
5. Stuart, *Zulu Rebellion*, 360–361.
6. Rudyard Kipling, 'M.I. (Mounted Infantry of the Line)' in *Rudyard Kipling's Verse: Inclusive Edition, 1855–1926*, London: Hodder and Stoughton, 1927, 455–458.
7. Many aspects of this narrative were to be contested. This is my considered reading of the evidence.
8. PAR: AGO I/1/317, Statement by Mhaqwa, 13 December 1906. 'As the impi approached the Mtandeni kraal with the whiteman, the impi sang a war song, when the impi formed into a circle, then the impi sang the great War song of the Qwabe tribe.'
9. PAR: AGO I/1//317, Deposition by Madevu (here given as Madoju), 23 February 1907.
10. BPP: C.3247, No. 27, McCallum to Elgin, 12 July 1906, Enc. 2; *The Natal Mercury*, 7 July 1906.
11. Stuart, *Zulu Rebellion*, asserts that 6 000–7 000 were present on the evening of the 2nd and 'vanished' (383) because of the militia's actions on the 3rd and the days following – an interpretation which has to be characterised as a deliberate misinterpretation of events made to enhance the 'military' reputations of his sponsors.
12. Stuart, *Zulu Rebellion*, 372. This is my reading – but it is clear that the troops fired before the charge. The number of four hundred is Stuart's and might not be correct.
13. Stuart, *Zulu Rebellion*, 381.
14. PAR: RSC I/1/96, Rex v. Macabacaba and others, Statement by William Collins, 5 March 1907.
15. Thanks to Muzi Hadebe, Vukile Khumalo and Steve Kotze for undertaking the trip with me to Izinsimba which raised so many of these questions, and gave some answers, to just what happened on 8 July 1906.
16. W. Bosman, *The Natal Rebellion of 1906*, London, 1907, 153.
17. *The Natal Mercury*, 17 July 1906.
18. Information given to Muzi Hadebe by Gezephi Zulu (widow of Ndlovu's son) on 14 December 2001 and PAR: RSC, I/1/95, Statement by Sifo kaZwenyani, 9 April 1907.

19. For accusations of atrocities see BPP: C.3027, No. 100, Elgin to McCallum, 16 July 1906 and the reply No. 102, McCallum to Elgin, 17 July 1906 in BPP: C.3027, No. 37 and C.3247, No. 55, McCallum to Elgin, 14 September 1906 and enclosures.
20. BPP: C.3247, No. 27, McCallum to Elgin, 12 July 1906.
21. PAR: CSO 2599, Confidential Minute Papers 1906-7, Diary of Field Operations . . . Umvoti Field Force, Entries for 5, 23 and 19 July 1906.
22. KC: American Board Mission: (microfilm) Reel 127, Vol. 24 , Adams Mission and outstations, Reports.

Part Two

LAW

5

Conquering courts

The trial of Meseni kaMusi and Ndlovu kaThimuni, 16–17 July 1906

As the most prominent rebels in the Maphumulo division, Meseni and Ndlovu were marked men and feared that they would never survive an attempt to surrender to the authorities there. But they knew the ground on which they had grown up. Although, in the dreadful fortnight that followed the abandonment of eMthandeni, the troops did everything they could to find them, they were unable to do so. But the chiefs also knew that they could not stay in the bush indefinitely. On the night of 12 July they crossed the Thukela and began to make their way to Eshowe, in the hope that they could surrender in safety to the Commissioner for Native Affairs of the Zululand Province, Charles Saunders. They were captured on the way, placed under escort, and returned to Maphumulo on the evening of 14 July, exhausted but alive.

They were brought before a court set up under martial law on 16 July. It consisted of some of the leading members of Natal's legal fraternity, now serving as officers in the militia. The four presiding officers included Lieutenant-Colonel James Wylie, of the Durban firm Shepstone, Wylie & Binns, while Captain W.S. Bigby of the Attorney-General's office prosecuted. A Pietermaritzburg solicitor and lieutenant in the Natal Carbineers, Hubert Walton, defended. It was alleged that on 18 June chiefs Meseni and Ndlovu had taken up arms with the intention of overthrowing the

Meseni and Ndlovu in gaol after their surrender.   (PAR: C4891)

government; they had attacked a military convoy on 19 June and His Majesty's and militia forces at Pheyana on 27 June, and murdered the storekeeper Adolf Sangereid, Trooper Albert Powell, and a civilian Oliver Veal.[1]

Physically the accused chiefs were exhausted. They had been living in the bush, hunted by the militia, and had had only one day to recover from their attempt to surrender in Eshowe. At that moment, beyond the building in which they stood on trial, the troops were on the rampage, burning homesteads and looting cattle. The dead lay unburied, and barbed wire coops had been filled with rebels on their way to the magistrate's court where they appeared in batches to receive sentences of flogging and imprisonment with hard labour. Fear and death filled the air. But the chiefs showed remarkable resilience. A journalist described them as

> clothed in shirts and shabby short coats, which did not cover their bare legs. I defy any white man to have looked dignified in such a garb, but these two men seemed the very embodiment of dignity.[2]

Meseni denied the substantive charges. He had killed no one and had taken up arms only 'as I understood I was going to be killed'. Ndlovu admitted that he had taken up arms, but not to overthrow the government, and he denied the charges of murder.

Beyond establishing that arming and acts of violence had taken place, the prosecution witnesses did little to assist the case against the chiefs. The chief Swayimana said that, although 'the whole country' had taken up weapons, he had never seen Meseni armed and Meseni had never tried to persuade him to arm. The Norwegian missionary Michel Tvedt gave evidence that on 19 June Ndlovu had told him

> 'You may stay here with your wife and children and then no one will harm you.' I asked if I might go about my work and he

said 'Yes but do not go far from your house, and I will leave a man to see that no one touches the Mfundisi or his property.'[3]

Then came the storekeepers, Thomas Oglesby and his son Fred. Thomas gave evidence that Ndlovu had not been present when Powell had been killed and that it had been the chief's intervention that had saved his life. 'His treatment was humane and he was in control of his people.' Fred Oglesby told how Ndlovu had sent men to stop him and his father from running away, and to get them back under Ndlovu's protection. He also reported Ndlovu's explanation for what had happened on 19 June, thus giving voice, some believed deliberately, to the chief's defence: Ndlovu

> said he was sorry I was in the plight I was, but it was owing to circumstances over which he had no control. He said they had risen for 3 or 4 reasons. One. That some had been imprisoned. Others. That some had been thrashed. Some had had their cattle taken. The Poll tax had been very heavy on them. They had made up their minds to rise and try and get some of that money back. They were not going to war with any people who had nothing to do with the troops. To use his own words 'With any Storekeepers or Civilians.' They had also made up their minds that no children, no females should be touched or killed. He also said that he would try and put us in safety.[4]

Beyond establishing the facts of the case, no evidence was led that was particularly damaging as far as the two accused were concerned personally, or which implicated them directly in the killings. Meseni had not been present at the violent clashes, and although Ndlovu had been, he had taken the opportunity to intervene and save lives. No questions were able to extract from witnesses the reasons why the individual whites had been killed, and no witness knew anything about the need for body parts for medicine – if such a thing did happen then it belonged to the world of the *izinyanga* who were the specialists in this field.

Then it was the turn of the chiefs. Meseni declined to be sworn but spoke strongly in his own defence. The journalist present felt it was a 'masterly history of the whole troubles from his own point of view' and 'an absolute and complete vindication of his position'.[5] Not only had Meseni not been present at the poll tax meeting where all this had begun, but the reason for his absence was that he was imprisoned at Stanger – a punishment for which he had never been tried. Then, without trial again, his people living on private land had been removed from his jurisdiction. Not only was the magistrate antagonistic to him, but the troops had burnt one of his homesteads. It seemed to him a deliberate provocation. Unable to prove anything against him in court it 'was burnt because they wanted to make me fight'. His people had gathered around him to protect their *inkosi* to whom the authorities were so obviously hostile: 'I was not treated as a man, but as a mere "thing".'

> I was simply treated as a mere nobody by the Magistrate who has charge of me. I then became convinced that I was regarded as a rebel by the Magistrate and that the army was to be brought against me.
>
> And that is the reason that I have just killed myself – because I understood that an army was being brought against me.[6]

Ndlovu spoke in his own defence, invoking the same principles of good governance that he had spelt out to Stuart in 1902. He and his fellow chiefs of the Maphumulo division had brought to the attention of the magistrate the reasons why it was impossible for them to persuade their people to pay the poll tax, and asked that their views be relayed to the authorities in Pietermaritzburg for consideration. It was the duty of government to consider such a request. Instead he had been told 'that the Government had spoken and that was the end' and, 'troops were poured in and were an enemy to us because we refused to pay the tax, instead of it being put in the right way and saying "we had not the money to pay".' The troops had maltreated his people: the men they came across on the road had been whipped and women abused. His deaf and dumb relative had been shot. Ndlovu had been called to the Stanger court in error, and had nonetheless been gaoled for nearly a month without being charged. It was clear to him that the authorities could find no reason to charge him.

> . . . I was told that I was now to be liberated and the Govern-ment hoped that I should attend in future and not despise the authority of the Government. I asked how I had despised the authority of the Government and the Magistrate said 'Go'.

Ultimately, in such conditions and under such treatment, it had been impossible for him to keep order amongst his people. They had been maltreated for too long and were too angry. In the end they simply decided that they would make up their losses by taking cattle. He had followed and, in doing so, had been able to keep them under some control and save lives:

> I admit it [going to Thring's Post with an armed force] because it was the will of my people. It was against my will that I went there at all. If it had been my will would not the man on this side of the Otimati [Oglesby] and the missionary [Tvedt] have shared the same fate?[7]

In essence Meseni and Ndlovu put forward the same defence. The legal framework in which they operated as chiefs, and which underlay many of the questions put to them by this court, assumed they were members of a system of a responsible and consultative administration. But in their experience this was not so. It had not been government at all but rule by bureaucratic fiat which, in the end, had been imposed arbitrarily and at gunpoint. This had forced their people to protect themselves and their chiefs. The crimes of which they were accused were the consequence of the abandonment of the principles of just government by the Natal authorities.

It was an eloquent defence made with courage and dignity and it impressed even the military officers conducting the court – but it would be naïve for us to accept it without qualification. It was a moral defence based on a partial presentation of the evidence, constructed by two men who had themselves spent their lives adjudicating disputes, and were very aware that beyond the walls of the court was the firing squad. Meseni's men had not gathered merely to protect him, their *inkosi*; and Ndlovu had not followed his people only to control them. Talk of rebellion and armed resistance had been everywhere – but there had also been practical, perhaps insurmountable, difficulties in advancing beyond defensive mobilisation in Meseni's case, and a raid in Ndlovu's – unless, of course, Zulu forces north of the Thukela had mobilised in their support. Without this, whatever rebellious intentions they had had in their hearts, a whole range of factors had made it impossible to carry them out fully in action. A defensive strategy had suited Meseni, whose homestead eMthandeni was more exposed to military attack. Ndlovu, with the impenetrable bush at his back had had more freedom to attack the military, although it had been impossible to sustain the offensive. Both Meseni and Ndlovu were *amakhosi*, men of spirit and authority commanding loyalty and held in great respect by their followers, and, although there can be no doubt that they had to adapt to the anger and demands of their people, they were not men to lose control over them.

The court found both chiefs guilty of attacking His Majesty's forces with the intention of overthrowing the government. Ndlovu was also found guilty of the murders that had taken place in his area. Both were sentenced to death by firing squad. But their composure in the most trying of conditions, and the confidence with which they presented their argument that it was bad administration and military harassment that had provoked their people, made an impression on the military tribunal, and it recommended clemency. It felt that

Meseni and Ndlovu under guard.   (PAR: C727)

in view of the evidence given by the two prisoners as to the
manner in which they had been governed and dealt with in the
past and had practically been driven to take up arms in self
defence as they thought, and in view of the humane and civilized
manner in which they carried on operations after they had armed

the sentence might be remitted to one of imprisonment.

The court's decision was passed to the militia's commandant,
Lieutenant-Colonel Duncan McKenzie, who refused to endorse it:
the firing squad was what these two chiefs deserved. The Governor,
however, accepted the court's recommendation and sentenced
Meseni kaMusi and Ndlovu kaThimuni to life imprisonment with
hard labour.

Martial law

Earlier in the year when the Governor remitted one of his sentences passed under martial law, McKenzie had written, 'If you continue to upset death sentences our work will be pointless':

> I do place on record however my opinion that if this golden opportunity of inflicting the most drastic punishment on all leading natives found guilty of treason is lost the opportunity may never recur.[8]

Martial law had been promulgated in Natal in February 1906 and it was lifted in October. Most of the officials, civilian and military, had had experience of it because it had been widely and controversially used in the South African war. It was essential to the prosecution of the 1906 campaign because it provided the military with cover to act without restraint, secure in the knowledge that they could not be effectively challenged so long as martial law was in place, and that before it was lifted, an act of indemnity would be passed to protect them from any subsequent legal action. Martial law was promulgated by the Governor, who then delegated authority to the chief military officer, who passed all death sentences to the Governor for ratification. Duncan McKenzie objected strongly when the Governor baulked at imposing the death sentence because, for this hero of settler Natal, it was imperative that capital punishment be used to demonstrate where power lay in the colony.

This was not how London saw it. In 1864, in a case still referred to in the Colonial Office in 1906, Edward Eyre, Governor of Jamaica, had used martial law to crush what he saw as a rebellion in Jamaica, and in so doing had provoked a debate over race and social justice which proved to be one of the nineteenth century's most significant legal controversies. In 1906 the Colonial Office published as an appendix to the Natal *Correspondence* the circular containing the regulations produced in the aftermath of the Eyre case.[9] The imposition of martial law was that 'lamentable alternative to the anarchy and social confusion which would otherwise ensue'. To declare martial law was to abandon the rule of law – in order to save it. The 1867 document contained recommendations – demands were unenforceable in a situation in which all authority had been handed over to the Governor – to be exercised through the commander-in-chief of the military. It attempted to put forward a number of guidelines that the authorities should follow when martial law was promulgated, and to clarify the relations between the various levels of authority and the courts under martial law. It pointed to the enormous responsibility that martial law placed on the Governor who could thereby exercise and delegate authority unchecked. It urged restraint when this was possible: the military should avoid attacking the unarmed, or burning crops and houses. The prime objective of martial law was to restore the rule of law; it was not to provide the military with the opportunity to punish and exact retribution, except insofar as this expedited the termination of the crisis.

Natal either failed to understand or ignored this fundamental principle.[10] The declaration of martial law allowed the militia to pursue without restraint what it saw as the enemy.[11] When London made some feeble efforts to question Natal's actions, it met with vigorous assertions of independence and the charge that a responsible government's autonomy was being threatened by imperial interference.[12] London countered with the argument that, as long as Natal still depended on a regiment of imperial troops for its defence, this necessarily implicated Great Britain in the colony's military activities. But Natal ignored or avoided such arguments, and responded with reactions so extreme that London decided not to risk a confrontation. Thus, when a court set up under martial law sentenced twelve men to death at the end of March, and the Colonial Office asked for more information before approving the action, the Natal ministry threatened to resign. Rather than provoke a constitutional crisis, in a situation where the suspension of the rule of law in a colony with responsible government had created vast areas of legal uncertainty, London backed down, the Natal ministry withdrew its resignation, and the Richmond twelve were shot.

Those seen as the ringleaders of the rebellion were brought before martial law courts presided over by officers with a legal background – as in the case of Meseni and Ndlovu discussed above. The rank and file were dealt with by magistrates in their own courts, but with extended jurisdiction under martial law. Once the gathering of men in the Maphumulo division had been broken up early in July, an order was given for those who had rebelled to give themselves up, and those who had not to report to the magistrate's office.[13] The militia hunted down those in hiding. An attempt by London to remind Natal's Minister of War that only those under arms should be taken prisoner was side-stepped and thousands of men were brought before these courts. Some were indeed captured under arms but most were rounded up while trying to hide from the militia. From 16–19 July it was announced that people in the Maphumulo and Lower Thukela divisions could surrender in safety. Prisoners were sent into the bush to announce this, and many men came in, to discover that while surrender gave them some protection from being summarily shot, it also enabled the authorities to detain them, bring them to trial, and sentence them. Once the period of grace was over, the troops moved in again – confident that those who had not taken advantage of the amnesty were rebels.

The net was cast very wide. Amongst the hundreds of men in the barbed wire cages around the magistracies were some who had resisted, some who had fought, some who had just been caught up in events, others who had fled into the bush to hide. And there were those who believed that they had supported the government and had come in to the magistracies when the cessation of violence had given them opportunity to do so – and were arrested.[14] Once there, they were grouped according to their respective chiefs, brought into court in batches, and charged with high treason. Most admitted they had armed, which was treated as a plea of guilty.

When witnesses were called, they were very often men who had proved in earlier cases their usefulness in identifying the accused as having been armed at the centres of resistance or during a particular phase of the rebellion. Other witnesses were men who had just been convicted and were used to give evidence against their comrades. Those accused were given the chance to defend themselves, but most just pleaded guilty. They were sentenced, usually to two years imprisonment with hard labour, on the docks at Durban, in the mines of northern Natal, or on government projects, usually after a cruel flogging.

Pleading not guilty or hiring a lawyer could work, but it was dangerous, for the penalties were increased if the plea failed – as it usually did, except for the few who found white employees to vouch for their alibis or their loyalty. Men of rank, or holding positions of responsibility within the administrative system, were 'held back', and brought to trial later, when they received stiffer sentences.

One puts down the martial law note books weary at the carefully kept record[15] of misery and injustice. The evidence led against the accused very soon becomes mechanical and repetitive. Some of the accused appear fearful, some desperate, others resigned. Some argued that they were forced to join the rebels, others that they had been framed, some denied any involvement at all. Others remained defiant and took the consequences angrily. Accused after accused, in their hundreds, were marched into the dock, pleaded guilty of arming, received their sentences, and were marched out to be transported to the gaol compounds.

No matter how they responded to the charges made against them, they deserve more than the obscurity of the martial law record book. For example, the old man, caught up in events, who tried to satisfy both sides, and lost to both:

> I have no reply to make to the charge against me, I am stabbed
> to the heart finding myself in the position I am now in. When
> I heard of the arming of Natives I went out to the kraals to see

if it was a fact. I found the Natives were all away from home – their kraals were closed up. I was overcome with fear thinking they would kill me, I armed myself and went into the bush at the Headquarters of the rebel camp at Nsimba. I was not present at any fight with Troops. I am an official witness in our tribe. My chief is Tshingumuzi. It is a long time since the natives spoke of rebellion. It is long since that the natives turned their hearts against the Government. It was first spoken of when the Poll tax was proclaimed. After that time, the natives had no peace in their hearts, and any native who spoke in favour of paying the Tax stood in danger of losing his life. Even I had to suffer for supporting the Govt. in telling our tribesmen to pay.[16]

There were the defiant:

I admit the charge which has been laid against me. I am an Induna in the tribe. We armed to fight the white people because of the poll tax. It was our intention to wipe out the white people and take back the country which the responsible members of our tribe said it belonged to Shaka and therefore it was our land.[17]

And there were those who were convinced, even in the dock, that they had been provoked by the authorities:

We went to war against the Government because the Troops met us when there was no war and beat us. We armed but we did not leave our headquarters.[18]

And it is what is implied in these records that is shocking: at the number of fathers who had lost their sons, and sons their fathers, at the stock responses which concealed what was felt, at the unspoken grief around these courts of those who had been left behind to mourn the missing and the dead, left without the resources to repair what had been destroyed.

On 1 August the Governor reported – again – that the rebellion, to all intents and purposes, was over.[19] For many people of Natal the time of suffering was just beginning. Although those seen as ringleaders were in gaol waiting confirmation of their sentences, and thousands of the rank and file in the process of being tried, there were still many men at large. Rumours that men were still hiding in the most inaccessible retreats of the middle Thukela valley were to be received for months, and reports of men alleged to have been rebels but who had never been brought to book, were to worry the authorities for years.

The continuation of martial law was, however, impossible. Not only was there pressure from London to have it lifted but it also involved Natal in a contradiction: self-congratulation and cele-bration at the successful crushing of the rebellion could not be convincingly maintained as long as the colony remained legally in a state of war. On 2 October 1906 Governor Sir Henry McCallum abrogated martial law in Natal and at the same time approved the act of indemnity against any prosecution for actions taken while it was in force.[20]

War through the courts

The war was to continue for years however – no longer in the field, outside the law, but now in the courts following conventional legal procedures. The immediate objective was to find those considered as having escaped punishment for their actions in 1906; but this was within the wider context of the desire to create a deferent African population that recognised, without question or complaint, the supremacy of white authority. Already the officials were preparing the way for the legal assault on the last remaining vestige of African political autonomy – the Zulu royal house in the person of Dinuzulu kaCetshwayo for his perceived secret role in the resistance of 1906. Thus in many ways the courts were the final offensive in the attempt to create a subservient African population.

And so the conflict continued. The authorities refused to facilitate reconciliation by granting a general amnesty. As a result, significant numbers of men continued to live a secret existence as outlaws, a matter of great concern to their families and sympathisers who wanted them to return to the social fold, and for the Natal authorities determined to pursue and capture them in order to demonstrate publicly the consequences of trying to live beyond the boundaries the colonial society was trying to create.

Most immediate and most pressing of all was the authorities' determination to bring to court and punish those responsible for specific acts of violence in 1906, the killing of whites in particular. With the abrogation of martial law in October 1906, legal procedures had to be followed. They began at the level of the magistracy where the Natal police initiated the investigations and served warrants on suspects and witnesses. Brought before the magistrate who conducted the preliminary examination the suspects were allowed to respond to the evidence collected against them. These sworn depositions, together with the magistrate's summary of the case, were then sent to Pietermaritzburg where the Attorney-General decided whether to prosecute and in which court – which would open the case to the public and the press, and the possibility of a legal defence.

In the months that followed the smashing of resistance in July 1906, the investigations began. Courthouse spies got to work, informers made their reports, the police followed up rumours and beer-drink gossip, checking on the homesteads to discover who was still missing. But it was difficult to get convincing evidence. There was hostility and despair amongst the people. Many potential witnesses were dead, others were absent. Statements were collected from those who had been present at the major confrontations, checked and mulled over. Homesteads were raided and men hunted down in the bush.[21] This work was in control of white police officers but carried out by African subordinates. Many of them were local men who had amongst the people they were investigating, not only favourites, but also enemies. The temptation to get the approval of their superiors by bringing in suspects, and at the same time to settle old scores, was great.

Often the investigation led to men already serving sentences. They were, of course, vulnerable, not only to threats of further punishment if they refused to co-operate, but to offers of remission of sentence if they did. The temptation to work with the authorities was very great. Apart from suffering hard labour itself, prisoners were also beginning to see too many of their fellows wasting away from the diseases contracted in gaol. They got to hear of men still at liberty, some of them their chiefs, who they knew had been 'rebellious', but were now giving additional evidence against their old comrades. And they worried increasingly about what was happening back at home. Their possessions and their people were exposed, and they faced the real possibility that, even if they survived their sentences, they would return to find their property squandered, and their homes and families removed from their control. Information and evidence given against the right people at the right time might be used to their advantage, even to gain their liberation. Those involved in key events were often tempted to give evidence, even to concoct it. Though for many the years that followed the end of military action in Natal were a time of silent heroism and fortitude, for others they were a time of false accusation and the set-up.

Notes

1. PAR: RSC I/1/96, Rex *v.* Meseni and Ndhlovu ka Timuni, Notes of Evidence and Finding of the Court, 16–17 July 1906.
2. *The Mosquito*, 2, 48, 6 June 1907, 5.
3. PAR: RSC I/1/96, Rex *v.* Meseni and Ndhlovu ka Timuni, Evidence of Mikal Tvedt, Otimati Mission, 16 July 1906.
4. PAR: RSC I/1/96, Rex *v.* Meseni and Ndhlovu ka Timuni. Evidence of Fred Oglesby, 16 July 1906.
5. *The Mosquito*, 2, 48, 6 June 1907, 5.
6. PAR: RSC I/1/96, Rex *v.* Meseni and Ndhlovu ka Timuni, Statement by Meseni, 17 July 1906.
7. PAR: RSC I/1/96, Rex *v.* Meseni and Ndhlovu ka Timuni, Evidence by Ndlovu, 17 July 1906.
8. PRO: CO 179/233, 12460/1906, McCallum to Elgin, 16 March 1906, Enc. 2, McKenzie to Minister of Defence, 9 March 1906.
9. BPP: C.2905, Appendix 1, Circular, 26 January 1867. For a discussion in the Colonial Office on the relevance of the Eyre controversy to the situation in Natal see the minutes on PRO: CO 179/233, 14033. For a succinct statement on the Natal ministry's attitude to martial law see PRO: CO 179/235, 26738, McCallum to Elgin, 29 June 1906.
10. Although the legal and constitutional implications are controversial and complicated. See Arthur Berriedale Keith, *Responsible Government in the Dominions*, second edition rewritten and revised to 1927, (two volumes), Oxford: Clarendon Press. Keith was a junior official at the Africa desk at the time – and noteworthy for his criticisms of Natal's actions – for which he incurred the displeasure of Lord Elgin and was moved from the Africa desk.
11. The more extreme manifestations of this were kept out of the published reports. For example BPP: C.2905, No. 57, McCallum to Elgin, 16 March 1906. The complete correspondence can be found in PRO: CO 179/233, 12460/1906.
12. The essential documents were published in BPP: C.2905, No. 35, Elgin to McCallum, 28 March 1906; No. 36, Elgin to McCallum, 29 March 1906; No. 37, McCallum to Elgin, 29 March 1906; No. 38, Elgin to McCallum, 30 March 1906.
13. It is difficult to establish just what happened – little care was taken at the time to make adequate records and much was covered up – but for one man's account see PAR: AGO I/8/112, 2725/06, Rex *v.* Nogweja.
14. I base this description largely on the full (and, unlike those from Maphumulo, legible) martial law record books of the Lower Thukela (Stanger) Division in DAR: 1/SGR, 1/4/2/1–5.
15. But not, it is true in most cases: Maxwell's idiosyncratic script with its heavy lateral scoring makes it difficult to read the Maphumulo martial law record books. Shuter's transcriptions in the Lower Thukela division are in a much better condition and I have used them extensively.

16. DAR: 1/STG, Martial law notebook, 1/4/2/4, 100/06, Rex *v.* Nkabi, 29 August 1906.
17. DAR: 1/STG, Martial law notebook, 1/4/2/4, 94/06, Rex *v.* Matambo and others, Statement by Zwangendaba, 29 August 1906.
18. DAR: 1/STG, Martial law notebook, 1/4/2/5, 148/06, Rex *v.* Sidoi and others, Statement by Nqangi, 30 September 1906.
19. BPP: C.3247, No. 19, McCallum to Elgin, 1 August 1906.
20. BPP: C.3247, No. 62 and 63, McCallum to Elgin, 6 and 9 October 1906.
21. PAR: AGO I/1316, Memorandum, Sergeant Rehmann, Natal Police, Stanger to Sergeant L'Estrange, Natal Police, Maphumulo, 1 November 1906.

6

Investigation and examination

The killing of Veal

The Maphumulo and Lower Thukela divisions were key areas of investigation: it was here that there had been massive mobilisations of Africans and where a store had been looted, a convoy of wagons attacked, and three whites had been killed, two of them civilians. Two of the most influential chiefs, Meseni kaMusi and Ndlovu kaThimuni, had been found guilty in July and sentenced to death. But there were still rebels living in the bush who needed to be brought to book, and, most important in the eyes of the authorities, no one had as yet been punished for the individual acts of violence that had taken place: the 19 June dawn raid by Ndlovu's men on the Thring's Post store, during which the stock inspector and spy, William Robbins, had been severely assaulted and the young storekeeper, Adolf Sangereid, killed; for the attack later in the morning on the military wagons near Oglesbys' store when Sergeant Knox was stabbed and Trooper Powell was killed and his body mutilated; and for the killing, mutilation and decapitation of the civilian cyclist Oliver Veal at Meseni's eMthandeni homestead on Sunday 1 July.

It was the Veal killing that attracted most attention. While the rumours that he had been tortured were discounted after a time, he was a private citizen who had been publicly done to death in a particularly horrifying way. Once the police had done the investigations, it was magistrates Thomas Maxwell and Frank Shuter who were responsible for the preliminary examination, with Shuter playing the leading role. Nearly a year passed from the time of the killings before the accused were brought to trial, and scores of statements and depositions were taken during the investigations

---

Key events of the rebellion in the Maphumulo and Lower Thukela divisions

Tuesday 19 June
05:00:   Attack on Thring's Post store by Ndlovu's Nodunga and Ngqokwane's Mbedu. William Robbins severely wounded, Adolf Sangereid killed, cattle taken, store looted.
07:00:   Attack on wagon train by Ndlovu's men. Trooper Knox stabbed and Powell killed. Followed by attack by militia on Ndlovu's Ezintandaneni homestead. Many killed.

Wednesday 27 June
Militia provoke attack at Pheyana. Seventy defenders killed.

Sunday 1 July
pm: Capture of cyclist Oliver Veal by Nyuswa force guarding Mvoti drift.
c.16:00:   Killing of Oliver Veal.

Monday 2 July
am: Column attacked at Nsuze and Mthandeni abandoned.
pm: Attack by Mthethwa/Qwabe force on wagon train at Macrae's store.

Tuesday 3 July
Surprise attack on eMthandeni fails. Mvoti valley put to the torch.

Sunday 8 July
Attack on rebel force in Izinsimba gorge.

Thursday 12 July
Meseni and Ndlovu surrender.

16 and 17 July
Meseni and Ndlovu appear before martial law court.

upon which the charges were eventually based. Many of these documents still exist. Though they are often confused, misleading, obscure, and inadequately translated, they contain invaluable insights into the worlds of those involved in the rebellion of 1906. But they also have to be read with the greatest care. The earlier documents, from the last half of 1906, are often unclear and inconsistent but also useful because they are spontaneous and unscripted. The later documentation, including the evidence led in court in 1907, is more controlled and the narrative emerges with greater clarity; but this is because it has been sifted and worked over to provide the consistent account of events needed to send the accused to, or save them from, the gallows. And as the months passed and the authorities' determination to find the offenders became more apparent, so it became more urgent for those who feared that they might come under suspicion to distance themselves from the killings – physically if possible, by disappearing, assuming a false identity, losing themselves in the towns – but if this was not possible, to distract the investigators by laying down, if not false then at least different trails, leading to other culprits. And amongst the scores of statements of who was where and when, one gets on occasion a glimpse of the untold stories of people and their doings which would never be exposed to the light of official examination.

I deal with the cases in the order in which they were to appear in the Supreme Court: first, with the Veal killing on 1 July at eMthandeni, and then in the next chapter with the earlier killings of 19 June at Thring's Post and near the Oglesbys' store.

Investigation: Veal (July 1906 – February 1907)

Meseni versus Macabacaba

As far as the death of Oliver Veal was concerned, the two key witnesses and most obvious suspects were the senior men at the eMthandeni homestead at the time: Meseni kaMusi, the Qwabe *inkosi*; and Macabacaba kaMagceni, a leading *induna* and Meseni's official representative over the Qwabe who lived in the Ndwedwe division in the south. He had been a late arrival at eMthandeni, getting there on Friday 29 June, having been sent by the Ndwedwe magistrate to investigate the men from his division who, it was said, had armed in support of Meseni. But the presence of a man of such standing had greatly encouraged Meseni who had appointed Macabacaba *induna* of the armed force at eMthandeni.

Macabacaba had accepted. Meseni thus had as his most senior assistant a man of authority to keep order amongst factions at eMthandeni that had shortly before regarded one another with considerable hostility. Then, three weeks later, both men were in gaol at Maphumulo and beginning another struggle, the one pitted against the other.

A lawyer in military service, appointed to assist in Meseni's defence at his trial under martial law, scribbled down a note of what Meseni told him at this time. Macabacaba, Meseni said, had informed him that Veal had been captured, but when he, Meseni, had discovered that Veal was unarmed he had ordered his release. Macabacaba had replied that 'your subjects' would never agree to this as they thought the white man was a 'spy'. Meseni then left the homestead to dig for medicine on the hill behind his homestead. On his return he discovered that his orders had been disobeyed and that Veal had been killed.[1]

Also in the Maphumulo gaol in July, Macabacaba gave his different account of events. On Sunday 1 July he had been supervising the slaughter of cattle for the men assembled at eMthandeni; he had not seen Veal, did not remember who had been with the crowd that brought him in, and had had nothing to do with the killing. But he did say that it was common sense that 'The white man would not have been killed without orders from the Chief. I say that Meseni ordered the white man to be killed.'[2] Of this he was certain.

Thus statements, made within weeks of the event, by the two most prominent men at eMthandeni, held the other responsible, if not for killing Veal, then for authorising it. They confronted one another with their different accounts:

> I disputed with Meseni in the Gaol, Meseni asked me why I had not released the whiteman and let him go? I replied How could I let him go when the whiteman belonged to Meseni and did not belong to me.[3]

In the long months of investigation and in the trial that followed so their statements became more detailed, their differences more specific, more individuals were drawn in and co-accused, and more and more witnesses gave evidence to support these opposing points of view. But, no matter how the accounts were to be elaborated, Meseni and Macabacaba kept to the essence of these early statements: Meseni said that he had told Macabacaba to release Oliver Veal; Macabacaba denied this and stated that Meseni, as *inkosi* in whose homestead the killing had taken place, must have given the order for Veal's death. The details of their accounts were altered and extended, but they stuck to these basic positions on their long journeys through the prisons and courts of Natal, the one on his way to exile on St Helena, and the other to the gallows in the Pietermaritzburg gaol.

The men at the drift

The investigation also began to reveal information about others who had played a part in the events that led to Veal's death. The drift on the Mvoti near where Oliver Veal was captured had been guarded by Swayimana's Nyuswa. Swayimana himself had not been there: as a 'loyal chief' he had been housed in safety at the magistracy. But many of his followers had mobilised on the side of their Qwabe neighbours. Given the intensity of the dispute that existed between the Nyuswa and Qwabe, it was not an easy alliance, but shared anger and the impending arrival of the militia had given them common cause.

Sibeko kaNdindiyana, a young man of Swayimana's Nyuswa, and Sihlobo kaNgenge[4] had caught Oliver Veal as he cycled from Maphumulo down towards the drift. Sihlobo was afterwards killed in the conflict, but Sibeko was arrested and placed in the 'bird cage' at Maphumulo. On 29 July he had been brought before the magistrate to make his statement. He told how he had captured Veal because as one of the men patrolling the road he had been under instructions to do so.

There had been two senior *izinduna* present near the drift. Dludla kaSiyazana was in charge of the Nyuswa and was Meseni's representative with the force at the drift. Dludla's homestead was near the road. He had originally belonged to Meseni, but had gone over to the Nyuswa in their quarrel with the Qwabe. He was an older man with his own homestead, who early in 1906 had just completed a period of work in Johannesburg. He had joined his neighbours when they had armed and made for eMthandeni under orders, he said, from Swayimana – their 'loyal' chief. Dludla reached eMthandeni on 22 June. Ritually purified and strengthened, his dispute with the Qwabe for the moment forgotten, he had been given meat by Meseni and had joined in the activities of the armed force gathered at eMthandeni, including the hunt held soon after he arrived. On Sunday 1 July he had been in charge of the Nyuswa force at the drift on the Maphumulo-Thongathi road.[5] After the capture when the crowd had gathered and were threatening Veal, he had rushed down to the road and taken charge.

The other senior man there, Lukhukhwana kaMcaba, was well known amongst the Qwabe because his father had been a personal servant of Meseni's father Musi. He had been placed with the Nyuswa by Meseni as his 'eyes and ears', and was drinking in a homestead near the road when he heard the shouts that a white man on a bicycle was approaching. By the time he got to Veal he was surrounded, but Lukhukhwana had pushed through the crowd, insisting that orders be obeyed and the white man be taken to Meseni. Singing a song of triumph, the force began to move towards eMthandeni eight kilometres away. Veal found the going rough and he stumbled as his boots slipped on the stony path. Lukhukhwana placed his right arm through Veal's left to help him along.

Before they arrived the sound of their singing had reached eMthandeni. Then came the messengers who announced that a white man had been captured. Macabacaba ordered the Qwabe to form up on the open space behind the homestead, and, when the Nyuswa arrived, the circle closed with Veal in the centre, now hanging desperately onto Lukhukhwana's arm. For a moment the mood changed. The Qwabe began to sing their 'war-song'. The sources are in English and the translation is hostile but if the 'war-song' was, as I suspect, the Qwabe *ihubo*, then its emotional power changed the mood from the noisy rough and tumble of the capture and the march across the hills to one of solemnity as the ancestors were invoked and the links made between this moment and the deep Qwabe past. Ritual killing was not made in anger or hostility, but as a sacrifice of the enemy to gain strength over them.

Representatives of different faiths had been present to witness this. There were *amakholwa* – believers from surrounding Christian missions, including preachers, with the *shokobezi* hanging from their dark clerical suits, or stuck in their hats. There were also *izinyanga*: one with a name like Maqandaqanda occurs often in the records. There was Sibhoko, a Tonga who had treated patients in Natal for half a century and now added to the medicine powder from an unexploded shell fired at Pheyana on 27 July. It was to be disputed whether he had been the most important, or whether it was Mabalengwe who had just arrived with, he said, body parts of white soldiers to give power to the potions. There was Mgwaqo kaQanana from the southern parts of Meseni's chiefdom, elderly, a herbalist who some said was an *umthakathi*, and others said was insane. Those closest to Veal, in the midst of the crowd pressing closer to get a view, included the *izinduna* in charge of the escort, Lukhukhwana and Dludla; his captors Sibeko and Sihlobo; and Macabacaba, the senior *induna*.

Men at the drift

Dludla kaSiyazana: Nyuswa *induna*.

Lukhukhwana kaMcaba: Meseni's representative.

Sibeko kaNdindiyana: Captures Veal.

Charge . . .

At this point the evidence began to differ radically, as all parties sought to deny that they had witnessed the killing. Meseni was said to have kept his distance before leaving the scene entirely, and an old trusted *induna* Somfongoza had pushed into the crowd and shouted that Meseni ordered that Veal be released. Others denied this. The men who had caught Veal accepted that they had led the large party of armed men who had conveyed him to Meseni at eMthandeni and stood with him in the circle at eMthandeni. But there their responsibility ended, when they obeyed the order to disperse and Meseni and Macabacaba took over. Lukhukhwana said, for example:

> We all left to eat and the white man remained with Meseni, Macabacaba and those who captured him. I returned to my hut to sleep towards evening and heard the elderly men say 'The white man is killed'. I asked 'Who killed him?' the reply was 'Meseni killed him'. I was in the hut with Meseni and said 'Why was the white man killed?' Meseni replied 'I am the chief, I can do as I like'! Mtshume was also in the hut at the time. I cannot say that Macabacaba killed the white man. All the natives say and know that Meseni killed the white man. No one else would have killed him. I know nothing more about the murder.[6]

Then there was Sibeko:

> I caught 'Veal'. Meseni sent the impi from Swaimana's Tribe
> out to guard the road on that Sunday with instructions to take
> any white man to him alive.

The next day they had been told Veal was dead, and Sibeko had
been given a cheque and some cash taken from the cyclist's pockets,
in accordance with custom associated with hunting, which rewarded
the man who had struck the first blow. But he had not killed him,
and did not know what had happened after Veal had been left
with their *inkosi* Meseni and his *induna* Macabacaba.[7]

This was the broad outline of events as sketched by the end of
July 1906 soon after the event.[8] The police and the detectives now
had to get answers to the detailed questions: who had participated
in the killing of Veal, who had struck the final blows, and who had
mutilated the body; and which of the two interpretations of who
authorised the killing should be followed – the one which placed
the blame on Meseni as *inkosi* of eMthandeni, or the other, which
asserted that Macabacaba had ignored Meseni's instruction to release
Veal?

In October 1906 a more detailed story began to emerge. When
Veal had been searched a diary had been found. It had been passed
amongst the *kholwa* till one was found who could read it. Veal, he
had said, was a 'detective' who

> has come from Greytown, he is on his way through here to go
> to Tongaat and then return to Maritzburg, he has made a bet
> that he will go through without the rebels seeing him – and
> that he will receive a big sum of money if he gets through to
> Tongaat and thence to Maritzburg.[9]

Thus it was apparent that Veal was no innocent traveller. Mhaqwa
then began to identify individuals responsible for his death. Sibeko

and Sihlobo, he said, had pulled Veal away from Lukhukhwana and delivered the blows that killed him. 'I covered my eyes and went home.'[10]

Sihlobo was dead, but Sibeko and Lukhukhwana were traced amongst the prisoners in the compound at Jacobs in Durban and questioned again. It was an unnerving experience for them, not knowing what information their interrogators had at their disposal, but they kept to their initial accounts, reiterating the obvious defence

---

The main suspects at the end of 1906

This is a short list – nineteen were eventually charged – and it is impossible to trace all their histories here – nor those of the many men upon whom suspicion fell but were not in the end brought to court. I concentrate therefore on

Macabacaba: *induna* of Meseni, his official representative at Ndwedwe. Arrived eMthandeni 29 June and placed in charge of the armed force. Accused of disobeying Meseni's instruction to release Veal. Nine sons killed in the rebellion.

Dludla: Nyuswa *induna* at the drift and previously one of Meseni's men. Arrived eMthandeni c.22 July. Said to have reported capture of Veal to Meseni.

Lukhukhwana: Meseni's eyes and ears at the drift. 'Assisted' Veal on his march to Mthandeni.

Sibeko: Veal's admitted captor and alleged killer.

Mabalengwe: Meseni's 'great war-doctor'.

Mgwaqo: the *umthakathi*.

Muthiwentaba: Brother of Sibeko.

Sibhoko: *inyanga* (continually confused in the record with Sibeko), arrested later.

Maqandaqanda [?]: *inyanga* – never found.

– that is, they pointed upwards, to Meseni, the man in authority over them, whose instructions they believed they were obeying when they brought Veal to eMthandeni. Thus Lukhukhwana reasserted that when he had protested at the killing of a non-combatant, Meseni had replied: 'Am I not a chief?'[11]

The investigators then moved to the gaol at the Durban Point where Dludla and Macabacaba were detained. They also held Meseni responsible: as Macabacaba said, 'Chief Meseni is to blame for the murder of this white man as he could have stopped the men from doing any injury to him – he had great power during the rebellion. I was afraid of him.'[12] Another suspect from the Point gaol was also interrogated and went further. He was Muthiwentaba, brother of Sibeko, who was very explicit and alleged that Meseni had 'said that if we killed a white man at a battle we were to bring his testicles and head to him'.[13]

By December 1906 it was decided that although the incident had taken place in the Maphumulo division, the inquiry should be conducted from the Lower Thukela division under the control of Frank Shuter at the Stanger magistrate's office. The most important suspects, Macabacaba, Dludla, Lukhukhwana, Sibeko, and now Muthiwentaba, were moved from Durban to Stanger for further investigation. Mgwaqo – the man whom many thought to be an *umthakathi* (a witch or perhaps insane) and who had been under suspicion from the start and sentenced in August to five years and twenty lashes, a considerable punishment for a man over sixty – also joined those under suspicion for killing Oliver Veal.

They were all very frightened now and their reluctance to name names began to weaken. It was becoming clear that to protect themselves, they could not continue merely saying that they had obeyed orders and handed Veal over: they had to be more specific about what they had seen. But this also had its dangers: they were prisoners, dependent on imperfect information or gossip, and in the control of their warders, the police and the detectives who were in contact with the outside world. If the information they gave appeared to threaten others they might find themselves at the mercy of a counter-charge or even being framed. And as the investigation moved on from December into January, often in the presence of men who they alleged had also participated in the events, such a possibility became a reality.

Macabacaba now made a number of statements before Shuter that were much fuller and more detailed than any of his previous ones. He was also forced to amend aspects of his earlier statements,[14] but the essence of his evidence remained unchanged:

> I say Meseni is trying to put the blame on the people for the death of the whiteman. His conduct is different now to when it was at the Mtandeni Kraal, there he showed his anger for the death of the men who fell at the Peyana fight. Then it was his command to the impi to capture any whiteman and bring him to the Mtandeni Kraal. The impi brought the whiteman to the Mtandeni. There [at eMthandeni] the whiteman became the 'game' of Meseni. There [in gaol at Maphumulo, however] Meseni replied 'I told the people to release the whiteman and let him go'. I asked who was present when this command was given. Meseni replied that Mtwazi was present. When the authorities called Mtwazi and questioned him, Mtwazi said he had never heard such a command given. I said to Meseni 'Can an Induna do as he pleases?' Meseni did not make any reply. Meseni never said to me that the whiteman was not to be killed. I did not hear any command given by Meseni that the whiteman was to be killed – but I say it was Meseni who gave the command that any whiteman who was captured was to be brought to the Mtandeni.[15]

Macabacaba gave more details of events at eMthandeni. He had arrived on Friday 29 June and had therefore only been there for a short time when the killing took place on Sunday. He had come on instructions from his magistrate at Ndwedwe to investigate the large number of men who had left the district to join the men at eMthandeni. But on his arrival Meseni welcomed him as an ally and appointed him *induna* over the force gathered there. Meseni needed support from a man of Macabacaba's status and seniority. The mood at eMthandeni, amongst the leaders at any rate, had been most sombre: the engagement at Pheyana had taken place the day before and the consequences for those in positions of responsibility, Meseni especially, had been devastating. Many of the huts at eMthandeni were sheltering the wounded and the homestead was in deep mourning for the men who had been killed.

Macabacaba told how, before dawn on Sunday 1 July, he had received a message from Meseni that he was to order the men to turn out. The Qwabe and Nyuswa formed an *umkhumbi*, and Meseni and Macabacaba had entered it. Meseni had addressed the gathering. Up to then he had acted on the defensive, but Pheyana had changed that:

> 'Men, I am greatly grieved, my warriors were shot down by the Troops at the Peyana, but I was not fighting. Now I am determined against the Troops. If you find them, stab them, if you overtake a person, capture him and bring him to me. Go now men of the impi, you Lukhukhwana go and show the road which goes up the Umvoti and when you reach the main road, hold it.' Meseni charged the impi to assist him and be powerful against those who wished to kill him.

The force made off to their positions, and Macabacaba and Meseni had walked back to the homestead: 'I talked with Meseni, he was greatly grieved because of the men of the impi who had been killed in the Peyana fight. He was crying and tears were falling down his face.' [16]

Magistrate Shuter was impressed. This seemed to make sense. Defeated at Pheyana, and grieving over the men killed, Meseni had been overtaken by a desire for vengeance – and when that afternoon Veal fell into his hands, the moment seemed to have arrived. As Shuter wrote: a 'large number of Meseni's impi were shot in that fight and that fact caused Meseni to become greatly grieved, and made him to become evilly disposed towards the troops'.[17]

. . . and counter-charge

Thus by the beginning of 1907 the case against Meseni was growing stronger, more men were named as participants in the killing, and the magistrate was becoming more convinced that a case could be constructed against the Qwabe chief. Men associated with Meseni, both in and out of detention, were increasingly concerned that they might be the next named. They had to protect themselves. And, as they sought ways to do this, so the broad alliance, which in July 1906 had brought to eMthandeni thousands of armed men from different chiefdoms between Durban and Maphumulo, began to fragment. Macabacaba, the man in charge of the force, was from the Ndwedwe division to the south; the young men who had captured Veal were Nyuswa higher up the Mvoti and had long been in conflict with their Qwabe neighbours. Their version of events laid the blame for the killing on men who lived in the vicinity of eMthandeni – Meseni and the Qwabe most closely associated with him. This latter group, in turn, from the end of January 1907, began to present the investigation with another version of events – an opposing one – a coherent set of statements which sought to exonerate Meseni, and explicitly blame Macabacaba and the men who had captured Veal, for the white man's death.[18]

The man who led this counter-charge, at least the one who is best documented, for there were others in the shadows, was Zwezinye kaJacobe. He was related to Meseni, married to his sister, had some pretensions to being an *inyanga*, and had worked with other doctors at eMthandeni. He had been arrested, brought before the Stanger martial law court, but not convicted. He came under renewed suspicion at the end of the year when Lukhukhwana had mentioned his name before the magistrate as one of the men who had been present at eMthandeni. Shuter had him re-arrested, but he was released with instructions to remain ready to answer charges when called upon to do so.

Up to this point he had denied participating in the rebellion. Now he changed his statement. He admitted that he had been at eMthandeni and assisted in the rituals to purify and strengthen the armed force there, and said that he was prepared to give evidence against those who wanted to involve him further in what had happened, in the killing of the white man in particular:

> as I had failed in my original intention – to wipe all the whites off the face of the earth – I made a clean breast of it . . . What caused me to rebel was the poll-tax. What made me make the statement was because I become angry with others denying things which we actually did.[19]

Zwezinye had been out with a force watching the approaches on 1 July, when he had received a message from Meseni to take over the duty of guarding the entrance to eMthandeni, to make sure all newcomers were ritually purified before coming into contact with the men under arms. Zwezinye strengthened them by sprinkling (*ukuchela*) with medicine (*intelezi*) after which they were able to join the armed men. He had been outside the hut when the news of Veal's capture reached eMthandeni, and heard Meseni consulting with his advisers, including Macabacaba and Dludla:

> I heard Meseni say 'Had the whiteman any firearms?' The reply was made that he was riding a Bicycle. Then Meseni said 'No, I do not see, it would be right to return the man and the Bicycle to the road where the man had been captured. Go out Macabacaba, Go out Dhludhla. The man has not done wrong, he is only travelling – take him away Macabacaba, he was

travelling along the Government road and I do not know why
you Dhludhla captured him.' Macabacaba said 'We shall never
let the whiteman go, he is a spy'. 'We shall kill him'.

The argument went on:

Dhludhla said 'I agree with Macabacaba in what he says, why
should the whiteman be released after we have suffered the defeat
at Peyana?' Meseni said 'My last words to you are if you will
insist on not letting the whiteman go, do what you like with
him, I have finished.'[20]

Meseni then called his dogs, picked up an iron rod, and walked up
a hill behind eMthandeni to dig for medicine for a sick child.

Zwezinye continued, telling how Macabacaba and Dludla had
given orders for the men in the homestead to form an *umkhumbi*
and wait for the arrival of the armed party with its white game –
the *inyamazana emhlope* caught in the hunt. They had then
assembled, with Veal in the centre flanked by Sibeko and Sihlobo,
and Lukhukhwana still holding him by the arm. Dludla had been
present, with Macabacaba in overall charge. A final attempt had
been made to get Veal released. Somfongoza, a greatly respected
old man who had been *induna* to Meseni's father, Musi, had entered
the crowd and repeated Meseni's order that the white man had to
be taken back to where he was captured. But he had been ignored.
Veal had been taken from the circle, his coat and waistcoat removed
and the pockets searched. Macabacaba had given the order to 'Kill
him'. Sibeko and Sihlobo struck their blows, Veal tried to defend
himself before Sibeko killed him with a final assegai thrust.[21]

Zwezinye did not know what happened after this. But the next
morning he had seen Macabacaba, Dludla and Sibeko wearing
Veal's coat and hat, coming from the direction of the killing. They
had been accompanied by Sibhoko, Meseni's Thonga doctor. He
was carrying something wrapped in grass. They had made up a fire,

placed an *udengezi* containing medicine on it, and then added the contents of the grass parcel: 'it looked like flesh and had white fatty tissue on it.' Macabacaba was ordered to place assegais in the medicine, then Sibeko, then all the Nyuswa had to point their assegais towards the *udengezi*, followed by the Qwabe.

Afterwards Zwezinye had drawn Sibeko aside and asked him why he had killed Veal despite Meseni's orders. The reply was that he had been ordered to so by the *induna* Macabacaba. He also confirmed that a part of the white man had been added to the medicine, and that Sibeko had been present when the white man had been cut up – together with Macabacaba, Dludla, Sibhoko and Mgwaqo.

Here at last was detailed evidence of the killing. Corroboration came in steadily over the next few days and weeks in a series of statements made before the magistrate at Stanger. Although in essence they supported Zwezinye, they gave more names and added more detail. Madevu kaJalimana,[22] who had been second-in-command of the Qwabe section at the drift, was in the seventh month of his sentence in Dundee when he was named by Lukhukhwana and moved to Stanger. Here he decided, like Zwezinye, to admit what he had previously denied and make a statement about what he had seen at eMthandeni. He was frank about his motive – self-defence: 'Had they not mentioned my name I should not have said anything about it, but as they mentioned my name I was bound to mention their names.'[23] In addition to his general confirmation of Zwezinye's account, he gave further information on the activities of Sibhoko, Meseni's chief *inyanga*. After the fight at Pheyana he had added the contents of the unexploded shell to his *intelezi* and sprinkled the troops with it, saying 'There is Mabopa. The guns will fill with water.' And at the strengthening ceremony on the morning after Veal had been killed, when the assegais points had been placed in the medicine being heated in the *udengezi*, he had said, 'Here is the defeat of the white man. It is darkness for the white people.'[24] Ntshiyikane, another convicted rebel, was released from gaol on 30 January 1907, the day he made his statement. He had climbed a tree to watch, and he gave details of how the men around Veal removed his coat and led him away from the crowd where he was killed. Somfongoza, well into his seventies and counsellor to both Meseni and his father, told how he had been sent to repeat Meseni's message to the crowd to release the white man, but that he had not been obeyed. He was arrested, detained at Maphumulo for a few weeks, then moved to Stanger where he was promised he would be released if he gave evidence of his abortive attempt to save the white man.[25]

From now on it was the three younger men, Zwezinye, Ntshiyikane and Madevu, who were to work most closely with the investigating team. They stayed near the Stanger courthouse, on call, talking with the police, or travelling with the investigating detectives to identify people and places that had a bearing on the case.

The counter-charge was working. Here were Qwabe witnesses at the centre of events who could give detailed accounts of the killing and who was involved. Macabacaba and the Nyuswa men were not going to be allowed to hold Meseni responsible for the killing, and with him possibly those most closely associated with him at eMthandeni. For some officials this version, by exonerating Meseni, went against their favoured interpretation: for others the gains were considerable because it gave them such detailed evidence of events – evidence that they felt could form the basis of a convincing case before a court.

But it was only a start. Not only were there sworn statements that conflicted with this version of events, but one aspect was still not covered. The crime was not just one of murder – Veal's body had also been mutilated and had been used for medicine. Who had removed the genitals, the rectum, the viscera, the foot and hand, and the head? There were suggestions that two of the *izinyanga* were responsible – Sibhoko[26] and the obscure Maqandaqanda – one witness saying that he had seen him with entrails and genitals

---

Leading crown witnesses

Zwezinye kaJacobe: Rebel, but found not guilty at the Stanger martial law trials. Re-arrested. *Inyanga* and relative of Meseni. Treated newcomers at eMthandeni. Key witness.

Somfongoza kaMtambo: *Induna* to Meseni and his father. Gave the message to release Veal.

Mbulawa: Details of the killing, especially the *kholwa* involvement.

Madevu: Brought to Stanger after seven months in gaol after being named by Lukhukhwana. Witness to the capture of Veal.

Ntshiyikane: Not gaoled and agreed to make statement. Climbed a tree to witness the killing of Veal, wheeled the bike to eMthandeni.

Mhaqwa: Brought food to eMthandeni. Heard Veal's diary entry read.

---

on a stick, and holding Veal's head.[27] However, even if the statement were valid the suspects had disappeared.

And there was one other name on the list of wanted *izinyanga*. As early as 30 July 1906 Governor McCallum had told the Minister of Justice that he had information that the name of 'the witch doctor who had doctored the tribe' was Mabalengwe,[28] and had given instructions that everything should be done to secure his arrest. The military handed the matter over to the Natal Police who at the end of December reported that despite all their efforts they had not been able to find him. The breakthrough came early in 1907.

Mabalengwe, the spots of the leopard

On 27 February Zwezinye kaJacobe, by now the key witness in the Veal murder investigation, recognised a man sitting at the store near the entrance to the Stanger courthouse. He went under different names, but Zwezinye identified him as Mabalengwe, the spots of the leopard, the son of Mandlamakhulu, who lived at the Lutheran mission at Pinetown. Zwezinye called a policeman, the man was arrested and his haversack was searched. It was found to contain medicines.

The next day Zwezinye made a formal statement before Frank Shuter, the magistrate. Mabalengwe, he said, had been the war-doctor at eMthandeni homestead during the rebellion. He had arrived there with recommendations from Ndlovu kaThimuni and had in his possession powerful medicines. He said he had been with Bhambatha himself, and had assisted Ndlovu when he attacked the whites at Thring's Post. He had been, when Meseni was first informed of his presence in the area, attending to Mashwili and the *impi* at Izinsimba. When he had completed his work there, he accepted Meseni's invitation and went to eMthandeni. Here, on 25 June, under the *umGanu* – marula – tree, Mabalengwe and his three assistants had made *intelezi* – war-medicine – and placed it in an *udengezi* on a fire. He had smeared one side of Meseni's face with black medicine, the other with red, and had then produced what appeared to be flesh, which he placed in the *udengezi*. He had said that it was a portion of a white man's genitals he had got from the doctor who had been with Bhambatha. He had poured oil from a bottle into the *udengezi* and the armed men were ordered to pass through the fumes and then, having been sprinkled with liquid from another pot, to say 'It is darkness – *mnyama* – for the white-man'. A circle was formed and Mabalengwe had addressed the men, saying that he had worked for Bhambatha and obtained his medicine from him. All pigs and other animals had to be killed, no white clothing should be worn and all articles of European manufacture had to be removed from their huts. No one should wear the skin of the small antelope, the duiker. Mabalengwe remained at eMthandeni until 1 July. Then, immediately after Veal was killed, he had handed the war-medicine over to the witness, Zwezinye himself, and that night disappeared.

Shuter sent the statement to the Attorney-General that day. The contents of Mabalengwe's haversack were placed in sealed envelopes and taken to the government laboratory in Pietermaritzburg by the detective in charge of the case, William Milliken. Most of the items were nondescript pieces of animal tissue – blood and bone and teeth. But the item in envelope no. 3 was different. It was a portion of the right half of the tip of a human penis, coated with dried blood to which fibres of cotton were attached, and there was some light brown pubic hair as well, pulled out, not cut from the flesh.[29]

On 6 March the Chief Commissioner of the Natal Police reported to the Minister of Justice that a 'Native Doctor' had been arrested in Stanger, and 'in the Doctor's bag were found several bottles supposed to contain human fat, also a piece of a thigh joint and other portions of a body, either Veal's or Powell's. This Native is said to have been with Bamabata at the time of the attack on the Police at Impanza'.[30]

The breakthrough had been made. The Governor's seven-month-old order had been met. Mabalengwe's arrest and Zwezinye's statement indicated that there were links between the leaders of the rebellion in the Thukela valley – Bhambatha, Sambela, Ndlovu, Mashwili and Meseni: Mabalengwe had provided war-medicine for them all, and treated their men.[31] And these were links of the darkest kind – made of body parts, obtained by murder and mutilation, binding the rebels together by means of barbaric ritual and the promise of victory over the whites. Mabalengwe's activities provided the rebellion with a connected narrative of savage rites and practices, initiated by chiefs in whom the colony had once invested responsibility and trust, and carried out by men whose actions vividly demonstrated how thin the veneer of civilisation was spread over Natal's African population.

The witnesses who had previously given statements to the investigation were recalled to provide the necessary formal supplements to their evidence. Yes, they knew Mabalengwe. He

was the great war-doctor of the tribe. They had seen him at
eMthandeni on the day that Veal had been killed. He had been
wearing a baboon skin cape, and a hat of jackal skin. On this they
were all agreed. Mabalengwe, who had so far been referred to only
infrequently and in passing in the records, now became a fixture –
as did his baboon and jackal skin accoutrements, by which all the
witnesses identified him.[32]

Preliminary examination, March–April 1907

The arrest of Mabalengwe caused a stir amongst the top officials in
Pietermaritzburg. At last evidence was emerging of the savagery of
African beliefs in witch-doctors and their potions, and of the role
they had played in the rebellion. When made public, the activities
of a man like Mabalengwe, caught with body parts in his medicine
bag, would go a long way towards justifying Natal's interpretation
of events and its subsequent actions during the rebellion. The
Attorney-General made contact with magistrate Shuter. He sent
instructions for the preliminary examination to be completed
without delay. A draughtsman was on his way to prepare the
necessary diagrams. He should proceed with the case, and there
should be no limit on the number of men charged for being present
at the killing: 'I wish this instruction to be closely adhered to,
whatever number there may be of them.'[33] The Attorney-General
intended something of a show trial.

Shuter got to work. As the depositions collected so far were
'disjointed',[34] fresh depositions were needed for the preliminary
examination, and in March and April the witnesses recounted again
what had they had seen at eMthandeni. In the process the links
became stronger, the details became more precise, and the
corroborative elements more prominent. The Attorney-General
gave instructions that Meseni was not to be indicted. It was easier
to construct a more coherent case now that Meseni was no longer
a suspect and his supporters were assisting the crown. The
examination could focus on Macabacaba, with Mabalengwe's

journeys among Ndlovu, Meseni and Mashwili to doctor their men providing both motive and a dark and disturbing narrative structure to the events.[35]

When Shuter asked if Meseni could be used as a witness for the prosecution, the Attorney-General gave him a 'free hand' to conduct the examinations as he thought best.[36] On Shuter's specific request Meseni was moved from the Pietermaritzburg gaol to Stanger for two days. We can assume that, as well as giving information, Meseni was briefed on the evidence collected so far and on the strategy that was being developed by the magistrate and his key crown witnesses.

Meseni made his statement on 19 March.[37] In it he identified the suspects as men who had been present at eMthandeni and implicated in Veal's death. They included Macabacaba, Dludla, Lukhukhwana, Mgwaqo and Muthiwentaba. He made special mention of Mabalengwe: 'I had no war doctor until Mabalengwe came . . . He was my war doctor.' He then repeated his defence: he had given orders for Veal to be released but Macabacaba had refused to obey. That night his doctor, Sibhoko, had brought a smoking clay pot into his hut, saying that it was the *inyamazane* they had killed. Meseni had driven him away, saying 'do you not know that you have killed the whiteman and you have also killed me?'. He had never seen Sibhoko again. Nor had the police.

Meseni's statement was read, as was required, in the presence of the accused. Macabacaba confronted him, saying that it was he, Meseni, who had wanted *inyamazane emhlope* and had ordered his *inyanga* – in fact the crown witness, Zwezinye[38] – to prepare the body. Meseni denied it – it was Mabalengwe who had wanted the *inyamazane*. If he, Meseni, had ever wanted a white man there were enough of them living locally for him to have got one. Macabacaba should have obeyed his order and released Veal, 'but now he finds himself in trouble he puts all blame on me'. Meseni went back to gaol in Pietermaritzburg well briefed for the coming trial.

More witnesses were brought forward. One has to suspect that they were being coached or at least were learning from their interrogators' responses, ratcheting up the sensational aspects. Sambana, convicted as a rebel but now pardoned, remembered Mabalengwe saying:

> The rebels under Ndhlovu have conquered the white people, and I have whiteman's fat that I shall work with there. He said they had finished off the white people not even one remained. He said he wanted another whiteman's fat which would make our bodies bullet proof and would turn the bullets into water.[39]

Zwezinye made another statement, now telling how, when he had taken over responsibility for the rituals, Mabalengwe had cut off a piece of a penis for him to add to the preparation, 'saying it is portion of the penis of a whiteman. I examined it. It was smelling. He directed me to use it when sprinkling the war medicine ... He said he had procured one whiteman at Bambata's and that he had procured another whiteman at Ndhlovu's'.[40] Madevu stated that Mabalengwe had informed the men at eMthandeni that he had obtained from Ndlovu's *impi* medicine incorporating a white man's anus and testicles which would enable them to stand firm – *ukumisa* – against the enemy.[41] And it was Mabalengwe who had led the crowd in the cry of 'Ji!' it is finished, as the assegai killed Oliver Veal.

Sir Henry McCallum's term of office as Governor was coming to an end, and in the light of the criticism he and the Natal ministry had received for their handling of the rebellion, a trial which revealed to the public something of the inner secrets of the rebellion of the previous year and the horror which had been averted, would be a very suitable parting gift for him. It was decided that the case would not be referred to the Native High Court but would be heard at the next session of the Supreme Court of Natal.

Notes

1. PAR: AGO I/1/317, 'notes of precognition of Meseni, made by Lieutenant Smyth who defended Meseni at Mapumulo in July 06'.
2. PAR: AGO I/1/317, Statement by Macabacaba, Maphumulo, 18 July 1906. Macabacaba made another statement at the end of July which can be found in PAR: 1/MPO, 5/4/: 'Meseni must have ordered his death because the white man would not have been killed by the impi without orders from the men commanding them. viz: the Chief.'
3. PAR: AGO I/1/317, Statement by Macabacaba, Maphumulo, 22 January 1907.
4. In some sources they are named as brothers.
5. PAR: AGO I/1/317, Statement by Dludla, Point gaol, 10 November 1906.
6. PAR: AGO I/1/317, Statement by Lukukwana, Maphumulo, 29 July 1906.
7. PAR: AGO I/1/317, Statement by Seboko, Maphumulo, 29 July 1906 and by Lukukwana, Maphumulo, 29 July 1906.
8. With the exception of Dludla whose statement was taken later while he was detained in Durban, but while it gives interesting detail it does not alter the substance of what was collected in July at Maphumulo from the men with whom he had been associated.
9. PAR: AGO I/1/317, Statement by Mhaqwa kaDulela, 13 December 1906.
10. PAR: AGO I/1/317, Statement by Mhaqwa kaDulela, 9 October 1906. This young man's statement is important because Mhaqwa was not a prisoner possibly seeking remission of sentence, but had been at eMthandeni with his sister having taken food there for their father. He nonetheless, in the months to come, gave evidence that supported the prosecutor's line. I have been unable to assess the extent of his responsibility for establishing the crown's case.
11. PAR: AGO I/1/317, Statement by Lukukwana, Stanger, 28 December 1906.
12. PAR: AGO I/1/317, Statement by Macabacaba, Durban, 12 November 1906.
13. PAR: AGO I/1/317, Statement by Mutiwentaba, Durban, 10 November 1906.
14. Specifically, he now admitted that he *had* informed Meseni of Veal's capture.
15. PAR: AGO I/1/317, Statement by Macabacaba, Stanger, 27 December 1906, as continued on 22 January 1907.
16. PAR: AGO I/1/317, Statement by Macabacaba, Stanger, 27 December 1906.
17. PAR: AGO I/1/317, see Shuter undated, 40pp, summary of the case interleaved in the statements.
18. It is true that a few statements had been made towards the end of the year that tended to support this interpretation of events. Mhaqwa's evidence is significant, but only when it is considered in the context of all the evidence he gave, from his first statements through to his court appearance as a crown witness. PAR: AGO I/1/317, Statement by Mhaqwa kaDulela, 9 October 1906 and subsequent dates.
19. PAR: RSC I/1/96, Rex *v.* Macabacaba and others, Evidence of Zwezinye under

cross-examination, 15 May 1907. Although some of the detail had been suggested already by different witnesses, Zwezinye's evidence was important for its proximity to key events, its coherence, and the fact that it was soon corroborated and extended by a number of new witnesses. It is possible to work out a rough chronology from the scattered evidence in PAR: AGO, I/1/317 and 318, Shuter's undated forty-page summary in PAR: AGO, I/1/317 was based on evidence collected up to 15 January 1907. While writing this summary he announced that there was 'more information to hand' - and this seems to be the evidence provided by Zwezinye, and transcribed on 26 January 1907.

20. PAR: AGO, I/1/317, Statement by Zwezinye, Stanger, 26 January 1906.

21. PAR: AGO, I/1/317, Statement by Zwezinye, Stanger, 26 January 1906.

22. PAR: AGO, I/1/317, Statements by Madevu kaJalimana, Stanger, 6 and 22 February 1907, continued on 23 February 1907. I have chosen 'Madevu' for a man whose name is spelt in a variety of ways - Madefu, Madovu, Madofu, amongst the most common.

23. PAR: RSC, I/1/96, Rex *v.* Macabacaba and others, Madevu under cross-examination, 13 May 1907.

24. PAR: AGO, I/1/318, Statement by Madevu kaJalimana, 6 February 1907.

25. PAR: AGO, I/9/32, Shuter to Attorney-General, 7 and 9 February 1907; and RSC: I/1/96, Rex *v.* Macabacaba and others, Somfongoza under cross-examination, 15 May 1907.

26. See especially PAR: AGO, I/1/317, Statement by Zwidi ka Mpahleni, Stanger, 23 October 1906.

27. PAR: AGO, I/1/317, Evidence of Magalela kaJana, 10 December 1906.

28. BPP: C.3888, No. 20, McCallum to Elgin, 21 March 1907, Enc. McCallum to Minister of Justice, 30 July 1906. The original, and the subsequent correspondence can be found in PAR: MJPW 133. Two other names were given as rebel commanders, Malagati and Macabacaba. The chaos created by the archivists in Pietermaritzburg who dismembered the Government House series for binding make it difficult to discover who gave the Governor these names, but the date of the information, between the sentence of death passed on Meseni and the Governor's exercise of clemency, is suggestive.

29. PAR: RSC, I/1/96, Rex *v.* Macabacaba and others, Report by W. Watkins Pitchford, The laboratory, PMB, 8 March 1907.

30. PAR: AGO, I/1/316, 45/07, Chief Commissioner W.J. Clarke to Minister of Justice, 6 March 1907.

31. PAR: AGO, I/1/318, Shuter to Attorney-General, 28 February 1907.

32. For Zwezinye's initial statement see PAR: AGO, I/1/317, Statement by Zwezinye kaJakobe, 28 February 1907. In the same file Meseni on 19 March 1907 confirms Mabalengwe's presence, as did most of the other important prosecution witnesses on 8 March 1907.

33. PAR: AGO I/1/318, Attorney-General to Shuter, 8 March 1907.

34. PAR: AGO I/1/318, Shuter to Attorney-General, 11 March 1907.
35. KC, Stuart papers, file 14 contains an undated typescript (pp. 23–29) that summarises the evidence which supported what became the crown case with Mabalengwe as the great war-doctor playing the central role. It was fortunate that I studied the evidence on which the crown based its case, in its primary context, *before* reading the document compiled it would seem by Stuart as Intelligence Officer. This enabled me to identify and utilise for myself, independent of Stuart's covert but considerable influence, the key documents and witnesses.
36. PAR: AGO I/1/318, Attorney-General to Shuter, 12 March 1907.
37. PAR: AGO I/1/317, Statement by Meseni kaMusi, Stanger, 19 March 1907.
38. PAR: AGO I/1/317, Statement by Meseni kaMusi, Stanger, 19 March 1907, cross-examination page 18, Macabacaba pencilled in.
39. PAR: AGO I/1/317, Statement by Sambana, 14 March 1907.
40. PAR: AGO, I/1/316, Statement by Zwezinye kaJakobe, Stanger, 3 April 1907.
41. PAR: AGO, I/1/316, Statement by Madevu kaJalimana, Stanger, 4 April 1907.

7

Investigation and examination

The killing of Sangereid and Powell

Thring's Post, August 1906 to March 1907

Meanwhile investigations into the other killings in the Maphumulo division continued. These had taken place on 19 June when at dawn Ndlovu's force had joined with Ngqokwane's Mbedu at Thring's Post to raid cattle. They had also looted the store and attacked the men in the storekeeper's house. William Robbins, the spy/stock inspector, had been severely wounded and the young storekeeper, Adolf Sangereid, stabbed to death in the garden as he tried to run from the house. The reason for the attack on the civilians is not clear: at least part of the force had been under instructions not to harm non-combatants. It could have been uncomplicated hostility and the excitement of the moment amongst individuals in a large crowd of armed men over whom the leaders had momentarily lost control, but it was suggested at the time that it was to stop them sending a telegraphic warning to the militia.

A witness to the killing had been found early on in the investigations. He was Nkwantshu kaShimuni, under chief Ngqokwane of the Mbedu. In August 1906 he had told the authorities that he had been at Thring's Post at dawn and seen two men stab Sangereid. They were Ndabazezwe kaMditshana and Nkosi kaNoxula, men from his own district with whom he had grown up, and they were detained. Nkwantshu also said the men had boasted that later in the morning they had thrown assegais at a passing trooper, one of the weapons injuring his horse.[1] This was a reference to Trooper Koster who was at the time on his way from Maphumulo to Stanger and had taken a short cut to Thring's Post. Before getting there he had been attacked by a small party of armed men, but he had dismounted and fired at his assailants, who had then moved off.

As the weeks passed, so Nkwantshu remembered more of what had happened on 19 June, and the range of his experiences and the number of his identifications increased. At the end of October he made another statement expanding on the one he had made in August.[2] Robbins had been attacked by Gamalakhe kaSisekelo and Dabula kaMzwakali. He had been saved only by the order of Ndlovu, who was standing close by. Ndabazezwe and Nkosi had killed Sangereid and someone else had removed his trousers. In November Nkwantshu was sent to Maphumulo in order to identify witnesses,[3] but of the six named only two were found: 'All the rest are rebels. If I could get near enough to serve summons on them I could have arrested them long ago. They are all in the bush.'[4]

By the end of the year the Sangereid investigation had slowed, and in February 1907 Shuter felt that the case 'has come to a standstill owing to the fact that the remaining witnesses are rebels at large and cannot be secured'.[5] The Attorney-General was having none of it and wrote an angry minute demanding action and an indication of how to take the case further.[6] It was a dangerous thing to do, to apply pressure by demanding results. It increased the possibility of the fabrication of evidence and perhaps the settling of old scores. Nonetheless, while it might not have advanced the cause of justice, it did produce more witnesses. Dabula, the man who had struck Robbins, became a crown witness and corroborated Nkwantshu's statement that Ndababzezwe and Nkosi had killed Sangereid.[7] Ndabazezwe, it was said, had also been active in inciting rebellion and had afterwards boasted of looting the store and killing the white man. Nkwantshu produced a clutch of relatives and a neighbour who testified that on the morning of the attack they had been at Thring's Post where they had seen Ndabazezwe and Nkosi.[8]

The last witness was a man who had already been very active on the side of the investigating authority in Stanger – Zwezinye, the key witness in the Veal case. He swore that the first accused, Ndabazezwe, had given him a verbal account of his activities at the time. These included the killing of Sangereid and the subsequent attack on the mounted trooper.[9]

Oglesbys' store

The attack on the store at Thring's Post had taken place at dawn on 19 June. After this the Mbedu had made their way homewards with loot from the store, singing the song of triumph heard by Robbins as he lay wounded under the bushes where he had been placed by the men who had saved him. Ndlovu's men had gone back up the road with the cattle towards Maphumulo where, once the cattle had crossed the Otimati, they had moved to the right in the direction of Ndlovu's Ezintandaneni homestead. A portion of the force, however, had moved on ahead and set up an ambush for the convoy of supply wagons that had spent the night near the Oglesbys' store. It was then seven and the convoy was just moving off towards the Maphumulo magistracy when it had been attacked. Trooper Knox had made his dash up the road for the magistracy while Trooper Albert Powell had run off in the opposite direction down the road towards the Oglesbys' store. The two storekeepers, Thomas and Fred, father and son, had decided to take Powell to a hiding place in the krans over the hill behind the store. Powell and the elder Oglesby had begun to make their way up the hill and Fred followed once he had locked up the store.

News of their flight had been passed back down the road, and when it reached Ndlovu, he had given urgent instructions that the white storekeepers were not to be killed. The man who had conveyed the message was Ndlovu's *induna*, Luhoho, and he passed it on to Bhixa, who had once worked for the Oglesbys in Durban. Fred Oglesby had been reached first and told to return to the store, assured that he would not be harmed. Thomas Oglesby and Powell had just passed over the crest of the hill when they were overtaken by a crowd of armed men. Bhixa had got hold of the old man and hustled him through the crowd back down the hill. But not before Thomas Oglesby had seen Powell pinioned, his chest exposed, and an assegai driven into his heart.

Exhausted and terrified, Oglesby had not been able to identify the killer. This vital piece of information was now provided by Nkwantshu, the eyewitness to the killing of Sangereid, pardoned and released from gaol. He gave his evidence formally at Stanger on 22 March 1907, at the time when the Veal case was proceeding rapidly under the urging of the Attorney-General. After the Thring's Post attack, Nkwantshu said, he had stayed with Ndlovu's force and had been amongst the men who had followed the two whites, Oglesby senior and Trooper Powell. From the top of the ridge Nkwantshu looked down and saw the Zulu close on the two men. Oglesby had been rescued but Trooper Powell was stabbed twice by a man who had 'ripped the stomach down', taken his rifle and bandolier, and then made his way back down the hill where he handed over the weapons to Ndlovu.[10]

Nkwantshu named the killer as Sifo kaZwenyani (or Zwelinjani) Thembu. He was a man of some standing in this part of the Maphumulo division, in the vicinity of the magistrate's office. He lived on the Otimati river, down from Ndlovu, under Ngobizembe, now detained in Pietermaritzburg. Sifo had been employed in the pass office in Johannesburg, and he was a brash and confident man, determined to ingratiate himself with the authorities – in ways not always to their liking. Earlier in the year he had asked the Johannesburg Native Commissioner to send a message from Sifo to the people of his district advising them not to listen to 'foolish talk' and pay the hut tax.[11] A telegram was sent, but communication of this sort via officials did not follow protocol and raised some eyebrows. Nonetheless, on the recommendation of storekeeper Fred Oglesby, it was felt by the officials in Maphumulo that Sifo's presence would be to their advantage. One of his men was sent to Johannesburg to call him back home to work as an informer.

Sifo created a stir when he arrived at the magistracy in May. He had devised his own khaki uniform, with Sam Brown and cap, gaiters, red puttees and a yellow belt. But an imitation military uniform was not considered suitable dress for an undercover agent and Sifo was instructed to hand over some of the items,[12] go home, and make regular reports to Fred Oglesby who would pass them on to the intelligence officers based at Maphumulo.

Obviously, for Sifo to be named as Powell's killer was a shock to those who had recruited him. And as informer (now rebel) Sifo's fortunes declined, so rebel (now informer) Nkwantshu's improved. Sifo was still in detention: Nkwantshu, his accuser, had been pardoned and released. And freedom liberated not just the man but his memory, and the details Nkwantshu gave were quite shocking. After Sifo had handed over Powell's weapons to Ndlovu, he had gone back up the hill in the direction of the body. When he returned he had been accompanied by someone else – none other than the now notorious war-doctor, Mabalengwe. The two men had come

> from the direction of where the body of the soldier was lying. The prisoner Sifo was in possession of the penis and testicles with pubic hair of the dead soldier. He had it wound round his bayonet and was holding the bayonet like this. The prisoner Mabalengwe had something which he had tied up in grass.[13]

Once Nkwantshu had given the lead, other witnesses added the detail. Although none of them had actually seen the death blow, they did remember Mabalengwe saying 'he had a business to perform on the body of the deceased',[14] and they confirmed the triumphant progress of the two men down the hill, genitals skewered on the bayonet. In these accounts Sifo became more and more prominent, urging Ndlovu's men on, with Mabalengwe shouting, '"The men are running away, oh for the men of Bambata who never ran away" – He was wearing a baboon skin and had on a cap made of a Jackal skin.'[15]

By early April 1906 when Shuter held the preliminary examination, the story was almost complete. Here was a narrative that made sense of the hitherto inchoate attacks and murders at the end of June and the beginning of July 1906. Mabalengwe's activities provided the necessary connections and a framework upon which those men giving evidence for the crown could hang their stories. Sangereid had been stabbed by Ndabazezwe and Nkosi. Nkwantshu had seen them do it in the pre-dawn gloom of 19 June. He had then travelled up the road with Ndlovu's men to Oglesbys' store, and there, just over the crest of the hill, he had seen Sifo stab Powell to death, after which Sifo and Mabalengwe had exhibited Powell's genitals, to be used in the strengthening rituals. Mabalengwe had used them on Ndlovu's men before passing down to Mashwili's stronghold in the Izinsimba valley and then over to eMthandeni on 25 June. He had still been there when the men killed Veal on 1 July and had then handed over responsibility for doctoring to Zwezinye, now the key crown witness to events surrounding the Veal killing.

All that was left was to complete the final act. Mabalengwe had left eMthandeni after Veal's death to move out of the Mvoti valley, up over the high ground, across the Stanger-Maphumulo road, and down into the Izinsimba valley to rejoin Mashwili and encourage him to follow Ndlovu and Meseni's example:

He spoke and said 'Have you yet captured the white game (Nyamazana) for me?' The men of the impi replied that they had surrounded Macaes house but found no whiteman, that they had surrounded Tollners house but found no whiteman, that

---

Thring's Post

Key crown witness:	Nkwantshu kaShimuni
Accused:	Ndabazezwe kaMditshana
	Nkosi kaNoxula

Oglesbys' store

Key crown witness:	Nkwantshu kaShimuni
Accused:	Mabalengwe kaMandlamakulu
	Sifo kaZwenyani

---

they had surrounded the Police Camp but had not found any whiteman and that they had been to James Huletts house but had not found any whiteman. Then Mabalengwe said 'The people of Meseni are alright – they procured the white game . . . and now they are firm.' He said it would not be proper to doctor one body of men with the game procured by another body of men. He said you must get the game for yourselves. He then took the responsible men and Indunas to one side and he painted them with Medicine. He sprinkled the men of the impi. [16]

The bid to catch white game, this statement implies, had been made and failed finally when Campbell drove off the attacking force from the Izinsimba at the Macrae's store fight on the evening of 2 July. In amongst the obscurities and confusions of the many different accounts of the violence that had taken place on either side of the Stanger-Maphumulo road in June and July 1906 there was the strong, dark, fearful connecting thread. It had been woven by Mabalengwe, the great war-doctor, as he sought to excise the power of his white enemies, and transfer it to the men who opposed them. It was this that the crown prosecutors hoped would become apparent at the Special Criminal Session of the Natal Supreme Court in May 1907.

Notes

1. PAR: AGO I/1/316, Statement by Nkwantshu kaTshumini, Maphumulo, 9 August 1906.
2. PAR: AGO I/1/316, Statement by Nkwantshu kaTshumini, Stanger, 25 October 1906.
3. PAR: AGO I/1/316, Memorandum Sergt Rehmann Natal Police Stanger to Sergt L'Estrange NP Maphumulo, 2 November 1906.
4. PAR: AGO I/1/316, Sgt L'Estrange to Sgt Rehemann, Natal Police, 8 November 1906.
5. PAR: AGO I/1316, Shuter to Clerk of Peace, 1 February 1907 and Clerk of Peace to Attorney-General, 1 February 1907.
6. PAR: AGO I/1/316, Attorney-General to Clerk of Peace, 14 February 1907.
7. PAR: AGO I/1/316, Deposition by Dabula kaMzwakali, before Shuter at Stanger on 15 March 1907.
8. PAR: AGO I/1/316, Depositions by Ndabana kaTulumana, Malunge kaSomtshiyoze, Mqedi before Shuter at Stanger on 22 March 1907. Nkwantshu's role in recruiting these men was suggested in the trials that followed.
9. PAR: AGO I/1/316, Deposition by Zwezinye kaJakobe, before Shuter at Stanger, 22 March 1907.
10. PAR: AGO I/1/316, Statement by Nkwantshu kaShimuni, Stanger, 22 March 1907. Sifo was mentioned in his statement of 25 October 1906 but the reference was not specific.
11. PAR: SNA I/1/335, 435/06, N.C.C.D. to SNA, 10 February 1906.
12. PAR: RSC I/1/95, Rex v. Sifo and Mabalengwe, Evidence of John Ritchie, 28 May 1907.
13. PAR: AGO I/1/316, Statement by Nkwantshu kaShimuni, 22 March 1907.
14. PAR: AGO I/1/316, Statement by Mfuzi kaMcenti, 6 April 1907.
15. PAR: AGO I/1/316, Statement by Palafini kaSkunyana, 23 March 1907.
16. PAR: AGO I/1/318, Statement by Nkabi, 15 March 1907. In July the previous year, months before Mabalengwe became a major figure, someone of this name had been referred to as being at Izinsimba. See PAR: 1/SGR, 44/06, Rex v. men of Chief Mashwili, 30 July 1906. This is not to argue that this quotation is an accurate reflection of events – it does suggest, however, that there is some underlying validity in the account.

8

The Natal Supreme Court

Special Criminal Session, 13–21 May 1907

Murder in the Mvoti valley
The nineteen accused

It was decided that the men accused of the murders in the Maphumulo and Lower Thukela divisions in June and July 1906 should be tried in Pietermaritzburg at a Special Criminal Session of the Natal Supreme Court in May 1907. Justice John Dove Wilson would preside. He was born in Scotland in 1865 and practised in Edinburgh before being appointed to the Supreme Court of Natal in 1904.[1] There would also be a jury – of nine male colonists. Natal's Attorney-General, Gustave Aristide de Roquefeuil Labistour, would lead the prosecution team,[2] and all the accused would be defended by counsel.

The first case to be dealt with was the killing of Oliver Veal. As we have seen, the authorities wanted a trial that would not only punish the perpetrators but would retrospectively justify Natal's approach to the rebellion. Evidence led in the Supreme Court would demonstrate the sort of barbarity with which the Natal authorities had to deal: barbarity in the full sense of the word and comprehensible as such to all civilised people – not the sort of arcane offence suited to the Native High Court. It would be a trial that would publicise African atrocities and challenge any sentimental notion of progress and advancement. It would be a trial that should persuade those who accused Natal of hysteria and brutality to reconsider the charge. And the sentences would send a message to Natal's African population about the nature of colonial justice, and the perseverance with which those who defied it would be pursued and the severity with which they would be treated.

The Attorney-General had instructed Shuter to include amongst the accused as many of the people who had been present at the killing as possible. It was reckless to put pressure on the magistrate in this way, for he then leant on the police, who in turn put pressure on their spies and informers to demonstrate their insider knowledge by producing suitable suspects for investigation. In the end nineteen men were accused of Veal's murder.

The Attorney-General had never before prosecuted so many for one offence, and to facilitate identification he arranged for numbered cards to hang around the accused's necks when they entered court. They appear to have been selected to represent the main elements in the crowd around the unfortunate Mr Veal on that first Sunday of July 1906. The first five accused had been the prime suspects from the beginning of the investigation. Four of these had admitted that they had taken part in the capture of Veal but they rejected the accusation that they had gone on to kill him and mutilate his body.

One of the most deep-seated areas of concern and prejudice amongst Natal's settlers was the belief that behind the varied expressions of discontent were the 'mission-natives', 'half-educated' and 'partly-Christian'. Their presence was noticed and punished at all the centres of resistance, and *amakholwa* from mission stations in the Maphumulo division were said from the start to have been active at eMthandeni. Three of the accused were brought to court to represent all those who mixed Christianity and African beliefs with such horrifying consequences.

The bulk of the accused stood for members of the crowd who had gathered round Veal and witnessed the killing, although they might not have participated actively in it. Despite months of intense investigation, the detectives had been able to find only one representative of the class of men they most desired to bring to court – the 'war-doctors' whose need for white man's flesh lay behind Veal's death and the killing of Trooper Powell. He was accused number 15, Mabalengwe.

Some of those accused had been flogged, detained for nine months with hard labour, and removed for interrogation, and were continually anxious as they tried to discern the nature of the charges being developed against them and to work out a strategy to defend themselves. They had made a number of statements on different occasions, and at the preliminary examination had been given the opportunity to respond to the evidence that had been gathered against them. The most prominent of the accused, Macabacaba, responded with a vehemence still discernible in a badly translated and confused transcription:

Are these all the witnesses who have spoken against us? Where is Somfongoza? What I say is that Meseni & his doctors killed the whiteman because he sent the impi to look for him as he wanted him to doctor the impi with. I had no power to go against Meseni in his own kraal & kill the whiteman. Meseni said he would overcome the government with his doctors. If he did not want him killed he had plenty of other Indunas to have handed him over to. Meseni [now] sees death looking him in the face so he wants to kill other people who have done no wrong. He could have saved him [Veal, then] if he had wished to do so. Throughout all the land can any one say where an Induna killed a man against the orders of his chief? All his witnesses who have testified against me have done so because I pointed to their chief. They are doing this because they say why did I say it was Meseni who killed the white man. Why do they want my blood when I was not present when Meseni decided to fight. How is it they have not named any of the men of the Umvoti with whom they are living & where the rebellion started ... I was afraid to contradict or oppose him for fear of his killing me as he nearly killed Mbulelo an Induna of his whom he told to go & chase over the sea with Mr Shuter. Meseni took me from my own division where I had paid my taxes. I want to see him & speak to him personally. I leave myself in the hands of the court. This is all I wish to say.[3]

Dludla had been in charge of the Nyuswa force that had captured Veal and marched him to eMthandeni. Lukhukhwana, Meseni's eyes and ears, had led Veal to his execution. They reserved their defence. Sibeko was accused of striking the death blow. When confronted with the evidence he denied it:

It is a marvel that people should talk like this putting what Meseni has done on to us. I do not deny that I caught the white man. I was sent by Meseni to do so. I marvel at Madevu, who was the chief's representative, not telling his chief when the evil occurred, & Zwezinye too who was the sentry at the gate & the chief coming & looking & then not saving the white man whom he had ordered should be released. If I had been going to kill him he would have died at Gaillard's drift. We caught him at the place where no people were – the two of us only. We put him before Meseni & his doctor & went away to eat. This is all for the present till I go before the judges & meet Meseni.[4]

None of these men denied their specific roles in the events that preceded the killing, but they had been acting under Meseni's orders and they had not participated in the killing itself. Veal had been handed over to Meseni and his doctors.

For settler Natal the foolishness of those who believed education and Christianity would eradicate savagery, and the dangers inherent in mixing Christian spirituality with African superstition, were demonstrated by the participation of the *amakholwa* in the rebellion generally and Veal's murder in particular. They were represented amongst the accused by three men, two of whom were arrested on evidence given late in the investigation. Jonase denied that he had been at eMthandeni at all. Joseph had been working in Durban and Johannesburg, had come to Stanger on the advice of his employer to claim compensation for losses during the rebellion, and had been arrested there. Zwezinye identified him as leading the prayers said before Veal's murder, dressed in a black coat and hat, and wearing spectacles and the white ox tail of rebellion. Indeed the black clerical garb adorned with the *shokobezi* became as important as Mabalengwe's jackal and baboon skin: in the end one has to suspect that its ubiquity in the evidence was more a consequence of the encouraging reaction of the interrogators than a reflection of the prevalence of clerical dress at eMthandeni. July dressed as a minister, and had been in charge of a mission school at Mona. He admitted to being part of the force but was up in the hills guarding the access routes to eMthandeni when the white man was brought in.[5] He had been named by Meseni during his visit to the magistrate's office at Stanger and was brought from the Jacobs compound to Stanger to be indicted.[6]

The accused Mqwago was said to have been involved in the mutilation and had perhaps made off with the head. It was debatable whether he was a doctor, although he was said to have special knowledge of medicinal herbs. Elderly, disturbed, he was believed by some to be an *umthakathi*, a person possessed of evil powers, and by others to be *uhlanya* – crazy. It was also alleged that he had advocated rebellion, used the rebel password, and boasted of participating in the killing of Veal. There was evidence on record that he had stuffed the dripping head into his haversack,[7] but it was also said that in fact he had been stealing beef. Whatever the case he certainly possessed an unnerving logic. In response to the charge against him he replied: 'I have something to say and I have nothing to say, I have nothing further to state.'[8]

This was frustrating for the prosecution, for whom it was most important to get evidence on who was responsible for war-doctoring and mutilation. But while there was little specific information on who had mutilated Veal's body, there were many references to the mysterious doctors and their assistants who had gathered at eMthandeni and who had been seen with body parts. These men could no longer be found, however, and as a result most of the responsibility for 'war-doctoring' fell on Mabalengwe. It was his demand for white soldiers' bodies to strengthen the *intelezi* that explained the killings in the Maphumulo and Lower Thukela divisions and linked them with the rebellion as a whole. Mabalengwe, however, denied that he had been present at eMthandeni: he had never worn a baboon skin: he was being set up.

The Accused
(as spelt in the charge sheet of the court record)

Active participants
1. Macabacaba – the *induna* in charge
2. Dhludhla – *induna* of the Nyuswa
3. Lukukwana – Meseni's representative
4. Sibeko – stabbed Veal
5. Mqwaqo – *umtakhathi*

Amakholwa
8. Jonase
18. Joseph
19. July

Present
6. Mbezi
7. Magwazamanina
9. Mlomo
10. Nomatye
11. Nsini
12. Baleni
13. Mantyonga
14. Sandqula
16. Majareni
17. Mutiwentaba

War-doctor
15. Mabalengwe

The other accused, representing the hundreds of ordinary members of the crowd, had been unfortunate enough to be identified by those assisting the investigators at Stanger. Most of them lived in the coastal districts. Many had come to the magistrate's court on ordinary business to be pounced on by the detectives and the men working with them.

> They arrested me when I was taking the whiteman's money to Stanger. If I had not gone to Stanger with that money, where would they have caught me?
>
> They (Zwezinye &c) took me to their house & asked me to give evidence with them against those who were with us but I refused to give false evidence as I was afraid the Magistrate would imprison me.[9]

Others insisted that they were being framed to save Meseni. Thus Sibeko's brother, Muthiwentaba, continued the uncompromising line he had pursued from the start:

> I was present when the white man was caught. We had been sent out by Meseni. I am surprised to hear it was Macabacaba who sent the men out to fight. It was Meseni who always sent us out & he always [said] we were to go to the white people & if we caught one to bring him to him to tell him what had he (Meseni) had done. He said if you find a lot of them fight them & if you kill them bring me their testicles – and bring me the head of one of them to sit on so that I may overcome them . . . I will say the rest of what I have to say at my trial.[10]

The case for the crown, 13–16 May 1907

The trial of the nineteen men accused of murdering Oliver Veal began on Monday 13 May 1907 and continued through the week. Sentencing took place on the following Tuesday, 21 May.[11] The accused were defended by four Natal advocates with experience in African cases. Arthur Foss practised from Stanger and had previously acted for Meseni. On this occasion most of his clients were men from the coastal districts who had been arrested in February on the grounds that they had been part of the crowd at the killing. Cecil Yonge was a member of the legislative council and had a special interest in Zululand affairs. He defended most of the men more directly implicated in the killing, including Mabalengwe. Reginald Tomlinson was instructed by the crown to defend the three *amakholwa*, while Hosking had to defend Macabacaba, the man said to have refused to obey Meseni's instruction to release Veal, and to have given the order to kill him.

The crown called twenty-three witnesses. Much of the first day was spent establishing the context within which the killing had taken place: Veal's bicycle trip through the Mvoti valley, the nature of the ground at eMthandeni. James Stuart, who had examined the body and was also an expert on African custom, spoke of the use of body parts in the preparation for war, agreeing with modern authorities when he gave his opinion that there would have been no vindictiveness in the killing. What was unusual about the body was the extent of the mutilations: the excision of body parts might have been expected, but not the removal of the head, and the viscera in their entirety. In the afternoon he was questioned on the way in which the language of the hunt had been used, as when the victim was referred to as white game. Following this idea, Stuart confirmed that the person who struck the first blow in the hunt was rewarded – not just the one who killed the quarry. Dr Watkins Pitchford from the government laboratory gave evidence of his analysis of the contents of Mabalengwe's haversack, and told the court that, while it was apparent that the pubic hair was not African, he could not give the racial origin of the genital tissue he had examined.

The African witnesses were then called to give their evidence. Much of it was the consequence of the strategy which had emerged over the past few months at Stanger, and as a result it mixed experience of the rebellion with interpretations developed during the police investigations. Madevu gave a detailed eyewitness account of Veal's capture and the march to eMthandeni where he had been searched, and a cheque, cash and diary had been removed from his pockets. After this the *amakholwa* had knelt down and their prayers were led by the accused July:

> He had a coat and trousers on. He had his assegais, and the cattle, ox tails were tied round his neck, which all wore . . .
> He prayed, and he said 'Our Father, who art in Heaven, grant us the strength that we may fight and conquer the whites' . . .

The Attorney-General wanted more on this subject and proceeded to draw from the witness information on the *amakholwa*, which he then linked with Mabalengwe – to create the picture of savage Christianity at work at eMthandeni:

Q: Are we to understand that the Kolwas formed a regiment by themselves?
A: The Kolwa were called upon to withdraw themselves from the rest, and to form a body of their own.

Q: Who asked them to do that?
A: Macabacaba first spoke about it; and then the teacher was one of the Kolwas. He shouted to the others to sever themselves from the generality of the natives and to go together.

Q: Why was that done?
A: Because they had learned how to pray, and they were to tell us what their prayers were.

Q: We want to know what that means, because we do not understand it.

A: Because they should offer the prayers, and we, who were illiterate, would hear their prayers, and their prayers were to the effect to grant (the Natives) strength to master the white men with whom we were going to fight.

Q: Their prayers were to benefit the impi?

A: Yes, calling upon the Almighty to grant us, the armed men, strength to fight.

Q: Did they offer these prayers often?

A : Yes. We would be called together to form a circle in the morning, and at noon, and at night, and these prayers would be offered . . .

Q: Besides having the Kolwas to pray for you, you had also witch doctors there, hadn't you?

A: Yes.

Q: Is the accused no 15 (Mabalengwe) a witch doctor?

A : Yes, he is a great doctor. One of our great doctors.

Q: What are his functions?

A: He said that he had the power that while we were fighting with the white people the bullet would not come out of the gun, but if it did come out of the barrel, it would melt and became as water, and do us no harm.[12]

The day after the killing, the witness continued, Macabacaba had given orders that they attend the ritual where they placed the point of the assegais into the boiling mixture on the fire: 'He told us to enter the kraal where we would be blessed by our spirits as we were going to fight the white men . . .' The ceremony had been interrupted by the gun fire from the Nsuze valley and they had left to take up their posts guarding the approach roads. There had been no signs of the effectiveness of the blessing in the days to come.

Towards the end of the second day Meseni was called from gaol to appear as a crown witness. The court record suggests that he was a man of ability, able to exploit even this moment as an opportunity to promote his own case – that his people had mobilised to protect him – and also able to slip the traps the defence lawyers laid for him in their cross-examination. When, for example, Advocate Yonge tried to get Meseni first to admit that his motive in giving evidence for the crown was to ingratiate himself with the authorities, and then how his authority as chief necessarily implied culpability, Meseni effectively side-stepped his opponent.

Q: You are undergoing imprisonment; what is your sentence?
A: I do not know. I was simply told I should die in gaol.

Q: Are you very anxious to get out of gaol?
A: Is there anyone who would not desire to get out?

Q: Is your imprisonment wearying to you?
A: It is very painful.

Q: Have you given up the hope of some consideration being shewn to you?
A: I have given up hope. I am in a very painful position.

Q: You are very sorry for the course that took you where you now find yourself?
A: Yes.

Q: You are anxious that the Government should understand you are sorry you were such a fool as to join the rebels?
A: Yes.

Q: You will not miss any opportunity in future of showing that you are really sorry?

A: What am I, that I should be in a position to help the Government in any way.

Q: If you have an opportunity of showing your regret, you will take it?

A: I do not know what you are referring to. I can see no opportunity.

Q: If one presented itself, you would take it?

A: Yes.

Q: You are agreed that this was a terrible matter, – the killing of this unfortunate man?

A: Exceedingly so. I told them inasmuch as they had killed this white man, they had killed me.

Q: Are you a strong man, who knows his own mind?

A: I am an ordinary mortal; there is no man who can say he is very strong minded.

Q: You did not feel any doubt of your own power as chief?

A: No. The only thing that is painful is imprisonment for deeds I did not commit.

Q: You were considered strong enough to govern your own adherents?

A: Yes; anything I said they would follow; they would not disobey me, except in this one particular matter, and I blame Macabacaba for the whole thing.[13]

Zwezinye's evidence was vital for its description (inconsistent as the defence lawyers pointed out) of the news of Veal's capture, his arrival at eMthandeni and Meseni's reaction to it. As an assistant to Mabalengwe his evidence was especially vivid:

Q: When Mabalengwe doctored the impi after his arrival do you know of any particular ingredients he used?
A: I know that what he smoked us with was the penis of a white man, but what he sprinkled us with was just simply some herbs.

Q: How do you know that?
A: He told me at the time that I was fumigating, when he was going to Ndhlovu's, what he had used.

Q: You took over the sprinkling for some time, didn't you?
A: Yes.

Q: With the concoction prepared by Mabalengwe.
A: Yes.

Q: Were any pieces of a human body given to you?
A: He gave me a piece of a human penis.

Q: Did you use it?
A: Yes, I was using that medicine up till the end – till the destruction of Messeni's men and the location.

Q: Did Mabalengwe tell you where it came from?
A: Yes, he said that one he got from Ndhlovu, and the other he got from Bambata's impi and Dinizulu.[14]

It was Ntshiyikane who had the closest view of the killing – first from a tree into which he had climbed before moving down to the ground to get closer:

I then ran round by some other bushes to look and then I heard Macabacaba say 'Stab him.' Sibeko then stabbed the white man with an assegai. The white man seized hold of the assegai and struck at Sibeko with his fist. Then a native came with a cane knife and struck the white man . . . It was then that the white man let go of the assegai and Sibeko stabbed him. When he received the blow he fell down. Mabalengwe then came on the scene and ordered them to use the ejaculation ('Jee.'). Mabalengwe said: 'We are delighted to-day, inasmuch as we have got a white man we will now overcome the white men.' And he said Bambata had been successful in driving the white men away . . .[15]

The Attorney-General used Mbulawa to establish the presence of 'Ethiopians' in the crowd, and the way in which the *amakholwa* in the circle had combined Christian and Zulu ritual when they knelt in front of Veal asking God for strength and protection. July, he said, was a Wesleyan teacher at Mona. But the witness did not have a great grasp of his subject:

Q: What is Topia (mentioned by witness)?
A: It is called a Topia because it came from the Wesleyans.

Q: Is it the Ethiopian Church?
A: It is a white Church, and there is a white Minister over July. He is one of these teachers . . .

Q: What did he [July] do?
A: He went on his knees and offered a prayer.)

Q: Did you hear the prayer?
A: No, I was occupied by trying to read a letter of book which had been found, and I was called to read it . . . it was too much for me . . . July opened it, and it was too much for

him, and then he called somebody else to assist him . . . I
thought I would go and make an attempt, but it was beyond
me.

Q: Did you put on your glasses also?
A: No, I have no glasses. I am not a chaplain of the forces.[16]

Although the defence lawyers had to deal with the specific activities
of their particular clients, it is possible to discern a general strategy
in their cross-examinations. Firstly, attempts were made to cast doubt
on the general veracity of the crown witnesses: they were nearly all
convicted rebels who had been released on condition that they gave
evidence against their erstwhile comrades in arms. Secondly, cross-
examination tested their ability to identify nineteen accused and
give an accurate account of their different actions, explaining why
they should have chosen these particular men out of the hundreds
in the circle. Thirdly, the defence raised the matter of chiefly power
generally, and questioned why it was that Meseni, with his
undoubted personal authority, had not in this instance been able
to enforce it. And finally, the defence dealt with the obscurities,
contradictions and anomalies in the crown's evidence. For example,
had Meseni been in the circle at any time or not? Some witnesses
said that he had left before Veal's arrival and returned as the crowd
was breaking up; others that he had been present, but only on the
margins; while the accused said they had seen him in the circle
with Macabacaba. Then there were the many differences, minor
for the most part but with significant implications, as to just who
had held, searched, moved, and struck down Oliver Veal. And why
was 'Meseni's great war-doctor', Mabalengwe, who had played such
an important role, 'here, there, and everywhere' as Mbulawa said,
absent in the earlier depositions, before his presence was asserted,
suddenly, consistently and vividly, in all the sworn statements?

The defence, 17 and 21 May 1907

The crown closed its case on Thursday 16 May and the defence opened the next morning. It began by examining witnesses for the less prominent of the accused – those representing the ordinary members of the crowd at eMthandeni. A number of witnesses swore that they had been at their homes with the accused on 1 July and that it was impossible for them to have been at eMthandeni. The Attorney-General's cross-examination was unable to shake them. Other witnesses were called, some of them crown witnesses, and cross-examined on inconsistencies and misidentifications in their evidence which pointed to their general unreliability. By the end of the fifth day certain aspects of the crown case as to the presence at the killing of many of the men in the dock had begun to look shaky. The court was adjourned to reassemble again on the following Tuesday.

There must have been some urgent negotiating over the long weekend. When the court reassembled the following Tuesday, the Attorney-General announced that he wished to withdraw the charge against twelve of the accused. Judge Dove Wilson agreed and instructed the jury to return a verdict of not guilty. The twelve were acquitted. Most of them were from farms on the coast, but two *amakholwa*, Jonase and Joseph, were also released, as well as two of the men from Swayimana's Nyuswa chiefdom, Majareni and Muthiwentaba. The Attorney-General's attempt to use the case to punish the widest range of participants in an act of shocking barbarism had failed. But seven men remained in the dock – the five accused of being directly involved in the killing, the preacher, July, and of course, Mabalengwe. They were called to give evidence in their own defence.

Dludla was the first. He was the Nyuswa *induna* in charge at the drift on the day Veal was caught, but the accusation that he participated in the killing could be explained as a consequence of Nyuswa/Qwabe feuding:

It is these people of Meseni who have been round gathering anybody they could get and thrusting them into this case. Although we were there on that day we are people who are daggers drawn with these people of Meseni's.[17]

Macabacaba told his story again, led this time by his own lawyer. He had gone to eMthandeni under instructions from his magistrate. He had arrived on Friday and found Meseni in despair but also furious at the way he had been treated. The chief had rejected Macabacaba's attempt to persuade him to negotiate with the authorities. 'Did I ever go to the town?' Meseni had argued,

> 'Isn't it the white people who come down to me? Did I ever go to their part of the country? Isn't it they who have come in, armed themselves, and used their weapons in my district?' I was wearing this very coat. I said 'Come on, let us go off to the Court.' . . . 'Let us go to Maritzburg, and report ourselves.' He said 'I cannot go to Maritzburg, they had imprisoned me'. I said 'Well, what had we better do?' He said 'Be quiet, don't worry me. I am not going to have anything more to say about this. My people have been killed.'[18]

Meseni, he said, had followed him towards the circle with his doctors, and had seen Veal. 'Everybody was there looking on. Then I went to him. He said "Tell the people to scatter themselves".' This they did, and Macabacaba himself followed them when Meseni told him to select a beast and give the soldiers meat. Meseni had remained behind looking at Veal – together with his doctors and the two witnesses who had giving the most damning evidence against the accused, Madevu, and Zwezinye, 'the man who sprinkles the impi so that bullets shall not be able to do them any harm'.

The accused *kholwa*, July, could not tell the court what happened on that Sunday at eMthandeni because he hadn't been there. He had been on the ridge guarding the path from Pheyana. Unlike the rest of the accused, Lukhukhwana was under Meseni's direct authority and had been sent to the drift as one of his trusted men. He had thought that he would be able to confront his accusers directly in court and was therefore doubly resentful of what was happening. As he retorted to his lawyer: 'I heard what Meseni said, but I thought I would be granted the privilege of asking Meseni questions.' Lukhukhwana felt that he had treated Veal kindly, assisting him over rough ground, linking arms with him in the circle, and that in the end the white man had looked to him for more than physical support. The evidence against them all had been concocted. Thus the idea that Mgwaqo was an ' "Mtagati", it is something that has been made up against him by the people who have charged him. His body is all right, but his head goes round'.[19] He did not believe that Somfongoza had entered the circle to deliver Meseni's instruction for Veal's release. Meseni had been present in the circle, and Meseni as chief was responsible for what had happened.

Mabalengwe's evidence in his own defence was led by his advocate Cecil Yonge. He had grown up in the Maphumulo division some thirty years before but now lived on Lutheran mission land in the Pinetown district. He was not an *inyanga*, he had never performed rituals to strengthen any *impi*, he had not been at eMthandeni on 1 July, he had never worn a baboon skin and a jackal skin cap.

> Oh, my lord, I live in the neighbourhood of a mission. They do not wear these sort of things in Mission stations.
>
> Q: It is all lies?
> A: All lies.

The medicines that he had in his possession when he was arrested had belonged to an *inyanga* by the name of Noyisile and to his brother, Sondodo. He had gone to the Lower Thukela division, with a pass from the magistrate, because he had heard that his brother was dead. He had gone to his homestead and taken possession of his brother's medicines, as was the custom.

The passing references to Mabalengwe's brother, Sondodo, are suggestive but remain obscure. He was described by Mabalengwe's lawyer as Meseni's 'great doctor', who had been killed at the time of the attack on eMthandeni. One cannot but suspect that this hints at the way in which Mabalengwe had been stung – and also at the way in which aspects of the Veal killing had been covered up, effectively and perhaps ruthlessly. But many questions remain, one of the most important being, why, once he had introduced Sondodo, did Mabalengwe's counsel not follow him up?

It was while Mabalengwe had been on his way back home from collecting his brother's medicine and was about to take the train from Stanger that Zwezinye had seen him and reported him to the police. He had been ordered to accompany them to search for Veal's murderers, and when he said he could not as he had not been at eMthandeni, he had been arrested.

How, Yonge asked him, had 'the private part' of a 'human body' found its way into the medicines in the haversack?

I will explain to your lordship all I can, but cannot speak things that I do not know about. They said that as I would not turn out and help them to search in the bush for the persons who were concerned in this murder, that I was to pay the 5/- to Zwezinye which was due to him for this work. I said I could not do that because I lived a long way away at Pinetown, and then I was promptly arrested and put inside . . . Five days went by, and on the 6th a detective came up and he said to me 'there is something that they have found in your bag'. I said why were those medicines of my brother's opened up when I was not present, opened by people too, who did a bad thing at the Mthandeni kraal. I said wouldn't it be quite easy for those people messing about with my medicines, not in the presence of any white person, to go and slip something in there that was not in there at the time I handed the bag over. These medicines belonged to my brother and Noyisile, from whose kraals they were taken.

The different bags of medicine were produced in court. Mabalengwe protested: 'These medicines have all been tampered with by Zwezinye, and I do not know what has happened.' They now in fact contained not only his brother Sondodo's medicines but those of Zwezinye as well. It was Zwezinye who had organised the plan to 'come here and manufacture evidence against me'. Mabalengwe did not know most of the men who had given evidence against him, but he had grown up in the district and he did remember Madevu from that time thirty years before. There was one witness, however, with whom he had had contact – Zwezinye himself.

It started from this detective and Zwezinye. The detective said that Zwezinye must go round teaching people all over the place my name. For three months this man was teaching people my name.

Q: What man?
A: Zwezinye.

Q: The detective told him to do that?
A: The detective told him to do that.

Q: The white detective?
A: Yes.

Q: Mr Milliken here put him up to go and get up a case against you?
A: Zwezinye had something underlying it. Zwezinye wanted to get rid of me because I had some claim on him . . . My

father lent his father £20. My father died, and his father
died; and now he won't let me have it back . . .

Q: And therefore he wants to hang you?
A: Therefore he wishes to have me killed so that that property
will not be claimed.

Q: He does not want to get rid of you because you have been
a fraud of a doctor?
A: No, because I have never touched medicine at all. My brother
was a doctor.[20]

Mabalengwe believed he had been set up – and set up by the very
men responsible not just for the killing, but for the mutilation as
well. The portion of the penis had been placed there by Zwezinye,
and by 'those very people who killed that white man. I am very
much afraid of them indeed. They have slipped that in'.

The last accused to appear was Sibeko, the youth alleged to have
struck the death blows. He stuck to his story – he had caught Veal
and he had been rewarded for it, just as he would have been if he
had struck the first blow in a hunt – but he had been obeying the
orders of the chief Meseni. Questioned by the judge, he virtually
condemned himself:

Q: You say you well knew the purpose for which Meseni wanted
to have this white man brought to him – what was it?
A: The chief wanted him for his doctors.

Q: What were the doctors to do with him?
A: I don't know. That is in the work of the doctors. I don't
know how they use white people.

Q: Have you no idea?

A: No, I would not like to take upon myself the responsibility of suggesting what the doctors were going to do.

Q: Was it anything to do with the sprinkling, or doctoring of the impi?

A: Even if they wanted this white man for medicine for the impi I do not know in what way they were going to use him for making medicine.

Q: Were they to use him for making medicine?

A: I think they wanted him for medicine.

Q: And it was in order that he might be used for medicine that you took him to Meseni?

A: No, I only did it in compliance with the order of the chief, which was to the effect that if we came across a man alone we were to capture him and take him to the chief.

Q: You told us you well knew the purpose for which he was wanted?

A: I only knew that he wanted him, as he said if we came across a white man we should take him and bring him to him.

Q: You say you well knew the purpose for which he was wanted – what was it?

A: He wanted him for doctoring the impi.

Q: And you were willing to bring him to Meseni in order that he might be used for that purpose?

A: Even if I had not approved of it I would not have dared to let the white man go, because it would have meant death to me.

Q: Did you approve of it?

A: Yes, I won't deny anything just because I am before the Court.

Q: You did approve of the purpose for which he was intended?

A: Yes. I didn't like taking this white man up, because I felt in my heart that some harm was going to be done to him, but as the chief had said that I should do it, I decided that I ought to do it.

In response to Justice Dove Wilson's questions from the bench, Sibeko's answers were an implicit appeal for an understanding of his predicament, and in so asking for understanding, Sibeko condemned himself to death.

Macabacaba's lawyer ended the case for the defence by calling three of the men who had been found not guilty and released that morning. It was brave of them to appear. They told the court how Zwezinye and other crown witnesses had ordered them to identify prisoners as men who had been at eMthandeni, and when they refused, they had been accused and imprisoned themselves.

With this the defence closed.

The verdict

Justice John Dove Wilson's summing up took nearly two-and-a-half hours during which time he impressed upon members of the jury that their decision had to be made according to the law and on the evidence, not on their emotions. Despite this injunction, even he let his judicial wig slip on occasion, for example, on the efficacy of war-medicine:

it is extraordinary, I think, to find that men living in touch with civilisation – men of ability, should even now be found capable of believing stories of that kind; but unfortunately it appears to be only too true . . .

It was his task to instruct the jury on the law. He explained repeatedly, and with great emphasis, that for the accused to have committed the offence of murder they need not have struck a blow or participated directly in Veal's death. If the jury felt that it had been generally known by those who participated in the rebellion that the killing of the white man was to be expected as a consequence of rebellion, then they were, in law, guilty of murder:

> if the crime is one which is naturally incidental to the rebellion, which anybody joining the rebellion might reasonably be supposed to anticipate as a natural result of it, then everybody joining the rebellion is responsible for it just as much as the person who actually struck the blow. It is for you, gentlemen, to consider in the light of the evidence which has been laid before you whether or not this killing . . . was just such an act as any native joining the rebellion could reasonably be expected to know would be an ordinary result of that rebellion; and if, gentlemen, you think it is, then I am afraid you have no alternative but to find every one of these prisoners guilty.

What then of the evidence that had been laid before them? The defence had argued that it had been concocted. Judge Dove Wilson reminded the jury that statements taken at the preliminary examination could be accepted only as evidence of a witness's reliability and not as evidence of what had occurred. Although there were inconsistencies in the evidence given by specific witnesses, and amongst the different witnesses, Dove Wilson urged the jury not to place too much weight on this. It was recognised that it was difficult to recall consistently and accurately specific incidents that occurred amongst a wild and excited crowd on an occasion like the one with which they were concerned, and that so often incidents referred to in passing at the preliminary examination only gained significance later. Therefore, he concluded, 'Gentlemen, in my experience, I have rarely found that evidence as to such discrepancies was worth anything'.

Dove Wilson then went through the evidence led against the accused reminding them of its weight and the general points upon which the crown witnesses had agreed. He spent some time considering the arguments for the defence – whether rebels had been provoked and whether Meseni had in fact given an order to kill Veal – and then, as far as this case was concerned, dismissed them as irrelevant in law.

Dove Wilson took particular care to remind the jury of their responsibilities – and their limits. They were not there to sentence the accused, nor would their decision send them to the gallows. Sentencing was the prerogative of the judge, and the possibility of clemency that of the executive. If there were moral questions of motive, or arguments in mitigation, these were not the concern of the jury. The jury had to apply the law – and he had taken them through this – to the facts – and they had heard them in detail and at length. On the basis of the law and the evidence, and on this alone, they must decide if the men were guilty of murder.

One has to suspect that Dove Wilson was not as sure of the jury as he was of his own mind, and that his instructions sought to remedy this. In the end he left the jury with little choice but to convict.

It did so. It took minutes to find all the accused guilty by eight to one, with the exception of Sibeko who was found guilty unanimously. Dove Wilson asked the accused if they had anything to say before he passed the sentence of death. Macabacaba deferred to his authority:

My Lord, shall I give a judgment in face of the judgment your Lordship has passed upon me? Your Lordship has the case in your hands, I leave it to your Lordship.

Dludla did the same. Lukhukhwana, Meseni's trusted man, asked yet again to be allowed to confront his chief directly. Sibeko felt the judge must understand that he was being sacrificed so that the real culprits might escape:

People who know all about it remain untouched. I know nothing about this case. If I have been found guilty in this case I want to be satisfied that your Lordship has been satisfied why I caught this man who I am charged with killing. Is it likely that an individual belonging to a tribe or chief would do something in compliance with an order of the chief without that chief knowing something about it? What did he say when he heard that I had killed this white man when I was in his kraal? That is all I have to say. If your Lordship has heard that I have finished.

Too late, Mabalengwe protested that witnesses had not been called to establish that he had not been at eMthandeni. The chief war-doctor also took the opportunity to remind his Lordship of the liberal ideal of justice:

I do not wish to contradict your Lordship in the decision you have come to, but I say that the Courts, so we understand, were established for our protection, and I place myself in the hands of the Court for protection.

July, to the end, denied that he had been at eMthandeni. And the *umthakathi* or the insane Mgwaqo made his comment on the verdict:

I know nothing about it. I see a train running about, that is all I know about it. I see all sorts of things rushing about in front of me like cattle and horses.[21]

Judge John Dove Wilson passed the sentence of death by hanging on all the accused.

Notes

1. Stephen D. Girvin, 'An evaluation of the Judge Presidency of John Dove Wilson of Natal (1910–1930)', M. Laws, University of Natal, 1987.
2. Labistour had come to Natal in 1879 from Mauritius to practise law.
3. PAR: RSC I/1/96, Response by Macabacaba to depositions, Maphumulo, 27 March 1907. Legal technicality made it necessary for the accused to be committed for trial in both the Lower Thukela and the Maphumulo divisions. They therefore formally had to be given the opportunity to respond to the depositions on two occasions: their responses to the depositions were longer and more vehement on the latter occasion.
4. PAR: RSC I/1/96, Response by Dhludhla to depositions, Maphumulo, 27 March 1907.
5. PAR: RSC 1/1/96 has July indicted on 21 March. Meseni had named him on the previous day and he was also identified by Mabulawa.
6. The other named was a Wesleyan evangelist Selby Msomi whose detention had been the subject of distressed correspondence between a Wesleyan missionary from Stanger and the authorities, some of which implicated the clerk and Zulu interpreter at the Stanger magistrate's office. Meseni stated that Msomi had preached daily at Mthandeni during the rebellion. The fact that he was not indicted suggests that there was something to hide in Msomi's case. The evidence against Msomi was substantiated by the evangelist in charge of the Ethamuni mission, John Nhlonhlo, thought by some to be Maphumulo magistrate Maxwell's most trusted informant. And one of the witnesses is described as a resident on Nhonhlo's mission and wife of Nkwantshu – the name of the key crown witness and perjurer in the trials related below. In fact Msomi's case suggests the way in which Magistrate Maxwell of Maphumulo was manipulated by witnesses with agendas – but it is impossible to follow all these roads of investigations here – they are interesting, but the starting points as well as the destinations too often remain out of sight.
7. PAR: AGO I/1/317, Mamtoto 15 March 1907, Sibonkolo 11 March 1907, Masifike 11 March 1907.
8. PAR: RSC I/1/96, Mgwaqo's response to depositions read at Stanger, 20 March 1907.
9. PAR: RSC I/1/96, Majareni's response to depositions read at Maphumulo, 27 March 1907.
10. PAR: RSC I/1/96, Mutiwentaba's response to depositions read at Maphumulo, 27 March 1907.
11. PAR: RSC I/1/96, Rex *v.* Macabacaba and others, 14 May 1907.
12. PAR: RSC I/1/96, Rex *v.* Macabacaba and others, Evidence of Madevu, 14 May 1907.
13. PAR: RSC I/1/96, Rex *v.* Macabacaba and others, Meseni under cross-examination, 14 May 1907.

14. PAR: RSC I/1/96, Rex *v.* Macabacaba and others, Evidence of Zwezinye, 15 May 1907.

15. PAR: RSC I/1/96, Rex *v.* Macabacaba and others, Evidence of Ntshiyikane, 15 May 1907.

16. PAR: RSC I/1/96, Rex *v.* Macabacaba and others, Evidence of Mbulawa, 15 May 1907.

17. PAR: RSC I/1/96, Rex *v.* Macabacaba and others, Evidence of Dludla, 21 May 1907.

18. PAR: RSC I/1/96, Rex *v.* Macabacaba and others, Evidence of Macabacaba, 21 May 1907.

19. PAR: RSC I/1/96, Rex *v.* Macabacaba and others, Evidence of Lukukwana, 21 May 1907.

20. PAR: RSC I/1/96, Rex *v.* Macabacaba and others, Evidence of Mabalengwe, 21 May 1907.

21. The judge's charge, verdict and the responses are all from the court record in PAR: RSC I/1/96.

9

The Natal Supreme Court

Special Criminal Session, 27–30 May 1907

Murder at Otimati

The next two trials at the May Special Criminal Session of the Supreme Court dealt with the murders committed in the Maphumulo division that had preceded the killing of Veal. These had occurred on 19 June at dawn when armed men raided the store at Thring's Post, killing the storekeeper Adolf Sangereid, and two hours later when a convoy of wagons was ambushed and Trooper Powell was killed. Two men were accused in each case and again the crown depended on the evidence of witnesses who had participated in the events. There was one key witness in both cases – Nkwantshu kaTshumuni, of the Mbedu of chief Ngqokwana – convicted of high treason by the martial law court, and released because of the assistance he gave to the prosecution.

Thring's Post, 27–28 May 1907

The crown case in May 1907 followed in outline the statement Nkwantshu gave the Maphumulo magistrate in August 1906 soon after the event itself. He had seen Sangereid being stabbed first by Ndabazezwe kaMditshana[1] and then by Nkosi kaNoxula. Both men were under chief Ngqokwana and from Nkwantshu's neighbourhood – he had grown up with them. They had told

Nkwantshu that, on the morning of 19 June after the attack on
the store, they had thrown assegais at a passing trooper, one of
them injuring his horse.[2] The two accused were prosecuted by W.S.
Bigby of the Attorney-General's office, who led evidence to establish
that the attack had been made at dawn on the storekeeper's house
where Sangereid and the stock inspector/spy, William Robbins,
were staying. Robbins had been stunned and stabbed, but three
men had saved him, driven off the assailants, and left him hidden
in the back garden. Sangereid had run from the house into the
garden, been caught and killed. Other witnesses gave more detail:
Dabula, who had struck Robbins with his knobkerrie, was followed
by a number of men who had seen the accused at Thring's Post;
and then by some who had seen them strike the death blow.

Cross-examination exposed weaknesses in the crown case. For
Dabula to have assaulted Robbins on the one side of the house,
and to have seen Sangereid killed on the other, he must, suggested
one juror, have been able to see through walls. Defence attorney
Chick concentrated on the fact that that morning the moon had
gone down at 4:30 and the sun was to rise at 6:30. Robbins had
looked at his watch when he heard his door being tried. It was
5:00. How, Chick asked, could the witnesses have identified the
accused with such certainty in the dark? Nkosi's mother, who was
also Ndabazezwe's sister-in-law, gave evidence for the crown that
backfired – the two accused she said had joined the rebellion, but
only after the sun had come up on 19 June.[3] And what of
Nkwantshu's evidence that after the attack he had seen someone
carrying trousers and a shirt with (after a hesitation) bloodstains?
Sangereid's body was found clothed. The last crown witness was
Zwezinye, key witness in the Veal case. He now had to stiffen the
current case, but he could state only that he had heard the accused
admit to the killing subsequent to the event.

The defence brought in a string of witnesses, starting with
Ndlovu kaThimuni himself, who gave evidence that while he had
been at Thring's Post, he had not seen the accused there. Judge

Dove Wilson pointed out that this was essentially negative evidence. The accused, however, were in no doubt about the nature of the evidence against them.[4] They were being framed by a number of men with whom they were closely associated. Many were related in marriage, others had been their neighbours and drinking acquaintances, and most had long-standing differences with them. As Ndabazezwe said, 'these boys had got themselves together and got a scheme against me and I knew nothing about it'.

> Nkwantshu said to me that he had been prayed [sic] by three persons, the Magistrate being the third, to admit and to state that I had committed this crime, and it is beyond me [that] he can come to your Lordship and barefacedly state that he saw me do this crime, we being who hate one another, one not even put one's feet in the other's kraal. I don't know [how] Zwezinye has got hold of the story. He is a stranger and does not belong to that part at all. I don't know [how] Zwezinye has come into it at all. Nkwantshu, Palafini and Madoda are all relations, so you can understand it that way . . . they have got a grudge against me . . .[5]

Ndabazezwe told the court that he wished 'to reply to those people who have deliberately placed a burden on my shoulders which I know nothing about . . .' He had been in dispute with Zwezinye over money and had not spoken to him for two years when to his surprise he discovered at Stanger that Zwezinye had given evidence against him in this case. He had also quarrelled with the key witness, Nkwantshu, over an outstanding claim of cattle he had against his brother. Most of the other witnesses were associated with Nkwantshu and consequently, Nkosi asserted, 'these are the feelings which are strong enough in their hearts to make them come to your Lordship and tell a lot of lies'.[6]

Dove Wilson once again directed the jury carefully. Firstly, he pointed to the nature of the evidence and its implications for the law. In the Veal trial all those participating in the violence were legally guilty of murder since it could be shown that it was generally assumed that going into rebellion implied the killing of whites. In this case, however, evidence had been led, and not contested, that the force had been ordered not to kill unarmed whites. Therefore only those who had struck the blows could be convicted of murder, and this is what had to be proved.

Again he warned the jury not to be too concerned about disparities in the evidence taken down at the preliminary investigation and that led in court.

> One knows perfectly well that a man taking down evidence in longhand, when he is probably considerably pressed for time, is frequently apt to set down something which does not reflect exactly what has been said by witnesses; and I know in my own experience – I have had a great deal of evidence to take down, and I think I can fairly well say that I am fairly good at doing it – I have frequently found that on looking back upon the notes which I have taken that I have written down something which I know perfectly well is not what the witness said at all.[7]

He went through the evidence of each of the crown witnesses, pointing out the areas of corroboration and of dispute. Was it too dark to recognise the accused? Why had evidence been led about bloodied, looted clothing when the body had been found clothed? Could the jury accept the accuseds' vehement protests that the evidence against them was concocted? This was their decision to make, on the evidence before them.

It took the jury half an hour to find the accused guilty by 7–2. Dove Wilson sentenced them to death. *The Natal Mercury* reported: 'Both men remained unmoved, although Nkosi assumed a sullen look. Ndabazezwe[8] saluted in a full deep bass voice, Nkosi's salute only being audible.'[9]

Oglesbys' store, 28–30 May 1907

The last case dealt with the killing that followed that at Thring's Post – the death of Trooper Powell over the crest of the hill behind the Oglesbys' store on the road to Maphumulo. There had always been a witness to the killing – Thomas Oglesby, who had tried to show the trooper a hiding place in the krans, but who had never been able to identify the man who had thrust the assegai into Powell's heart. Here the case stuck until March 1907 when Nkwantshu kaShimuni – already key crown witness in the Thring's Post case – identified the killer as Sifo kaZwenyani, informer for military intelligence. Moreover, Nkwantshu asserted that after the killing Sifo, together with the great war-doctor Mabalengwe, had returned from the body exhibiting Powell's genitals on the end of a bayonet. In April Frank Shuter, magistrate at Stanger, completed the preliminary investigation, and Sifo and Mabalengwe were indicted for the murder of Trooper Albert Powell.

The trial began on Tuesday 28 May.[10] Dove Wilson presided and W.S. Bigby was again the prosecutor. He began by informing the court that, since Mabalengwe had already been sentenced to death for the murder of Oliver Veal, the charges against him in this case had been withdrawn. One has to suspect, however, that the prosecution dared not risk his appearance in the dock. Sifo was

Thring's Post	
Accused:	Ndabazezwe
	Nkosi
Key crown witness:	Nkwantshu
Oglesbys' store	
Accused:	Sifo
	Mabalengwe
Key crown witness:	Nkwantshu

defended by advocate Cecil Yonge whose request for the exclusion of any juror who had sat on the previous cases was granted.

After establishing the facts of the killing, Bigby led evidence that sought to depict Powell's death as part of a longer story of violent insurrection and savagery, which had in this case seen the body mutilated in accord with dark superstitious practices. Nkwantshu told the court how he had seen Sifo stab Powell. The trooper had fallen on his stomach, and then rolled upon his back, whereupon others stabbed him and Sifo had ripped him open, in accordance with Zulu custom. He had then carried Powell's rifle and bandolier down to the road where Ndlovu and his men were meeting with the recently rescued Oglesbys. Here Mabalengwe had reminded Sifo of a discussion they had on the previous day. They had gone back up the hill, in the direction of where the killing had taken place, and returned in triumph. Mabalengwe had an ominous grass-wrapped bundle in his hands; Sifo had Powell's genitals – testicles, penis and pubic hair – skewered on his bayonet.

Ndlovu and his men had then gone on to Ndlovu's homestead where they were ritually treated with 'war-medicine' by Mabalengwe by *ukuncina* – licking the potion off their fingers. Sifo had been put to one side as a 'warrior, he had killed a man', and following custom for men who had been heroes in battle, he and others wore the 'wild asparagus' plant *pingantloya*.[11] The ritual had been interrupted by the arrival of the militia but it was repeated the next day down in the thornveld away from the attentions of the troops.

By the end of the first day in court it was clear that Nkwantshu's evidence was causing difficulties. Sifo's attorney asked that Nkwantshu's cross-examination be postponed, and he was ordered to stand down. Two other witnesses were then called and closely cross-examined by the judge and the defence. They were particularly interested in the nature of the injuries to Powell's body.

At the beginning of the second day, Mfuze, a crown witness, was recalled and, while being examined by the court, fell into the trap.

Q: You said that when Sifo and Mabalengwe were coming back from the body of the white man Sifo was carrying something on a bayonet, what was that?

A: It was a penis and testicles.

Q: How was it being carried?

A: On the bayonet.

Q: How?

A: He had thrust the bayonet into it.

Q: In your examination-in-chief you said he was carrying a penis. What makes you say now that he was also carrying the testicles?

A: I was stopped when I had said penis, I hadn't time to say testicles.

Q: You intended then to have said testicles as well?

A: Yes, I should have ended up by saying that.

Then it was Nkwantshu who was recalled. Yonge began the lengthy cross-examination by going through his evidence-in-chief, before getting Nkwantshu to confirm that he had seen Sifo open Powell's body, beginning 'at the throat', and then with his genitals, 'everything complete', skewered on his bayonet.

The case for the prosecution was in disarray. Dr Howden, the medical officer who had examined Powell's body, was recalled to the witness box. The wound in Powell's chest had been small – only about an inch-and-a-half across – and although the front of the body was covered with blood, the clothing had not been removed and the abdomen had not been cut open. The cause of death had been the assegai thrust into the heart. The throat had been cut, but other wounds had been inflicted after death when pieces of flesh were cut from different parts of the body. The penis had indeed been amputated, but the testicles had not been removed. It was clear that the crown witnesses' descriptions of the killing and the mutilations were contradicted by the evidence of the medical officer who had examined the body.[12]

With the evidence of the crown's witnesses exposed as false, the defence was straightforward – Sifo had not been there on 19 June. He had stayed at his homestead. It was only after the rout of Ndlovu's force that he had made an appearance in the Timati valley, assisting the wounded and gathering together the people scattered by the militia. The Oglesbys, first father and then son, were taken through the events of the day again. At no stage had either of them seen Sifo. The younger man contradicted the crown's attempt to depict Ndlovu presiding over a circle of assembled warriors, receiving Powell's weapons after the killing. He had been resting by the roadside, making arrangements to secure the store and to take its owners to a place of safety.

Ndlovu's appearance in the witness box on the third and final day became something of a trial within a trial, with the chief determined to make use of the opportunity to present his own view of events, and the prosecution equally determined to depict him as a devious man who had played a major role in the horrifying events which culminated in the death of the trooper. Ndlovu won this court battle, emerging as a canny leader of undoubted ability.[13] When pressed, he was adroit at shifting responsibility elsewhere, especially onto crown witnesses. He made effective use of the inadmissibility of hearsay evidence. Attempts to extract evidence from him on the practice of ritual and killing for medicinal purposes, were also unsuccessful.

> Q:　When a native has stabbed somebody in a battle is he doctored in a special way afterwards?
>
> A:　No, I cannot speak for that, owing to the fact that as old as I am at present, I have never had anything to do with fights. I should not like to make a false statement on chance.

Q: Do you know this plant, the Pikinhlolo? [*pingantloya*]
A: You mean a plan[t] from outside in the country? Yes.

Q: Isn't that worn by natives as a mark of distinction?
A: No, I know nothing about that. I should not like to invent
    something out of my head for the pleasure of the Court,
    on something I had not seen.

Q: When a warrior has stabbed someone, does he eat the same
    flesh as the other people?
A: I cannot invent something I have never seen.

Q: Does he, or does he not?
A: I do not know.

Q: Is he separated from the rest until he has been through
    certain ceremonies?
A: I cannot say for that. I would not like to make a statement
    of anything I have not seen with my eyes.[14]

The defence counsel took him through the main events of 19 June.
The force that had attacked Thring's Post was in fact, Ndlovu said,
made up of two elements; his own men were there, but so were
men from chief Ngqokwane's Mbedu, and it was they who were
responsible for looting the store and for killing Sangereid – together
with most of the crown witnesses, led, of course, by Nkwantshu.
This divided leadership gave Ndlovu the chance to take cover when
the court's questions became too specific. He could not of course
deny that he had allowed his men to raid Thring's Post and then
attack the supply wagons. He had already been found guilty of this
under martial law. In any case, this was war: an attack on an armed
force that had already attacked his own people. He insisted that he
had not led his men on 19 June, but had accompanied them in
order to keep them under some control. They had been provoked

into action first by the imposition of the poll tax, and then by the action of the troops who had come into the area, looted cattle, burnt homesteads and killed a local man. His people were angry, demanding that Ndlovu take action. If he had not accompanied them, they would have gone without him.

Q: Were you in charge of the company?

A: I said at the outset that my plan was that we should not go and expose ourselves on the high-road at all. It was the anger of these warriors of mine, who were angered by hearing that some native had been killed by the white people, and they would insist upon doing things as they liked.

Q: Did you not hear that some of your men had stopped wagons on the road?

A: No, I did not know . . .

Q: Yet you were in charge of the impi?

A: I say that I had not control of that impi. I followed the impi because I saw it going out in a rage, owing to some native having been killed by the white people.

Q: Who was in command of the impi?

A: I said before that the Mabedwe people came down and persuaded my people to go with them.

Q: Who was in command of the impi?

A: Mpitimpiti.

Q: Wasn't he bound to obey any orders of yours?

A: No, because he didn't belong to my tribe.

Q: What was your position there then?

A: I was a person who was running along because I was angry.

I didn't wish my people to go and kill white people. I was angry about it.

By going with his men, he had succeeded at least in saving the lives of the storekeepers and the missionary and his wife. It was while Ndlovu was arranging this, at the side of the road which joined the store and the mission, that Powell had been killed over the crest of the hill behind him. He had been told of this only much later. He had seen Mabalengwe at a distance, but had never seen Sifo. The claim that they had exhibited parts of Powell's body was a fabrication. He had received a revolver, which had belonged to the younger Oglesby, and a rifle and bandolier had been handed to him. In the excitement and rush of the moment he had not enquired where they had come from, and the speed with which he was attacked soon afterwards by the militia had precluded further investigation.

Q: You received a rifle and bandolier?
A: I admit that, I held it with my hand.

Q: Did it not occur to you to inquire where that had come from?
A: I no longer had anybody to ask. It was no sooner handed to me than the individual who handed it to me passed by in a hurry.

Q: Did you not call him back?
A: No.

Q: Why?
A: They were not standing, they were passing in a hurry.

Q: Had you no power as a chief to command that man to come back and tell you where he had got it?

A: I no longer had any influence over these people. They even said to me: 'You pay your taxes by us and these white people kill us.'

Q: Then you were a chief without any power among your own people?

A: Yes, I was just a chief by word of mouth at that period, and I say that I had still a little authority when they did not kill these white people.

Q: If you had no power over your own people how could you prevent them killing these people?

A: They just happened to obey me. It was an act of God.

The crown case had been built on the idea of unprovoked, armed uprising, characterised by barbaric ritual, and there was no place in it for an attempt by a responsible leader to control an angry people goaded into rebellion. Time and again the prosecutor came back to one point: if Ndlovu had had the authority to intervene and save some white lives, why had he been unable to control the attacks on the store and the wagons, and the killings there?

Q: You were able to prevent the impi from killing the white man, but yet you were not in command of it?

A: I reproved these people for what they wished to do and I said 'You are treading dangerous ground now by the attitude you are adopting to the white people, but if you have made up your minds, and there is no turning you back my advice to you is that you do not touch any unprotected white people. If you want to fight go for the soldiers'.

He made no attempt to evade that accusation that he had not opposed the killing of members of the militia, given that they were in a state of armed conflict. But this was not the prime objective of the attack. It was a narrow line to walk, but Ndlovu kept his balance:

Q: One of the reasons you went out was in order to kill any soldiers in arms, wasn't it?
A: I didn't understand that myself.

Q: You had no objection to your impi killing members of the white impi?
A: Why should I stop them doing that?

Q: Well, was there any reason, if they did that, they should conceal it from you?
A: They kept that from me, I think, on account of this order which I had given to them, that if they shot any white man who was just coming along that I would shoot that fellow myself.

Q: Even although that white man happened to be an armed soldier?
A: Well, if he was a white soldier coming along by himself, that was quite a different thing from the regiment, or the enemy. But soldiers – I told them to go to the soldiers.

As a defence witness Luhoho, Ndlovu's *induna*, brings to the court record a calm precision and authority, mirroring, it seems, his actions on the day of the attack. It was he who had given the order to Bhixa to rescue his ex-employer, Oglesby senior, which he had done by pushing aside the armed men and bringing him safely back down the hill to Ndlovu. Luhoho's evidence proved to be key for the defence. He rejected the crown witnesses' accounts of what had happened on 19 June. They were fabrications. He had not seen Mabalengwe – he knew what he looked like, as he had been pointed out in the magistrate's office after his arrest – and he did not believe he was present on 19 June with or without a baboon skin and jackal

---

Rex *v.* Sifo for the murder of Powell

Key crown witness
Nkwantshu: Witnessed killing.
Howden: Medical officer. Examined body but gives initially mis-
leading information on the nature of the wounds.

Defence witnesses
Oglesby: Oglesby jnr did not see Sifo and Oglesby snr, who
witnessed killing, contradicts **Nkwantshu**.
Ndlovu: Did not see Sifo.
Bhixa: Did not see Sifo.
Luhoho: Did not see Sifo and gives evidence of rivalry between
accused and key crown witness.

---

skin hat. Sifo had never been ritually purified and honoured after
the killing; there had not been time for such a ceremony before
they were scattered by the militia. And in Luhoho's evidence, even
in translation, a distinction appears which is rare indeed in these
transcripts – a distinction between 'doctoring' and 'war-doctoring':

Q: Did you ever see him at any doctoring?
A: Do you mean war doctoring?

Q: Yes?
A: No, I never saw him war doctored.[15]

Luhoho had been surprised by the arrival of the militia at Ndlovu's
homestead and had scattered with the rest of his people down into
the valley. His foot had been shattered by a bullet, and he had lain
still amongst the dead. Then, when the militia had gone, desperate
with thirst, he had dragged himself towards a stream. He was
washing the wound when Sifo had come up to him and asked what
had happened earlier in the day. Luhoho was convinced that Sifo
had not been present when Powell had been killed.

How then, counsel asked, could Luhoho account for the evidence of the crown witnesses, which situated Sifo so clearly at the killing, and for Nkwantshu's declaration that he saw Sifo strike the death blow?

A: I say it is on account of ill-feeling they have towards Sifo.

Q: On what account?
A: They simply make up lies against him because they say he killed a white man.

Q: What is their object?
A: On account of a feeling of jealousy, because he was chosen by the girl.

Q: Who is the particular person?
A: I think it is Malunge who had a dispute with him and they came to words.

Q: Is that the man who has given evidence here?
A: Yes.

Q: Do you suggest that Malunge is at the head of the conspiracy with two or three others who have given evidence here against this man?
A: Yes.

Luhoho spoke with authority and Bigby's cross-examination failed to unsettle him. The evidence that a prosecution witness and the accused had previously quarrelled over a woman was not effectively contested. A number of men came forward insisting that Sifo had been at home and not in the vicinity of the store on 19 June. And Oglesby might have been terrified, exhausted and confused but his account of the assegai thrust with precision into the heart was clear and in accord with the medical officer's description of the body.

The crown witnesses' evidence on the other hand was not only sensational in the extreme but in direct conflict with the medical evidence. There were just too many anomalies. The prosecution was losing its case.

Sifo was called to give evidence on his own behalf. He denied any knowledge of the killing. He was being framed, and framed over a girl. Nkwantshu had even told him in gaol what he intended to do, not only to Sifo, but to the men sentenced for the murder of Sangereid.

> I have one word to say. I say, is it lawful because there is a person who goes and makes love to what belongs to me, that that person should turn round and send me to death. Because it appears that I have committed a crime by taking this girl to wife and paying lobola for her myself. Before the Government I have no crime at all, because I have helped the Government a great deal. Whilst I was a boy I used to work for the Government, when I was a little boy like that (indicates), whilst my father was alive. I have never committed a crime. Now, today, I have got a crime thrust upon me, on account of somebody who wishes to have something of mine; because the reason why I came down here is because I was summoned from Johannesburg . . . Now, today I am under these red cloths (curtains) which adorn this place, and I have blood upon my head on account of a wrong which I know nothing of, which is caused through illfeeling. I have nothing further to say.[16]

The jury took ten minutes to find Sifo not guilty and discharge him.

Aftermath

The Governor of Natal, Sir Henry McCallum, was due to leave Natal at the beginning of June 1907 and wanting to depart with something of a flourish. A number of events were organised to mark the end of his term of office and vindicate the manner in which he had dealt with the rebellion. The Supreme Court trials, however, had failed as an exhibition of Civilised Justice at work – even-handed yet unflinching in the face of murder, magic and mutilation. However, in his last week in office, McCallum did succeed in sending into exile chiefs who had been found guilty of treasonable offences during the rebellion. The Natal ministry had for months been pressing the British authorities to agree to their exile to another part of the empire as a counter to the insidious rumours amongst Africans that His Imperial Majesty's government disapproved of Natal's actions in the recent rebellion. On 1 June, twenty-five chiefs began their journey into exile on St Helena, and *The Natal Mercury* reported:

> The gang of prisoners, as they marched out of the gaol gates, presented an interesting spectacle. Dressed in drab, ill fitting gaol clothes, liberally besprinkled with broad arrows, and with numbers and sentences imprinted on their sleeves, it was difficult to imagine that these were a big proportion of the men who, just twelve months ago, turned the Colony into a military camp, and who had raised the standard of a revolt which might have possibly spread throughout South Africa. The majority of the prisoners were middle-aged or elderly men, and there were a few grey beards among them . . . One man, whether from fright or illness it was impossible to say, collapsed almost immediately he got outside the gaol, and had to be supported by two of his comrades.[17]

Amongst their number were Meseni and Ndlovu.

Having thus demonstrated the consequences of chiefly disloyalty, McCallum on 3 June rewarded loyal chiefs by allowing them into his presence for consultation. S.O. Samuelson, under-Secretary for Native Affairs in Natal, and Charles Saunders, Commissioner for

Rebel prisoners leaving Durban.   (*The Natal Mercury Pictorial*, 12 June 1907)

Meseni, Ndlovu and Tilonko arriving at St Helena.   (*The Natal Mercury Pictorial*, 14 August 1907)

Native Affairs of Zululand province, were there. The Governor's opening remarks reflect the tone:

> In the proceedings to-day, I want them to look upon me as their father, in the same way I look upon them as my sons. I want them to speak freely and frankly, and say whatever is in their hearts.

It is unnecessary and tedious to go on with this. McCallum was as blind to the dynamics of colonial power and African perceptions as the chiefs were wary of saying anything that might offend the authorities. They thanked the Governor for the privilege of bidding him farewell. A few expressed their hopes and fears, but hints of criticism and deviations from formal expressions of gratitude and deference were promptly corrected. The officials of the Native department had prepared McCallum's closing address so that most of the chiefs received a personal message – praise for some, a caution to others, thanks for those who it was believed had acted un-equivocally on the side of the authorities in 1906, and a warning to those who had not shown as much enthusiasm. He ended with

> one or two words of parting advice – don't let the people listen to the ill words of agitators, and kick out the witch doctors – they are devils in disguise. They led a lot of people astray during the last rebellion, and thousands have lost their lives through the evil speaking of witch doctors.
>
> Another person to avoid is a lawyer. Keep out of the hands of lawyers. There is no occasion for them, especially in matters of administration. They will only bleed the natives, who can get no sounder advice and more beneficial to themselves than from their rulers.[18]

McCallum had been able only to begin reviewing the sentences in the Maphumulo trials, and the process was completed by the Acting

Administrator, Justice W. Beaumont. Very different groupings
hoped to influence their decisions. In London radical MPs had an
audience with Elgin and kept up pressure on the under-Secretary
of State, Winston Churchill. When he heard that seven men had
been sentenced to death Churchill did not hold back:

> It is my duty to warn the Secretary of State that this further
> disgusting butchery will excite in all probability great disapproval
> in the House of Commons . . . Surely the slaughter of so many
> thousands in the 'rebellion' may atone for the murder of Mr.
> Veal. The score between black & white stands at present at about
> 3500 to 8.[19]

Even the Natal jury was discomforted by the role that it had played,
and asked for commutation of the death sentence for all those
sentenced in the Veal case[20] – except for Sibeko and Macabacaba.
Acting Administrator Beaumont tried to persuade the Natal
ministry to find reasons to reduce the number of men to be
hanged. In the end Dludla, in charge of the Nyuswa force that had
captured Veal, and July, said to have led the prayers, had their
sentences commuted to life imprisonment. They were followed by
Lukhukhwana's and even that of the *umthakati*, the disturbed
Mgwaqo.[21]

   This left Mabalengwe, Sibeko and Macabacaba. On 13 June six
of Macabacaba's wives arrived in Pietermaritzburg for a final
meeting with their husband. Afterwards, 'greatly distressed', they
pleaded for the commutation of their husband's sentence.[22] Then
from the depths of the condemned cell Macabacaba made his own
voice heard. As a last request he was allowed to make a petition for
pardon. It was taken down and supported by an old acquaintance,
Walter Acutt, Justice of the Peace and an official of the Native High
Court. It would be, Macabacaba continued to claim, an act of gross
injustice if he were to hang. He was the victim of his decision to be
open and straightforward with the authorities: he had named

Meseni – who, with the Qwabe leadership, had devised a plan to save themselves from being tried for Veal's death, with Zwezinye playing the pivotal role.

> I was a stranger in the tribe. I was brought up by Meseni's father.
> My nine sons were killed during the rebellion. I want it known
> that what has been done was by the order of Meseni. He and
> the doctors ordered the whiteman to be killed.

The petition was rejected.[23]

In the end the Natal authorities were deprived of the judicial massacre they had intended when they put over twenty men in the dock for murder. Five men went to the gallows, nevertheless: Ndabazezwe and Nkosi for the killing of Sangereid at Thring's Post; Macabacaba, as the man who gave the order that Veal should die; Sibeko for striking the blow; and Mabalengwe, the mighty war-doctor, whose desire for body parts of the enemy had given meaning and shape to the rebellion in Maphumulo in June and July 1906 – or, at least, a rebellion as the settlers of Natal were able to comprehend it.

McCallum left Natal on 6 June confident that he was 'leaving the colony with native matters fairly flattened out'.[24] Historians have found the phrase apposite[25] as did Winston Churchill: ' "fairly flattened out" is a good expression, & does justice to the wisdom & humanity that have inspired, no less than the beneficent results that have attended the native policy of the Natal Government, & Sir Henry Macallum.'[26]

But the Natal authorities were still not satisfied. The execution of those who it was said had murdered whites, the exile of chiefs said to be disloyal, over three thousand dead and three thousand in gaol, the refusal to consider an amnesty for those in hiding, the cattle seized, property looted and homesteads burnt were still, incredibly, not enough. Even as McCallum left, officials were planning further punishment and suppression, paying particular attention to Dinuzulu kaCetshwayo whose standing amongst Natal's Africans only seemed to increase in direct relation to the intensity of Natal's efforts to reduce it.

Natal had in fact not been flattened out. The colonial dream of conquest, the creation of an African population both subservient to and appreciative of alien rule was never – could never – be attained. And explanations had to be found for this, external explanations, independent of the settler psyche, in the deep, dark plots of the men who had sought to subvert civilisation and restore barbarism; men like the half-civilised, half-educated, spoilt, indolent but dangerous descendant of the Zulu house of kings – Dinuzulu kaCetshwayo.

The Natal authorities now turned their malevolent eye on Dinuzulu. After intense investigations, the office of the Attorney-General persuaded itself that it had sufficient evidence to show that Dinuzulu was deeply implicated in the 1906 rebellion. He was brought to trial in 1908, and in 1909 found guilty on a few of the minor charges. He was released from detention in 1910 by the new government of the Union of South Africa, but confined to a farm in the Transvaal. Since it was feared that this act would appear to Natal Africans as favouring the Zulu royal house, the order was given for the exiles to be repatriated from St Helena to Natal, but not allowed to return to their homes. Meseni was confined in the Ixopo division, and Ndlovu to the Swartkop location outside Pietermaritzburg.

Notes

1. Alias Nzimela alias Mahakana. He is often referred to as Nzimela in the records but was charged under the name Ndabazezwe.
2. PAR: AGO I/1/316, Statement by Nkwantshu kaTshumini before Thomas Maxwell at Maphumulo on 9 August 1906.
3. I have not followed the complex and contradictory role of Nozingogo who was Ndabazezwe's sister-in-law and Nkosi's mother, in this case.
4. Ndabazezwe said that his father had just died and he was still in mourning and consequently could not have gone into rebellion. Much of the cross-examination of witnesses was on this point.
5. PAR: RSC I/1/95, Rex *v.* Ndabazezwe alias Nzimela alias Mahakana and Nkosi, Evidence of Nzimela, 27 May 1907.
6. PAR: RSC I/1/95, Rex *v.* Ndabazezwe alias Nzimela alias Mahaka and Nkosi, Evidence of Nkosi, 27 May 1907.
7. PAR: RSC I/1/95, Judge's charge, 28 May 1907.
8. Nzimela in the text.
9. *The Natal Mercury*, 29 May 1907.
10. For the court record see PAR: RSC I/1/95, Rex *v.* Sifo and Mabalengwe, 28–29 May 1907.
11. Bryant, *A Zulu-English Dictionary*, 503.
12. Medical Officer Howden's reports were inconsistent. The original medical report states that the penis was removed (PAR: RSC I/1/95, Medical Officer Howden to PMO, Militia, Pietermaritzburg, 22 June 1906). But this report went astray, and at the preliminary investigation on 4 April 1907 Howden made another statement in which he stated that penis and testicles had been removed (PAR: AGO I/1/316, Annexure 5). Subsequently his original report was found, and in his evidence before the court, when recalled, he stated unambiguously that the testicles had not been removed from the body.
13. Except perhaps in his final comment to the court, when, with exaggerated and unconvincing expressions of surprise, it dawned on him that the rifle that had been handed to him could have belonged to the dead soldier.
14. PAR: RSC I/1/95, Rex *v.* Sifo and Mabalengwe, Ndlovu as defence witness gave evidence and was cross-examined on 30 May 1906.
15. PAR: RSC I/1/95, Rex *v.* Sifo and Mabalengwe, Evidence of Lohoho, 30 May 1907.
16. PAR: RSC I/1/95, Rex *v.* Sifo and Mabalengwe, Statement by Sifo, 30 May 1907.
17. *The Natal Mercury*, 3 June 1907.
18. BPP: C.3888, No.41, McCallum to Elgin, 5 June 1907, Enc. 1, Notes taken at interview, 3 June 1907, 100–101.
19. PRO: CO 179/241, 18285, McCallum to Elgin, 23 May 1907, teleg. Minute by Churchill, 25 May 1907.

20. Referred to in Shuter to the Attorney-General, 9 July 1907 in PAR: AGO I/9/33.
21. PRO: CO 179/241, 24335, Beaumont to Elgin, 9 July 1907 informed the Secretary of State of the commutation. But in PAR: MJPW 125, 1048 they are reported hanged on 12 July 1907. One has to hope that this was an error in reporting not administration.
22. PAR: SNA I/1/370, 4343/07, Statement by Uzikoli. Chief wife of Macabacaba Ndwedwe division, 13 June 1907.
23. PAR: SNA I/1/371, 1803/07, Statement of Macabacaba, Central Gaol, 27 June 1907 and associated documents.
24. BPP: C.3563, No. 26, McCallum to Elgin, 1 June 1907.
25. Shula Marks, *Reluctant Rebellion: The 1906–8 Disturbances in Natal*, Oxford: Clarendon Press, 1970, 340 and Ronald Hyam, *Elgin and Churchill at the Colonial Office 1905–1908*, London: Macmillan, 1968, 253.
26. Churchill's minute on PRO: CO 179/241, 19723, McCallum to Elgin, 1 June 1907.

Part Three

WAR, LAW AND RITUAL

10

War, law and ritual

History and histories

This book has depended heavily on legal records – rich, indispensable but hazardous historical material. The use of convicted prisoners as prosecution witnesses, and the offer of amnesty in return for co-operation, makes it particularly difficult for the historian to work confidently with their accounts of events. Although the use of participants in the alleged crime by the prosecuting authority is a theme intrinsic to the history of law, such witnesses should be subjected to effective cross-examination.[1] It might be argued that they were in the trial of Sifo for the murder of Powell – but this did not happen in the Sangereid case where two men were hanged on the evidence of a man whose capacity for invention in a capital case was subsequently exposed in court. Again it is not the injustice of the case that I am attending to here – it is the bearing on history of the fact that it can be shown that in the most important cases evidence, then legal now historical, was concocted with the deliberate intention to convict.

It is impossible to decide how aware men like Shuter were that their key witnesses were manufacturing evidence in the cases they brought to the Supreme Court. Did they deliberately frame selected men or were they caught up in, and persuaded by, plots planned and decided elsewhere? I have suggested how this could have been done – but have followed the trails only a certain distance. To have continued would have made the narrative impossibly long and increasingly tentative. By the nature of the process it is unlikely that there are definitive accounts of how various men were set up to take the blame, and we can only speculate on what the records imply. And one must suppose there is some blurring of the boundary between devising a sound case and fabricating one – indeed the ability to move with confidence in this shifting, shadowy terrain might well define a good criminal lawyer – but there can be little doubt that all parties were aware to a greater or lesser degree that evidence was being invented, and that certain of the individuals indicted for the murders had been framed.

Much of the evidence in the Supreme Court cases was manufactured at a fairly low level of the colonial administrative hierarchy – amongst the African policemen, the court officials and interpreters, the indunas, whose arrogance and inefficiency were so resented by ordinary people. Fred Oglesby, who had reason to know, held them much to blame, hatching their plots as they sunned themselves on the steps of the courthouses watching the passing crowd: so many of the men convicted of rebellion, he believed,

> were pointed out by men that sat at the Courthouses, and I can only think that it was for devilment that they were so pointed out by men that on dozens of occasion had a 'knife into them' and this was a grand chance to get a bit of their own back.[2]

But such minor members of officialdom were also under pressure from those immediately above them – the detectives in the CID of the Natal Police, who in turn were being watched by the magistrate, upon whom the Attorney-General leant for results which he could report to the Natal ministry. The news of Mabalengwe's arrest with body parts in his possession was of sufficient importance to reach the desk of the Minister of Justice within days. And Mabalengwe said at his trial that Detective Milliken had spread his name about for three months before he was set up for the sting which saw him at the doors of the Stanger courthouse with a haversack full of

medicines. It was the Governor who had first named Mabalengwe
as the war-doctor responsible for Veal's death – and in doing so
might well have given voice to a rumour which his subordinates
felt should be promoted to the rank of prophecy.

War-doctoring

To repeat, having noted their importance as histories, we have to
remember that the trial records are hazardous source material. Their
being in English creates huge problems. Even at the most basic
level this raises difficulties that go way beyond the more obvious
ones of transcription and translation. To take just one example,
the tendency, without thought or justification, to prefix 'war' to
nouns – hence war-doctor, war-song, war-hut, war-dance, war-dress,
war-paint, war-medicine. This all-pervasive practice not only justified
the flogging, fining and imprisoning of hundreds of men at the
time, but also closes off vast and crucial areas to historical understanding and analysis.

There was an overwhelming tendency to characterise all rituals
as 'war-doctoring'. James Stuart did just this is in his official history
of the rebellion – and used as his source the legal report of the trial
of those accused of organising the ritual held at eNkanini in 1905
with which I begin and end this book. He drew the conclusion
that:

> There is no act, passive in its nature, which a Native can commit
> that betrays hostile intent more plainly than being doctored for
> war. Once such ceremonies are held, all that remains is to await
> the signal for a simultaneous rising.[3]

There is no evidence to suggest that these rituals created ceremonial
time-bombs which then waited for the opportune moment to
explode. This illegitimate reduction of a healing and strengthening
ritual to a simple ritual preparation for war reflects colonial opinion

of the time. In Stuart's case, however, it was put forward by the leading expert on native customs and it is difficult to see how it could not have been done deliberately to deceive. From here it entered the ethnographic literature on the 'military organization of the Zulu'.[4] But thirty years before, John Colenso, the Bishop of Natal, had criticised just such abuse of evidence in order to prove 'doctoring for war', when he analysed the court record and the newspaper accounts of the trial of Langalibalele kaMtimkhulu Hlubi for rebellion. Colenso's conclusions in 1873 can be applied usefully to the court records of 1906 and reveal very similar problems of transcription and translation – indeed the vocabulary and the turns of phrase are often the same.

Colenso examined the way in which the Zulu word, *intelezi*, a potion, was rendered as 'war-medicine' even though the qualifier 'war' – *intelezi yempi* – was not originally used. This supposed 'war-medicine' was then associated with *ukuchela* – sprinkling – and rendered as 'strengthening them for the war'. It was clear to Colenso – the compiler of a dictionary whose examples of idiomatic usage have influenced Zulu dictionaries ever since – that the extension of 'sprinkling' to 'war-medicine' to make 'a preparation for war' was an addition to the evidence by the interpreter or the compiler of the court record:

> The fact is, that the phrases 'strengthened for war,' 'prepared for war,' 'war-preparation,' are not the usual Zulu phrases, and would not proceed naturally from the mouth of any native.

Colenso investigated the nature of the rituals that had been cited as examples of Langalibalele's 'doctoring for war'. It was usual for such ceremonies to be held after a mysterious event – an inexplicable death, an untoward happening, an omen, a lightning strike – an *umhlola*. In this case they had taken place years before, after Langalibalele's brother had died unexpectedly. Langalibalele spoke with Colenso on the subject of *ukuchela* and *intelezi*. He was himself an *inyanga* of great repute – with particular skills in rain-making and the use of medicinal plants. For this reason, and because the sources are generally so dominated by the colonial abuse of these terms and practices, I give *inkosi* Langalibalele space by quoting him at some length on the subject:

> Well! that sprinkling took place in order to 'bring back the spirit' (*buyisa idhlozi*) according to the native custom, that, when the master of the kraal has died, an ox is killed, a mixture (*ubulawu*) is rubbed together, the people are sprinkled with medicine (*intelezi*), and strengthened to be firm, and so the spirit of that dead man will be brought back home. It is not true that they were prepared for war. There is no force (*impi*) which, when once sprinkled for war, is allowed to go and stay in their kraals or mix with women . . .
>
> According to native custom the spirit was charmed (*lungiselwa*) in the great kraals. Therefore, since Uncwane had died because those three willed it – the ancestral spirits of the tribe through whom he had lived – in all those kraals these were addressed (*bongwa*) – *viz.* those three, and the late Uncwane – that he might return home to the tribe.
>
> This was the manner of their sprinkling. The doctor was called to rub together *ubulawu*, that Langalibalele might be sprinkled with it, and be white, as he had long been black with fasting. The people – that is to say, only the men of each kraal and the neighbourhood – were summoned and sprinkled with that *intelezi*, after the spirits had long been addressed; for the addressing of the spirits begin with speaking, then the ox is slaughtered, and the act is called *ukuluma* or *ukulumisa*, to sprinkle the men, so that the evil is taken away and they are strengthened.
>
> The war-medicine (*intelezi yempi*) differs essentially from the *intelezi* for death, and for any mysterious event (*umhlola*), and for the sky (lightning-stroke). That *intelezi*, with which the men were sprinkled when the spirit of Uncwane was brought back, was

the same as that used for the sky. Langalibalele knows well the composition of that *intelezi*; and he knows well too the war-medicine, *i.e.* its component parts, being himself a doctor. And those doctors whom he called – he called them because it was necessary that they should charm, and he too was continually helping them by pointing out the necessary herbs. (He began to describe the plants used for war-medicine: but, as his nomenclature was not very scientific, I could not identify them.)

The sprinkling with war-medicine takes place outside the kraal, not within it. Again, men who have been sprinkled with it must never return to their kraals and mix with their women, since thus, it is said, the *intelezi* loses its power.[5]

Always thorough, Colenso sought for confirmation and asked friends to interview men from different parts of the colony and the Zulu kingdom. They confirmed Colenso's essential point: *ukuchela*, sprinkling with *intelezi*, was used in different contexts to strengthen the community, and once the ceremony was over people returned to their homes; *ukuchela* with *intelezi yempi* was a ritual most obviously distinguished from others by the fact that the participants did not return home or associate with women but proceeded directly to fight.

And we have other contemporary accounts of ritual preparation for war at different levels of social organisation, from the African chiefdom[6] to the Zulu kingdom. In the latter case the ritual was large in scale, more elaborate, with the killing of a black bull as the central dramatic ritual performance, after which the participants went directly into battle. The killing of a bull was never a feature of the rituals in 1906. There were, however, fundamental principles manifested in the ceremonies carried out during the rebellion, which are apparent in accounts of rituals deep in the Zulu past, and are still familiar today.

In the rebellion of 1906 we find evidence for a range of rituals from purification and fortification, to strengthening against the

A 'witch-doctor' through a colonial lens.   (*The Natal Mercury Pictorial*, 30 May 1906)

Supposed movements of Mabalengwe.

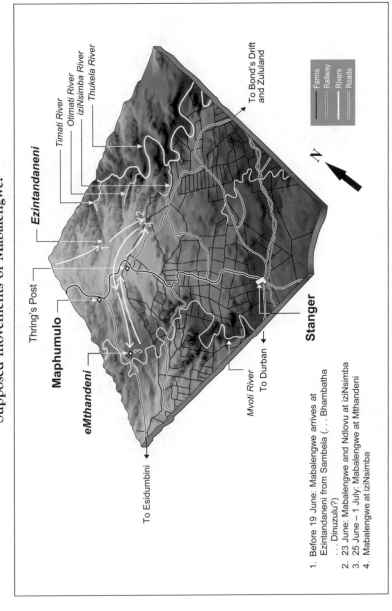

1. Before 19 June: Mabalengwe arrives at
   Ezintandaneni from Sambela (. . . Bhambatha
   . . . Dinuzulu?)
2. 23 June: Mabalengwe and Ndlovu at iziNsimba
3. 25 June – 1 July: Mabalengwe at Mthandeni
4. Mabalengwe at iziNsimba

threat of attack, to strengthening for attack. After some of these, the participants returned to their homes strengthened and purified, but not ritually prepared for violent conflict. During the rebellion men who had armed against the authorities and gathered at a stronghold or chief's homestead were secluded until they had been treated by a doctor, using ritually prepared medicine. When the situation allowed it they were also treated immediately before violent action. But to apply the phrase 'war-doctoring' to all such cere-monies is to use the concept of the colonial enemy.

Inventing witch-doctors

Mabalengwe, murdering and mutilating, taking physical possession of the masculinity of those whom he sought to overpower, was essential to the colonial vision of the rebellion. It was Mabalengwe the war-doctor who linked the different aspects of the resistance in the Maphumulo and Lower Thukela divisions together into a cohesive narrative structure. He had come from Dinuzulu and Bhambatha, via Sambela, and was present at the centres of resistance – at Thring's Post, the Oglesbys' store, and eMthandeni and the Izinsimba gorge – seeking body parts of the enemy at each place. Mabalengwe proved that Natal faced rebellion of the most barbarous kind.

I suspect that this Mabalengwe did not exist – at least not in the form in which he was presented in the Supreme Court trials. Mabalengwe was invented: by some of those suspected of killing Veal who needed a fearsome witch-doctor to deflect and absorb the official determination to find such a creature; and by the officials themselves as they sought to comprehend in their own terms the confused and contradictory story of the rebellion. In their version Mabalengwe provided a coherent plot in which a great war-doctor sought human bodies to practise his barbaric art. He was created during the police investigation and the magistrate's preliminary examination, and he was destroyed by the hangman in the Pietermaritzburg Central Gaol.

This Mabalengwe did not exist outside the legal process. Tragically, the man Mabalengwe did. There is evidence that there was an *inyanga* known as Mabalengwe who came from Sambela and worked in the Maphumulo division in the area between the Stanger-Maphumulo road and the Thukela in late June and early July. This evidence is slight but significant because it dates from a time before there was an opportunity for crown witnesses to develop any major conspiracy. Whether he was the man who, it was said later, had come from Bhambatha, or even from Dinuzulu, to Ndlovu at Ezintandaneni, then to the Izinsimba, had moved across the main road to eMthandeni, then back to the Izinsimba, wearing baboon and jackal skins, encouraging the pursuit of white game and using it when it was hunted down, is, however, most uncertain; whether he played the central role in all the attacks made on whites at this time, and in the mutilation of two bodies is very doubtful.

One has to suspect that the activities of a number of *izinyanga*, some invented, some half-remembered, some deliberately forgotten, at different places, were consolidated into the persona that the prosecution so desperately desired: one powerful, highly mobile, war-doctor. As a lawyer, confused by evidence of his continual reappearance at different places, asked during the trials, 'How many doctors were there by the name of Mabalengwe during the rebellion?'[7]

This is no reason to doubt that there were *izinyanga* of differing rank and reputation at the various gatherings of armed men during the rebellion. Ritual and religion are key themes in the rebellion and were practised at every meeting and before each mobilisation. Purification and strengthening ceremonies were strictly observed, and new arrivals were isolated until they had partaken in such ceremonies. The *izinyanga* who organised these rituals were mysterious, powerful, often fearful presences. Bryant's comparison of *inkosi* and *inyanga* is typically overblown but contains a useful truth:

Compared with the sleek and imposing personality of the chief the medicine-man presents quite a mean appearance, though picturesque and awesome withal.

Along with the chief he shares the greatest power in the savage tribe – not, it is true, the power of supreme authority, but a power over life and death not less effective and real, though hidden and mysterious. His well-wrinkled features bear the unmistakable stamp of a thinking mind, and his intelligent eye has that flash of deep cunning so well suited to one who has often been the accomplice, behind the scene, to sinister deeds. His lean, wiry frame betokens a life of toilsome, if well-rewarded, activity rather than of luxury and repose – an activity consisting mainly in constant arduous journeyings throughout the land, and frequently even into the foreign lands of adjoining tribes.[8]

Izinyanga moved from one place to another, and as members of a peripatetic profession, they melted away when pressed too closely by the enemy. Their names appear in passing in the court record: Sibhoko,[9] Maqandaqanda, and the obscure but perhaps most significant Sondodo, Mabalengwe's brother. Mabalengwe came to stand for these *izinyanga*, the men who knew too much – of the rebellion, of its participants, of custom and tradition, of the lie of the land, of the authorities' desire for retribution – to stand trial themselves. Mabalengwe the war-doctor, although identified by African witnesses as a major force in the rebellion, was the invention of white fears.

Such acting out by Africans of colonial perceptions of Africa might have been a consequence of deliberate strategy on the part of those in authority, but it was also quite possibly the result of the unconscious or even accidental transmission of white perceptions and prejudices. Consider the matter of the plant *'pingantloya'* which Shuter, in his official summing-up of the preliminary examination, said was worn by Sifo and others and, according to tradition, had identified them as heroes in battle.[10] To confirm this custom he referred to the entry in Bryant's dictionary published the year before, which reads: 'Wild asparagus – a long-stemmed thorny plant . . . often used by Europeans for Christmas decoration, also worn stuck in the head by a native who has killed a man in war time.' Key crown witness Nkwantshu made the same identification in court: it was 'that plant white people collect when they wish to decorate their buildings'. One has to wonder whether, in so doing, Nkwantshu was independently confirming Zulu tradition and settler custom, or whether he had access to Bryant's dictionary either indirectly through a passing reference, or directly through coaching. It certainly wasn't a shared tradition: Ndlovu said he hadn't heard of it and a defence witness dismissed the whole idea – the plant when set alight could be used as a torch but he didn't think it could be worn – 'It has thorns in it'.[11]

But the most vivid example of Africans reflecting colonial perceptions of African practices has to be the attempt to convince the court that Sifo had not only removed Powell's genitals but exhibited them impaled on a bayonet. This story was first recorded by Nkwantshu and then repeated by the witnesses associated with him. Medical evidence, however, showed that it was an invention, but it was an invention that, again, had its origins in settler fears – and male nightmares.

Although Trooper Albert Powell was killed in the excitement of the chase, there was a calculated, deliberate quality in the act itself that is significant. He was caught, held, his tunic was pulled aside, a probing hand felt his chest, and the assegai struck between the between the fourth and fifth ribs into his heart. After this his throat was cut. Powell was not slaughtered as in battle but as in a sacrifice. In Zulu tradition the abdomen of a man killed in battle had to be opened: the subsequent well-being of the assailant demanded this. The crown witnesses assumed that this had happened, and were exposed as liars when confronted with the medical evidence. The blood which drenched the front of Powell's body had come from the wound in his heart and the doctor conducting the post mortem examination had to unbutton his clothes to examine the abdomen which had not been touched; Powell's trouser leg had been slit open to remove his penis.

The horror of the killing cannot be disputed, but a corpse 'ripped open' and parts of the body exposed in triumph was not part of it. An important analysis of present-day killings to acquire body parts suggests that they are carried out as a necessary sacrifice of an individual for a greater social goal, and that there is 'conceptual continuity' between such ritual killings and 'ritual acts of less grim kinds which nevertheless have the attainment or preservation of collective well-being as their main purpose'.[12] Despite obvious differences created by the fact that the Powell killing took place at a time of armed conflict and in the heat of direct physical confrontation, the evidence is not incompatible with this analysis.

Veal's corpse was too mutilated to allow a similar observation, but its condition does suggest that it was treated as an animal slaughtered rather than as a man killed in battle, and James Stuart gave evidence that supports the idea of a killing carried out in the spirit of a sacrifice.[13]

It is possible to detect, in the confused and contradictory evidence on the arrival and the departure of Oliver Veal from eMthandeni, suggestions that there were sacred elements in his violent death which were hidden in subsequent accounts. On 1 July the atmosphere in the Mvoti valley was grim: the armed men gathered there had suffered severe losses, and the troops were approaching from all sides. The sense of impending catastrophe was lifted for a moment when down the road came a white man pedalling furiously towards Thongathi. The Nyuswa marched him to eMthandeni, and the Qwabe gathered there heard them singing as they came over the hills. (If only we had direct evidence of the songs sung, and the dances danced in the rebellion, our analysis would be so enriched. All we have of this occasion is a fragment in the legal record – 'the snake which is not trod upon'.) On arrival a circle was formed with Veal and his captors in the centre. There was a pause, and a silence.

The Qwabe sang, probably the Qwabe *ihubo*, their clan anthem, invoking the ancestors and their part in the history of the Qwabe, a history that was about to change forever. It was at this solemn moment, poised between the memory of an independent African past and the certainty of an oppressive colonial future, that the *amakholwa* invoked the assistance of another god as they knelt in front of Veal and prayed: 'Our Father who art in heaven, give us strength this day to defeat our enemies the white people who oppress us.' Veal was then struck down.

The killing took place in a moment of calm within the disturbed atmosphere of approaching catastrophe. Although Powell was killed in the heat of the chase, the act itself was clinical and the mutilation done in secret. The account by the African crown witnesses of the triumphant exhibition of his genitals was a fabrication. It might have been deliberately inserted into the narrative by the detectives or officials to create antagonism towards the accused and to heighten the dramatic intensity of the trial. I think it more likely that it was developed in a process by which, in response to the wide-eyed and open-mouthed reaction of the interrogators, accounts of violence and mutilation were exaggerated incrementally until a quick, clinical, covert killing and excision of body parts became a barbaric slaughter followed by the exhibition of severed, male genitals. In the end the invented story of triumphant, public sexual mutilation was so powerful in its confirmation of their deepest fears that it convinced the interrogators themselves, overwhelmed the contradictory medical evidence and became essential to the prosecution's case. It was told in court under oath – before its rebuttal brought the crown's case crashing down and released the accused.

'Nature's noblemen': Ndlovu and Meseni

And yet, and yet . . . reading and re-reading the evidence, one glimpses more details of the historical events which lie behind these invented stories told in court. Sifo was said to have impaled Powell's genitals on a bayonet. Bayonets – written phonetically as 'benetu' or 'spenetu', occur often in the sources and in violent contexts.[14] It is possible that bayonets had become available at this time as loot or army surplus after the South African war, but there is a suggestion that the role of the bayonet went beyond that of a utilitarian, improvised replacement of the traditional assegai. Nowhere is this more apparent than in the mysterious, obscure but nonetheless significant references in the records of the Stanger martial law trials, to the arrival of 'Bayonet' in the fastness of Izinsimba after the killing of Powell and the seizing of his rifle. Not only are there references to 'Benetu who is Ndhlovu',[15] but also one of the rare allusions at this time (July 1906) to Mabalengwe. Mahagawu had just arrived at Izinsimba:

> I went along and then I was told to go and sit down at a distance. I was told the Doctor would come to me and then I would be permitted to go amongst the people and eat meat – there were about 40 fires going at the same time, and cattle were being slaughtered all the time. I remained seated for a long time and I saw all the things which they did. Then Msuduku (No. 9) came along he was the doctor. Just then I heard Ndhlovu ka T[himuni] call out 'Fall in' he gave the command twice. The people said 'Do you not hear uBenetu?' I did not understand the meaning of uBenetu. On the call of 'Fall in', Msuduku No. 9 left me – then the people gave their war cry which was 'Hehe, what has turned you, have turned because of the poll tax, qa qa'? and immediately the people came swarming out of the bushes . . .

> x-examined by the Court: All the people were armed with Assegais. Shields . . . knob sticks and axes. The Chief Ndhlovu carried a Rifle with bayonet fixed . . .

> Msuduku No. 9: I ask why does Mahagau say I was the doctor. The doctoring was done by Mabalengwe of Sambela. I was only to assist Mabalengwe.[16]

Ndlovu kaThimuni, in the account I give of him in this book, was a man acutely aware of what had happened to his people after sixty years of colonial rule, and desperately concerned about their future. Determined to act with responsibility, and in accordance with his ideas of good government, he was nonetheless forced into rebellion. He responded bravely and intelligently when brought before the colonial courts. We must not, however, let his obvious qualities push us towards treating him patronisingly and sentimentally – like the colonial journalist who described Ndlovu and Meseni as 'not only Nature's noblemen, but nobles by birth, the descendants of kings'. He had been a rebel leader – the Bayonet – ordering his men to 'Fall In!' and undergo ritual strengthening for violent conflict. Between the time of the attack by the militia on 19 June and his arrest on 12 July, he was active in organising resistance in the broken bush-covered terrain away from the road and towards the Thukela. To the west, upriver, was Sambela, who had kept men in the field, and women, children and livestock in safety, despite a number of attempts in July by the militia to drive them out. Ndlovu's territory had also been successfully defended after the initial attack of the 19th, although it suffered a number of subsequent drives by the militia. To the east was the Izinsimba where Mashwili had been in hiding with his Mthethwa and Ntshingumuzi's Qwabe. They had been massacred on 8 July, an action which McKenzie attempted but failed to repeat in Ndlovu's and Sambela's territories in the west. The militia's failure is an indication of Ndlovu's and Sambela's defensive success.

We must not let our legitimate rejection of the exaggerated and sensationalist and even invented accounts presented in the court cases lead us also to reject the evidence of effective resistance. Ndlovu argued in court that he had been forced by his men into participating in the attack on Thring's Post. I suspect that this applies to the timing of the event rather than the action itself. When he intervened amongst his people, as he did in saving the lives of non-combatants, he did so decisively, and it is hard to accept that Ndlovu was unaware of the pressures amongst those around him to make use of the most powerful medicine possible, medicine that required body parts from the enemy. Ndlovu denied knowledge of such practices in court, but it is very difficult to accept this from a man so closely linked to Zulu tradition and who had taken an expressed interest in Zulu history.

A similar argument can be used for Meseni, although his situation was significantly different from Ndlovu's. He was the ruler of a far greater number of people, and they were spread over a much wider extent of territory. He was deeply angered by the serious and undeserved antagonism of the authorities but, unlike Ndlovu, Meseni did not have the terrain upon which to fall back in order to protect his people and stock from the militia. His military strategy was a defensive one, and his people came to eMthandeni to protect their chief. By 1 July Meseni at eMthandeni could have been playing the final act of a Shakespearean tragedy. His people, with others in support, were gathered around him. He was grieving for those already killed. The columns of troops closing in were armed with weapons of mass destruction to which Meseni had no material answer. As a participant recounted:

> When we went to fight with the whites, I said to some of the impi we are doing wrong, and it is useless us going simply with practically naked hands, and think that we can do anything . . . Some of them agreed with me, and said it would be impossible for us to get the upper hand.[17]

There were, however, non-material strategies, spiritual ones, upon which Meseni insisted and in which his people actively participated: sacrifices to the shades; appeals that they look on their descendants with favour; rituals of purification to prepare the people at eMthandeni for the coming conflict; medicine to weaken the enemy and darken its path. Meseni's *impi*, spiritually cleansed and fortified, and armed with assegais, waited for the arrival of the columns of militia with 15-pounders loaded with shrapnel, Maxims, and Mark V bullets in their rifles. But they also had other weapons – weapons forged by history, tradition and custom and struck in rituals understood and practised, with different aims and degrees of intensity, by everyone in the resistance. They would achieve ultimate effectiveness if they were mixed with physical parts of the enemy. This was widely accepted, to such an extent that it did not have to be questioned or discussed. Indeed it was best left to those who had the knowledge and the skills, and the urgent need for the effective utilisation of every possible means to give strength to the Qwabe in this terrible moment in their history overcame any hesitation.

Meseni, like Ndlovu, was a successful and adroit leader. They were both men who, when pressed, acted decisively. They were political strategists who had kept their positions amongst their people in the most difficult of situations, utilising both African custom and the colonial political and legal system. Like politicians throughout history, they knew the importance of distance and deniability. When Veal was brought to eMthandeni, Meseni left. When Veal was dead, he returned. He knew little and saw nothing. He made sure of that.

Records of ritual

Purifying, fortifying rituals in their different forms were a feature of all mobilisations and actions in the rebellion. When a newcomer arrived at a place of mobilisation, he was kept apart until purified, cleansed and strengthened. These were standard practices and an intrinsic part of the rebellion. The mobilisation of rebels took place in an atmosphere of religious preparation. Aid was sought from the ancestral shades in song and dance and from medicines licked from the fingers, sprinkled by a doctor and absorbed from fumes and smoke. Records of rituals are found throughout the source material, but their significance is obscured because they are so often presented as 'doctoring for war', 'war-songs' and 'war-dances'.

For example, I refer in the text to the singing, at especially solemn moments, of the *ihubo*; the evocation in song of the shared history of the living and the dead. To characterise it as a war-song is misleading – at least out of context. The evidence suggests to me that the violent element in these rituals increased with the violence of the events themselves. In the months before the rebellion, ritual expressions of commonality and resistance remained expressions, but with the outbreak of hostilities they became overt. The violent circumstances demanded it, prompting the procurement of the body parts of the enemy for use in the rituals.

Amongst the participants this was both known and not known. As Sibeko said, in his pathetic and fatal answers to Judge Dove Wilson, casting his mind back from what Sifo called 'this place of red cloths' to recall how he felt as he marched the white buck to eMthandeni:

> I didn't like taking this white man up, because I felt in my heart that some harm was going to be done to him, but as the chief had said that I should do it, I decided that I ought to do it.

The pursuit and slaughter of a human being were referred to, and not referred to, in the use of the image of the hunt, the capture and killing of the *inyamazane emhlope*. Even if we cannot be sure of the accuracy of the historical sources, we can sense in them the shape and the significance of the ritual associated with these killings. A hunt had been held at eMthandeni on Friday 22 July, an event that would have brought many men together in social action for the first time and would have been accompanied by various rituals to ensure safety and success. Bryant, in his important description of hunting for big game, describes how

> the whole body of hunters formed themselves into a circle, round which the medicine-man passed, both in front and behind, sprinkling each man with an asperge on body and legs with his

own special prophylactic. A fire having then been kindled in
the centre of the circle, and the medicine-man having sprinkled
thereon his own patent mixture, each huntsman passed thereby
and, as he did so, thrust the point of his spear into the smoke
'for luck'.[18]

It is easy to discern common features in this and other strengthening
rituals depicted in this book. This description seems especially
pertinent when we consider accounts of the ceremony that took
place at eMthandeni on the morning of 2 July at which men were
strengthened not for a hunt for big game, but for a confrontation
with an even more dangerous enemy closing in on eMthandeni.
They are grouped around a fire with medicine heated on a *udengezi*
and in which there is fat, which it is strongly suggested has been
taken from Veal's body. They are ordered to 'Point your Assegais
to the pot (Udengezi) that they may smell the odour from the pot',
and to say, 'It is darkness for the whiteman'. [19]

The accounts of this ceremony were made in circumstances
which encouraged distortion or even invention – it was after all
an episode in the crown witnesses' narrative of the arrival of
Mabalengwe at eMthandeni and his role in the killing of Veal in
order to obtain parts of his body. Their description of the application
of this medicine to the assegais of the combatants, regardless of
their factual accuracy as accounts of a particular ceremony, do reflect,
it seems to me, the importance and the nature and rituals of the
time, and the thinking of the men involved. It is possible to discern
the contours of historical events and attitudes even behind the
clouds of obfuscation that drift over the legal records.

Responsibility

So far I have dealt mainly with questions of evidence and the
interplay of sources when seen from historical and legal perspectives.
But there is another feature of this history which is perhaps less

obvious but more insidious and revealing: this is the fact that the legal processes initiated against the twenty-two men accused of murder treated them in terms of their individual culpability. The nature of their involvement differed, from those who struck the blows, to those who gave the orders, to those who participated in the events merely as spectators. Nonetheless, they were indicted as individuals and had to defend themselves against charges of individual participation.

The killings were not, however, individual acts – they were shared social ones. This made the pursuit of individual culpability a search for something that did not exist. Thus the man accused of striking the death blow was outraged at the way he had been deserted by those whom he believed had given the orders, and based his defence on the fact that he had been obeying instructions: 'People who know all about it remain untouched . . . Is it likely that an individual belonging to a tribe or chief would do something in compliance with an order of the chief without that chief knowing something about it?'

Ndlovu and Meseni as chiefs were, of course, responsible for what happened on the Maphumulo road and at eMthandeni when the men under them raided the stores or armed to resist the militia, but to make them individually responsible for acts carried out by the forces under them proved impossible. Apart from the legal complexities of defining and proving criminal responsibility, and of those created by the fact that they had already been convicted under martial law, both chiefs were clever men, with a lifetime's experience in adjudication themselves, and who covered their tracks, literally and metaphorically. But in so doing they exposed the men under them who argued, understandably, that they were under orders and obliged to obey their chiefs.

Because the rebellion was a social action characterised by general rather than individual participation, there is some (but only some) sense in Dove Wilson's instruction to the jury that, if the death of whites was an expected outcome of rebellion, then all rebels were responsible in law for Veal's death and guilty of murder. In practice, however, all this interpretation did was to give the jury the confidence to pass verdicts of guilty on all those eventually accused in the Veal case. There was no deeper consideration of the evidence as to degrees of responsibility, autonomy and culpability.

Those accused, and those who feared they might be accused, pointed their fingers elsewhere – up or down the political hierarchy or sideways at other groups – either at those who gave orders or at those who carried them out. The tragic consequence of this was that broke it up the broader unity based on opposition to the colonial authority, which had been a feature of the rebellion, and in the process created new factions organised for survival within colonial structures. It set up individuals or groups of individuals against others, and the bitterness of betrayal and division, marked by accusations and counter-accusations, cast a divisive shadow over the memory of the rebellion itself. The Qwabe pointed at the Nyuswa; others drew closer to Meseni to accuse those from the south like Macabacaba; Ndlovu as chief of the Nodunga held the Mbedu responsible for disobeying his order; and the Mbedu turned against men like Sifo whose chief was Ngobizembe. These were all divisions amongst members of different chiefdoms. There were also divisions amongst local groupings: the relatives and drinking friends of Nkwantshu gave evidence against neighbours with whom they were in dispute – evidence which sent them to the gallows; Mabalengwe believed that Zwezinye and his co-witnesses had concocted their story against him not only to save themselves but to terminate a long-outstanding debt; and then there was the rivalry over a woman that the Supreme Court accepted lay at the root of the crown's attempt to blame Sifo for Powell's death. Kinship and politics, ambitions and disappointments, neighbourly alliances and rivalries, new loves and old debts, the stuff of social existence, were transformed into weapons and used unscrupulously and at times with deadly effect. The result was the fragmentation of social cohesion forged in a time of common distress, by a socially destructive legal process which transformed allies into victims offered up to protect certain individuals and to satisfy the colonial demand for vengeance.

Tragic as this process of accusation and counter-accusation was, and significant as the evidence it generated is, it was never sufficient. The authorities remained unsatisfied, and in an important sense never could be satisfied. The colonial goal of a simultaneously subservient and appreciative colonised population was, as I have already said, an illusion. For those in authority, the hangings and the humiliations notwithstanding, the punishments were still felt not to have been sufficient and the lesson the masters intended to teach had still to be learnt.

This was apparent in the number of men who had escaped the authorities' net. Official estimates of casualties on the rebel side are virtually useless but we can get a rough idea from a journalist who was a participant in these events in the Maphumulo division. He estimated that eight thousand men mobilised, one thousand five hundred were killed, one thousand surrendered and one thousand taken prisoner. Of the four thousand five hundred remaining, one thousand were in hiding and the rest had 'melted away' and gone back to their places of work.[20] 'Melting away' suggests a passive process, but it could not have been so. For thousands of men to escape in this fashion, in these times of martial law, patrols and a battery of pass laws, implies a knowledge of the landscape, its peoples, organisation, subterfuge, careful planning and a steady eye and hand when confronted by officialdom.

Hundreds of men were in the vicinity when Powell was killed. One man was indicted, an informer, and he was found not guilty. There were hundreds of men gathered together at the killing of Veal, and instructions were given to indict as many as possible: nineteen were accused, twelve were released, seven were found guilty on the evidence of participants in the crime, and three of these hanged. In neither case were those who had mutilated the bodies discovered. This again points to the existence of a network that set up systems to protect those under threat from a vengeful authority.

It could be argued that the witnesses for the crown in the Maphumulo trials were part of such a network and that many of the men accused in the Veal and Sangereid trials were offered up to make sure that inquiries were not pursued further and that no one delved deeper. Despite months of investigation the *izinyanga* in the cases were not found – except for Mabalengwe, whose role is obscure and guilt is doubtful. Ndlovu protected those he could by naming people who were dead, and his example was followed by others. Meseni did not: the investigation pointed far too clearly in his direction, and he named others to save himself and those close to him, or perhaps, in a more generous reading of the evidence, to stop the investigation proceeding further. For it is clear that most of those who participated in the killing at eMthandeni, active and passive, escaped prosecution – some through death, most by 'melting away'.

Although the war in the field was over, with terrible losses in the Maphumulo division, and despite the appearance of leading figures in the war in the courts, resistance continued. The authorities knew this, and for them the explanation had to lie, not in themselves and their impossible dream of total domination, but in the existence of an even deeper and more devious plot being planned against them. Natal had been 'fairly flattened out' but, apart from its borderlands, Zululand had escaped, and there in the north lived the son of the last Zulu king, Dinuzulu kaCetshwayo. Even as the Natal chiefs were being transported to St Helena, fresh reports were being received of his continued activities against the state. Means were being devised to bring him under control – but this is another story.

Contending communities

It is possible to discern in the activities, statements and rituals of those who rebelled, different visions of the forces that united them, and what they hoped to achieve. At the centre for many was the known community, the clan and the lineage, all those descended from a common ancestor, the living and the dead. Thus, in the Qwabe ritual held at eNkanini by acting-chief Ntshingumuzi and Mbombo in 1905 with which I begin this book, it was the community, based on the patrilineal lineage, which was mobilised for ritual cleansing at a time of distress. During the ritual at eNkanini there was a return to a shared past, and the assistance of the ancestors was invoked for healing and for strength in a time of trial. The singing of the *ihubo* evoked in the inglorious present the splendour of an autonomous past. The making of the *izinkatha* repaired the broken links in the lineage, consolidating its powers, the better to confront its enemies.

The word 'lineage', however, is such an inadequate, technical term for these deep spiritual bonds. The people who gathered at eNkanini were related and knew the links of blood and marriage that connected them, and which were confirmed and strengthened in the shared ceremony. They belonged to a community of the living whom ritual placed in close communion with their shades. It intensified the powerful sense of community by descent – perhaps still the most powerful of all social bonds – but although it was deeply rooted, it was also narrow, limited to those descended from a common founding ancestor.

The chiefdom was a wider structure that incorporated different discrete lineages under the authority of a dominant chiefly one. It was with the chiefdoms that Shepstone had made his initial accommodation and upon which Natal native policy had depended since the founding of the colony. Later, in changed times, a major objective of the colonial authorities was to reduce what autonomy remained with the chiefdoms and their chiefs. Once the rebellion began, however, those chiefs who associated themselves with resistance became the focal points of mobilisation, and in some cases they extended their authority, now not just as chiefs but as rebel leaders. The prescribed borders between chiefdoms broke down as followers of apparently loyal chiefs joined those in rebellion. Between the main road and the Thukela, Ntuli, Mbedu and others were led by Ndlovu and his Nodunga Zulu, and after the devastation of the Nodunga by the militia on 19 June their neighbour Sambela of the Ntuli came to their assistance. Mthethwa and Qwabe dominated those gathered at Izinsimba under Mashwili and Mahlanga, but all the chiefdoms of the Lower Thukela division had representatives there. The Qwabe and Nyuswa dominated those who mobilised around eMthandeni, but they were joined by men from different chiefdoms stretching all the way to Durban. The range and pervasiveness of Meseni's perceived power is reflected in the way in which his orders to workers to leave Durban and gather round him at eMthandeni were described: 'His word was heard just like thunder is heard': 'That word was like thunder in Durban'.[21]

United in resistance, chiefdoms still fought and prayed separately. It was the Mhlali contingent that suffered at Pheyana, the Nyuswa that guarded the Mvoti drift, the Mbedu that left Thring's Post with their loot, the Nyuswa and the Qwabe that sang their own songs and formed up in different segments of the *umkhumbi* with Veal in the centre, and the Mthethwa and Qwabe that occupied different parts of the Izinsimba gorge. But as armed rebels they shared a vision of resistance. These were new alliances amongst people for whom a half century of divide and rule had created intense animosities. In the winter of 1906 the divisions were, if not forgotten, for the moment overcome.

Although more inclusive than organisation around the lineage, mobilising under local chiefs was still limited, and this local, rural vision of community left its adherents vulnerable on a number of levels. It restricted the tactical options open to the leaders; it brought workers out of urban environments into rural areas to defend their chiefs, thereby exposing them time and again to the fire-power of highly mobile, heavily armed militia, who once they had broken up the large concentrations of men, were able to move at will amongst non-combatants and their resources, destroying the basis of rural existence; and it meant that plans for attacks on urban centres did not materialise. The idea of 'our land' and 'their towns' still dominated, and militarily it was disastrous. As Meseni, for example, protested:

> Did I ever go to the town? Isn't it the white people who come down to me? Did I ever go to their part of the country? Isn't it they who have come in, armed themselves, and used their weapons in my district?

Ironically, while this acceptance of segregated authority restricted rebel tactics, its termination was the major objective of the authorities. It had been intrinsic to Shepstone's policy of indirect rule but now had to be brought to an end. No chiefs would be permitted to retain such misplaced notions of autonomy: the pretensions and powers of chiefs were to be reduced, and authority would now be exercised unequivocally from the colonial centre.

Shepstone's system of segregation recognised African chiefly authority but then divided it in order to maintain control. The incorporation of chiefs under a single African authority, as in the case of the Zulu kingdom, was seen by him as an intolerable threat, and a dominant feature of his later years was his attempt to bring about destruction of that kingdom and the creation of local chiefly rule on the Natal model.[22] But the very intensity of the Natal attempt to destroy the power of the Zulu kings only strengthened their standing in the eyes of Africans as the consequences of colonial exploitation increasingly ravaged their lives.

This was a long process. There are hints of it from the time of the 1879 invasion of Zululand when, although large numbers of Africans from Natal were drafted into the invading forces, there were also expressions of regret for the passing of a formidable, autonomous African state. Such feelings intensified, and by the early years of the next century the living representative of the Zulu royal house, Dinuzulu, now confined to a single district in northern

Zululand, exercised an increasing influence over the people of the colony. The history of the founding and rise of the Zulu kingdom was a history with which they were all associated, on one side or another. It was an independent history, a history of resistance, a history of African independence. As was frequently said, Africans in Natal had submitted to white rule believing that they would escape tyranny. Sixty years of colonialism had proved them wrong: they had only exchanged an African conqueror for a foreign tyrant. It was now time to reclaim their African, their Zulu, heritage.

The incorporation of this view of the past, broader and more inclusive than that of the lineage and the chiefdom, was a powerful motivating and mobilising factor in the rebellion – I would suggest, the most powerful. It was a history just a century old: a history in which their grandparents had participated, a history still accessible to those without reading and without books, the links being made by oral communication. It was a claim to the land of Shaka, and Zulu autonomy, to the legacy of the man who had been in authority when the white newcomers had arrived. He and his successors had negotiated a settlement with them, but their descendants had revealed their inadequacy as rulers and should now return to their land over the sea from where they had come. It was a claim for the restoration of the land to the people united by the founder, Shaka kaSenzangakhona. When William Robbins opened the door to the veranda at five in the morning on 19 June, he was greeted by the Zulu royal cry of 'Usuthu' and an assegai thrust. The wearing of *shokobezi*, the white cow tail insignia of the Usuthu, became for the authorities legal confirmation of rebellious intent. At their trials rebels testified how hesitation to confront the colonial forces ranged against them was overcome by the news that the army of the Zulu kings was about to sweep down from the north and assist them.

Mashwili, grandson of Dingiswayo, flanked by his son, Langalibalele, and Mahlanga of the Qwabe, the leaders of the armed force in the Izinsimba fastness, gave voice to this wider vision of Zulu history when he admonished John Boziana for having bought and sold their mutual heritage, thus turning his back on the African community to which he belonged.

> You are alone now. You have bought land which belonged to Shaka, you seek to become like the animals of your white people, you drive off the Natives and give the land to Coolies – then you told the young men to pay Poll Tax – you influenced them.

Mashwili's vision was one of an all-encompassing resistance: the arrival of forces from Zululand would allow rebels to leave their hideouts in the rural areas and attack the towns:

> The Chief Mashwili gave it out that Dinuzulu was expected to help them. Their plans were to sweep off Stanger – it was said Mqhawe had swept off Verulam, and that Greytown had also been swept off and it was intended the impi should go as far as Durban. The Chief said the white people were oppressing the Native. He said the Natives had to pay Rents and Taxes for land which belonged to Shaka. The rebels replied 'Yes – we are thankful for the words – the land is ours'.[23]

To the end Ndlovu and Meseni believed there was a chance that Dinuzulu would give the order for mobilisation. Day after day men moved out from the Izinsimba fastnesses to watch for the arrival of the Zulu regiments at Bond's drift. They were still waiting when McKenzie's columns trapped and massacred them on 8 July.

But there were other visions of the world as well, wider than those contained in the history of the Zulu kingdom – visions open most directly only to those who could read, and available in the book which they were most used to reading, the bible. Natal and Zululand had experienced intense missionary activity from early in the nineteenth century. The mission reserves and the men and women who lived in them were a significant presence in the colony, economically active in agricultural production for the market, transport and trading, and beginning to demand, as Christian, civilised men and women, a greater share in the social and political life of the colony. To the colonial authorities these *amakholwa* – believers – were anathemas. Assertive, ambitious, pretentious, they resisted classification as members of an identifiable tribe under a compliant chief. As the nineteenth century drew to a close, so the official attempts to curb their independence and restrict their activities increased. By the turn of the century they were showing signs of resistance both to the state and to the churches in which they had been educated. Many of the *amakholwa* had broken with their founding mission churches. Some had left to form parallel institutions, others, disillusioned with the disparity between what their preachers preached and what they practised, had broken away to form independent sects.

Among the colonists there was little understanding of and no sympathy for African converts of any kind. Africans who wore western dress, spoke English and were reluctant to show the deference that settlers demanded, clearly had illegitimate aspirations to equality. Hostility to 'Ethiopians' was particularly intense as they were associated with the slogan 'Africa for the Africans', which expressed a view of the future that threatened and infuriated settler and official alike. There was a tendency to lump all *amakholwa* together and, when scapegoats were needed, to condemn them as 'Ethiopians'. In his first official communication on the outbreak of the rebellion Governor Sir Henry McCallum had his explanation: it lay in

> the unfathomable unrest which has been observed among the natives of South Africa during the last two years was intended to culminate in simultaneous and concerted action; that Ethiopianism, which has for its cry 'Africa for the Blacks,' is the mainspring of the movement . . .[24]

The presence of *amakholwa* at eMthandeni and the significance of their role in the rebellion became the subject of acrimonious debate between the authorities and the American Board missionaries in particular. We know that there were many *amakholwa* at eMthandeni and others with the men guarding the access roads, but the nature of their relations with the missionary societies or the independent churches and sects is difficult to establish. Meseni said that the *amakholwa* held prayers every morning during the mobilisation, and others said that they were organised in their own regiment. They were present at the ceremony that preceded the killing of Oliver Veal; one of them read his diary, and they prayed that they would be given strength to overcome their enemy. While I have accepted some of this in the narrative I have written above, I have treated the evidence with caution, because the records also suggest that the presence of the three *amakholwa* amongst the accused was brought about by the official desire to have 'Ethiopians' represented in the dock. And not just laymen, but ministers dressed in clerical black, with spectacles indicating their pretensions to literacy, all exterior manifestations of an inadequate interior. Again, this does not mean that their presence was invented. I would suggest that 'believers' of different persuasions were present and that they played their part in the invocation of spiritual allies. But whether they behaved in the manner suggested in court is less certain – the image of bespectacled men, in sombre clerical dress, kneeling before the condemned Oliver Veal, joining Mabalengwe in his jackal skin hat and baboon skin cape in prayer to their different deities, presents such a vivid realisation of the interplay of religion and ritual, tradition and innovation, sanctity and profanity, at a moment of dramatic intensity, that, once evoked, it is difficult to exclude it from the imagination.

We must not deny the *amakholwa* presence because the colonial authorities sought to exaggerate it. They were there and did play an important role. But as had been the case with the other participants – the *izinyanga* and the spectators – the authorities had been unable to bring them to court and prosecute them successfully.

This was a consequence, not only of the terrible casualties in the days that followed the attack on eMthandeni, but also of the networks of resistance which hid their identity from the detectives then and historians now. The participation of *amakholwa* – be they members of conventional or independent churches – is significant, for these were people who had access to print and writing – to the books, newspapers and letters through which they were able to join other communities of the African oppressed: those who lived in forced exile, at work in the cities and longing for home, those who had lost their land and were labouring for those who now possessed it, and those all over the world who sought the return of their heritage, of Africa to Africans. Such a vision, no matter how it was understood or formulated, was one that had the potential to create links amongst all believers, not the face-to-face links of orality but the remote, non-personal – what have been called the imagined – bonds created by the written word.

These connections made it possible to move between African beliefs as evidenced in the rituals that invoked the favour of the shades, and the elements of Christianity that appealed for the intervention of a supernatural deity. This capacity for spiritual mobility between different belief systems and the world of protest and political demands was demonstrated in the use of the word *uhlanga*. Literally it means the starting point, the place of beginning, as when a new growth branches off the main stem of a plant, or the source of growth.[25] This was extended to signify the founder – of a family, a lineage, a descent group, people.[26] It appears that this was the meaning of the word as it was used in the mid-nineteenth century, but by the beginning of the twentieth century it was being used in a wider field of reference. While the sense of originator was retained, it began increasingly to be used to distinguish the founding or native peoples from, by implication, the newcomers, the settlers; to distinguish those who had a right to the land as first people from those from over the sea who laid claim to it. This shift in meanings of *uhlanga* under the impact of settler colonialism in the nineteenth century seems to be comparable to the development of the meaning of the word 'nation' in European languages, from denoting origin or birth to conveying a sense of a wider community of peoples.[27] In Natal in the early 1900s, men associated with the Natal Native Congress founded a newspaper called *Ipepa lo Hlanga*. This can be translated as 'The Paper of the People', but in context it meant much more: the Paper for the people from Here – Africans. As someone said before the Native Affairs Commission: Ethiopians 'spoke of themselves as representing the "uhlanga" (Aboriginals)'[28] – again making the distinction between natives and newcomers.

Official disapproval closed *Ipepa lo Hlanga* but it was replaced by *Ilanga lase Natal*, 'The Sun of Natal', founded in 1903 by one of the great names in South African history, John Dube. Dube's father had been a minister with the American Board Mission and his son had travelled to America and returned with a vision of African progress through education and self-help. As editor of *Ilanga* he had been hauled before the Governor in 1906 and told to moderate his opinions. His sympathies were with the rebels, but he disapproved of tactics that could only lead to the shedding of African blood, further alienation of the races, and with it fewer opportunities for African advancement. His vision for the future could be seen in his renowned school and industrial training centre. It was called *Ohlange* – perhaps evoking the place where it begins – an initiative resonating sonorously with other beginnings in an African past.

Meseni and Ndlovu: Changing while staying the same
The intention of those who prosecuted the violence against those they saw as rebels, was to terminate amongst the colonised unacceptable manifestations of independent thought and action: the questioning of authority; the pretensions of chiefs who still maintained they shared power in Natal; the demands by educated Africans for recognition of their achievements and for incorporation into existing political structures; the demands of

believers who combined an African spiritual awareness with their Christian practice. All such pretensions to autonomy, to independence, all protests, were put down with extraordinary violence. But they were not extinguished. Instead, like the rebels who melted away, they disappeared only to reappear in different but recognisable patterns. All the social features and developments mentioned in the previous section remained factors in subsequent histories: religious belief with differing emphases on its Christian and African features; the links, structured by the lineage, between the living and the ancestors; the dominant role of the *inkosi* in this. In the case of the Zulu royal house the hostility of the authorities only had the effect of increasing its prestige in African eyes. In the end it had to be incorporated into the colonial power structures – reviving in a new context Theophilus Shepstone's system but no longer as a political accommodation of African patriarchs. Rather it was an assertion of white racial political dominance through African administrative structures – and called segregation. Religion, kinship and Zulu cultural identity continued to play their parts in the struggle now for human rights, and carried out by men, women, citizens and workers, within the ever-growing, expanding, kaleidoscopic variants of Zulu, South African and African nationalism.

Much of this, of course, not all, can be seen in the lives of the two men whose activities in 1906 and 1907 are recounted in this book. On their repatriation from St Helena in 1910, Meseni and Ndlovu were not allowed to return to their homes in the Maphumulo division. After the rebellion a concerted effort had been made in Natal to terminate once and for all the essential features of the pre-colonial African system of government. Instead of the prime social bond between the *inkosi* and his followers being defined by a pledge of personal allegiance – *ukukhonza* – it would now be defined by territorial occupation: a 'ward' system by which a chief's authority was restricted to those domiciled in his bounded territory.[29]

After the exile in 1907 of the chiefs convicted of rebellion, a ward had been created out of their territories in the Maphumulo division. This new Ngubane chiefdom was placed under Sibindi, the Bomvu chief who had committed himself so vigorously to the colonial side in the rebellion that 'for his services he was appointed an hereditary chief'.[30] But Sibindi and his successor were unable to extinguish the loyalties of the people over whom they had been appointed. Meseni was not given permission to return to Maphumulo while he was alive, but his people insisted that he be buried there and the funeral was a demonstration of Qwabe loyalty to their hereditary chief.

Despite his exile, Meseni had been able to retain and even extend his influence over his followers. While on St Helena a prophet had appeared to him in a vision – none other, his widows said, than the most famous Zionist prophet, Isaiah Shembe of the Nazerite church. In a ritual at his grave, Meseni became a member of Shembe's church.[31] The continual influence of older beliefs was also apparent. In 1920 an *inyanga* was hanged for murdering a young man and using his body parts for medicine which was meant to return the Qwabe chieftainship to Meseni's descendants.[32]

After his repatriation from St Helena, Ndlovu used his considerable political acumen to put pressure on the authorities to secure his re-appointment as chief. It took time, but in 1918 the Chief Commissioner asked the Secretary for Native Affairs to allow the chief's return to the Timati valley:

> on the distinct understanding that he returns as a Commoner, and that any interference by him in tribal control will lead to his being again removed from the division. His conduct in 1906 was such that he should under no circumstances be reinstated as Chief.[33]

But the Chief Commissioner's instruction was overcome. In 1921 Ndlovu kaThimuni – labour recruiter's policeman on the diamond mines in the 1880s; actively involved in history and politics after he succeeded his father as *inkosi*; critic of the colonial administration; 'Benetu', the bayonet of Izinsimba and saviour of non-combatants at Otimati in the 1906 rebellion; reprieved from the firing squad and returned from exile in 1910 – was reinstated as chief of his people, the Nodunga of the Zulu. And he continued to protest. Soon the Maphumulo magistrate was expressing concern about the chief's unauthorised travels away from his territory, his active involvement in Zulu politics, and his personal attendance on Solomon, the son of Dinuzulu of the Zulu royal house. In 1927 Ndlovu consulted a Durban lawyer to see if he could take legal action against this magistrate.

Ndlovu kaThimuni died on 20 November 1928 at Ezintan-daneni, the homestead from which he had been driven by the Natal militia 22 years before.

Back home. Ndlovu kaThimuni with the Otimati mission in the background, and gun bearer. (From the photographic collection of the Norwegian Missionary Society)

Notes

1. I am drawing here on Stephen Sedley's review of John Langbein, *The Origins of Adversary Criminal Trial* in the *London Review of Books*, 25, 18, 2003.
2. PAR: SNA I/4/113, F. Oglesby to S.O. Samuelson, 22 October 1907, confidential.
3. Stuart, *Zulu Rebellion*, 347, n., in which he refers to *Decisions of the Native High Court from March 1907, to December 1907.*
4. In E.J. Krige, *The Social System of the Zulus*, Pietermaritzburg: Shuter & Shooter, 1957, 272, n.3. See also Samuelson, *Zululand*, 139–140.
5. BPP: C.1441, *Langalibalele and the Amahlubi Tribe . . . By the Bishop of Natal*, London, 1875, 47–52.
6. H. Callaway, *The Religious System of the AmaZulu*, Cape Town: Struik, reprint 1971, *Intelezi for Soldiers*, 437ff.
7. PAR: RSC 1/1/95, Rex *v.* Sifo and Mabalengwe, Mgibini, cross-examination by Yonge, 28 May 1907.
8. A.T. Bryant, *Zulu Medicine and Medicine-Men*, Cape Town: C. Struik, 1970, 9.
9. After this section was written I discovered that in 1909 the police arrested an old, lame, deaf *inyanga* called Jakalazi or Sibogo (Sibhoko). Many of the same crown witnesses, including Zwezinye, were re-assembled and he was brought to trial in 1910 for the murder of Veal, found guilty, and hanged. I have taken cognisance of the trial, and used information from it, but the revival years later of the case produced evidence that by now was so dated and formulaic that no easy conclusions can be drawn from it.
10. PAR: AGO I/1/316, Shuter to Attorney-General, 10 April 1907, Summary of Evidence.
11. PAR: RSC 1/1/95, Rex *v.* Sifo and Mabalengwe, Mjezi, cross-examination by Bigby, 30 May 1907.
12. Harriet Ngubane, 'The predicament of the sinister healer: some observations on "ritual murder" and the professional role of the inyanga', In *The Professionalisation of African Medicine* (eds. Murray Last and G.L. Chavanduka), Manchester: Manchester University Press, 1986, 197.
13. 'Q: Would you look upon it as an act of barbarism, or a thing done for a war purpose?
A: Most decidedly done for a war purpose, and done entirely in accordance with custom, I should say. I do not believe it was done in a vindictive spirit.' PAR: RSC I/1/96, Rex *v.* Macabacaba and others, Evidence of James Stuart, 13 May 1907.
14. For example in PAR: AGO I/1/318, Evidence of Mapakete and Nkabi, 26 April 1907.
15. DAR: 1/SGR, Martial law note book, 1/4/2/2, 56/06, Evidence of Mahagau, 2 or 3 August 1906.
16. DAR: 1/SGR, Martial law note book, 1/4/2/1, 44/06, Evidence of Mahagau, 30 July 1906.

17. PAR: RSC I/1/96, Rex v. Macabacaba and others, Madevu, cross-examined by Foss, 14 May 1907.

18. Bryant, *The Zulu People*, 685–686.

19. PAR: AGO I/1/317, Deposition by Madoju [Madevu], 23 February 1907 and Zwezinye whose account of the same ceremony was made on 26 January also before Shuter at Stanger.

20. *The Mosquito*, 2 ,3, 26 July 1906.

21. DAR: 1/STG, Martial law notebook, 1/4/2/2, 65/06, Rex v. Meseni's people, Evidence of Mqibelo, 10 August 1906, and Evidence of Mahlemuka, 11 August 1906.

22. See Guy, *The Destruction of the Zulu Kingdom*.

23. DAR: 1/SGR, Martial law notebook, 1/4/2/1, 51/06, Evidence of John Boziana, 31 July 1906.

24. BPP: C.2905, No. 26, McCallum to Elgin, 16 February 1906.

25. See the examples in Callaway, *Religious System of the AmaZulu*, 2, 7, 9, 14, 16, 22, 31–33, 42–45, 82 especially. I am aware of the important discussion on the word as it appears in Xhosa history but cannot enter into the debate here. In fact I can do no more than hint at what seems to me the considerable significance of the word, its shifts of meanings, and the contexts in which this took place, for the history of African nationalism in South Africa.

26. Colenso, *Zulu-English Dictionary*, 'original source of a people, *inkosi yohlanga*, originator of a nation'. The use by the Colensos of the word 'nation' here is interesting but, obviously, problematic.

27. E.J. Hobsbawm, *Nations and Nationalism since 1780: Programme, Myth, Reality*, Cambridge: Cambridge University Press, 1990, 14ff.

28. *Native Affairs Commission, 1906–7*, Evidence of Charlie Sindane, 776.

29. See the extensive documentation in PAR: SNA 1/1/374, 2229/07. *De jure* this principle provided the legal foundation for policy – I suspect *de facto* its application has always been limited but this needs to be researched.

30. PAR: Maphumulo, Correspondence, 3/1/1/3, Magistrate Maphumulo to Chief Native Commissioner, undated. A revealingly contradictory phrase of course.

31. Bengt Sundkler, *Bantu Prophets in South Africa*, London: Oxford University Press, 1961, 313.

32. PAR: CNC 3392–3495, correspondence 380B.

33. PAR: Maphumulo, correspondence, 3/1/1/3, Chief Native Commissioner to Magistrate Maphumulo.

Epilogue

The eNkanini ritual, Rex v. Ntshingumuzi, Mphobeyana and Mbombo, Native High Court, December 1907

I began this book by describing the ritual that was held towards the end of 1905 at eNkanini in the Lower Thukela division. It was attended by Qwabe who were to mobilise and die in the Izinsimba gorge in July 1906, and was organised by Ntshingumuzi kaMkwetu, their acting-chief, and Mbombo kaSibindi Nxumalo, the *inyanga* from Osuthu. I want to end with an account of the ritual's aftermath, for it reflects revealingly on the story of the 1906 rebellion in the Maphumulo and Lower Thukela divisions.

Ntshingumuzi, it will be remembered, had employed Mbombo (the man in the photograph on page 2) to find a remedy for the illness afflicting his branch of the Qwabe lineage. Mbombo discovered that the *inkatha*, the sacred grass coil that embodied the spiritual strength of the *amakhosi*, had been destroyed, and he conducted a ceremony late in 1905 during which two new *izinkatha* were made. During the investigations after the rebellion, references to this ritual persuaded magistrate Shuter that 'there is a strong connection with Ntshingumuzi's act of doctoring the tribe and the rebellion',[1] and on further enquiry that 'the case against Ntshingumuzi is so serious as to warrant the breakup of his tribe' and 'all responsible Headmen, and Indunas of the tribe took part in the doctoring, and their aim was solely to provoke war against the Government'.[2]

The case against Ntshingumuzi then got lost in the myriad of issues the magistrate had to deal with in the aftermath of the rebellion, and it was only revived in mid-1907 when the investigators, pursuing war-doctors for the Maphumulo murder cases, came across the trail of an *inyanga* who had been at work in the Lower Thukela division before the rebellion and who had supervised the ritual at eNkanini. Investigations showed that his name was Mbombo. His home was in the Usuthu division and his chief was therefore Dinuzulu kaCetshwayo. In June 1907 Mbombo was brought to Stanger for investigation and detained.

Shuter, now humiliated by the substantial failure of the cases before the Supreme Court and by the criticisms of what he called, with lightly-veiled irony, 'wiser, and more capable minds'[3] felt that this was a case that might restore his reputation. The Attorney-General was immediately interested. Shuter was ordered to commit Mbombo for High Treason and Sedition and to 'enquire most closely into the connections of the accused with the Usutu and his antecedents'.[4]

The formal process of collecting evidence was extended to include the Qwabe leaders who had employed Mbombo – Ntshingumuzi, the acting chief, and Mphobeyana, half-brother of the late chief. Although the prosecutor was specifically to deny that evidence had been concocted or that there had been opportunity for collusion amongst witnesses, this was simply not the case. The pre-trial records show that there were many opportunities for the officials to select hostile witnesses, some already well-practised in other trials, and to identify members of the Qwabe lineage who were antagonistic to Ntshingumuzi's appointment as acting chief. There are also indications of coaching[5] and, as the time for the trial drew nearer, a discernible shift in emphasis in the various statements made to the officials about the eNkanini ritual. In 1906 the tendency was to testify that Ntshingumuzi and Mphobeyana had used medicine in a ritual to strengthen their people. This view is sustained in the evidence given at Mbombo's preliminary investigation in July 1907, but once Ntshingumuzi and Mphobeyana were included in the indictment, the evidence becomes repetitive. Certain incidents become standard: Mbombo is referred to as Dinuzulu's war-doctor, and the eNkanini ritual as a public declaration of the Qwabe intention to go to war with the whites.[6] The crown case was, I suspect, a selective compilation of incidents that occurred in various ceremonies that took place over an extended period before and during the rebellion.[7] Just as Mabalengwe came to represent the essential war-doctor, so the eNkanini ritual represented war-doctoring.

Detention in the Stanger gaol while preliminary investigations were going on was debilitating. Mbombo became seriously ill but when, in August 1907, he had to respond formally to his committal, he took the opportunity to ask that Harriette Colenso be informed of his detention. In the 1870s Mbombo had lived on church land at Bishopstowe and had become acquainted with Harriette Colenso, known throughout Natal as the friend and supporter of Dinuzulu and someone prepared to act on behalf of Africans. She had not been able to follow the Supreme Court trials in May because her time was taken up with assisting Dinuzulu, who was being harassed at the time by the authorities, and she was told of Mbombo's attempts to contact her only at the end of October. She instructed the attorney R.C.A. Samuelson to visit him, and Mbombo was released on bail of £100 and placed on a train to Pietermaritzburg where he arrived on 8 November. Shuter's project had run into an unexpected obstacle.

Harriette Colenso was shocked at Mbombo's physical condition and had his photograph taken to record the effects of five month's detention in a Natal gaol. He then went to Bishopstowe to be cared for by her sister Agnes Colenso. He had contracted consumption, and Agnes Colenso (and covertly the CID) watching over him anxiously, did what she could to ease the pain and allow him to gain strength for the court case. Their views on his medical condition differed. His diarrhoea worried her, but not Mbombo who, she reported, 'says it is clearing out the poison & that all his izito [lower limbs] are getting *so* comfortable'. The people at Bishopstowe welcomed him with gifts of beer and 'He wants crushed izimkobe [boiled grain] *with* his amas [sour milk] *now*. He says it was nice *alone* at first because his stomach having stuck to his backbone the amas slipped in easily between & ncibililika'd [melted, made comfortable] his heart!'[8] It might have been the effect of the chlorodyne, cough lozenges, and bronchial tablets, or perhaps just tact, that caused Mbombo, the famous *inyanga* from Mahashini, eventually to tell Agnes that 'He *does* believe in Umuti wabelungu now'.[9]

Mbombo Nxumalo, defended by attorney R.C.A. Samuelson, and Ntshingumuzi and Mphobeyana Qwabe, defended by the Stanger advocate A.E. Foss, appeared before the Native High Court from 3–13 December 1907. The crown called sixteen witnesses, most of whom were men (eleven) and women (five) who had attended the ceremony at eNkanini and who now asserted that it had been celebrated by Mbombo and organised by Ntshingumuzi, with the assistance of Mphobeyana, with the object of doctoring the Qwabe for war.

Nearly all the male witnesses had been convicted of High Treason in the Stanger martial law court eighteen months previously. Some of them had already been released in recognition of the evidence they had given for the crown in other cases, others hoped for this.[10] There was also an attempt from within the Qwabe lineage to discredit Ntshingumuzi and thereby remove him from his official position. The crown was certainly able to marshal antagonistic witnesses from the ruling lineage: four widows and two sons of Mamfongonyana, as well as a widow of Zidumo, gave evidence against Ntshingumuzi. For one of the witnesses, Friend Addison, who had also been a commandant of the Stanger militia during the rebellion, this was easy to explain:

the Zulu are adepts in bringing charges against men of note, when they are found guilty of the crime of treason, and it is a noted fact, that under their own Kings, they frequently gave false evidence to implicate a noted man, or King's Favorite.[11]

There were also indications that convicted crown witnesses believed they had been betrayed by their leaders. Many gaoled rebels felt that chiefs who in 1906 had not been unsympathetic to their arming, now distanced themselves from those suffering directly as a result of their actions. Moreover, it was part of a chief's duty to do what he could to protect his subjects: 'Ntshingumuzi ought to have said something in his favour, and he felt hurt that he did not do so.'[12]

The defence called sixteen witnesses. Soon the judges became impatient with the accounts of sprinkling and purging, and let this be known in their asides from the bench. The journalists in court tired as well and failed to record in detail what would now be important historical and anthropological evidence. Mbombo's attorney, R.C.A. Samuelson, although well-meaning and with an incomparable knowledge of colloquial Zulu, was also plodding and naïve, but his case was a good one, and he and his Qwabe witnesses had worked hard on it. They related how Mbombo had been employed as a doctor for individual patients at eNkanini, before being approached by Ntshingumuzi to treat the sickness in the chiefly line. Elderly men described the ceremonies in which they, as active soldiers in the Zulu kingdom, had been doctored for war, making clear the considerable differences between those rituals and the one that had been held at eNkanini. One woman under cross-examination by the crown insisted that Mbombo was a 'medicine doctor' not a 'war-doctor' and, on being pressed by the prosecutor, replied 'If they were only war doctors they would be out of work most of the time'.[13] Senior women and men testified to their participation in a ritual undertaken to strengthen the tribe and its chiefs against sickness, exhibiting at times a refreshing func-tionalism: 'The reason why brooms were used for sprinkling for fevers is that the dirt can be taken from the floors of a house and that way the broom is used to sweep away fevers.'[14]

The three accused all gave evidence. Ntshingumuzi's dealt with the political history of the Qwabe, but the journalist in court found it so tedious that he did not take it down. Mphobeyana spoke of the significance of the *inkatha* which was 'a sign of the tribe, and if any of the tribe went away it brought them back to the fold'.[15] Mbombo spoke in his own defence on 12 December. He was ill and weakened by his detention, and complained that his medicines and his possessions had been taken away from him, including his handkerchief 'which he wishes to get back, as he could not wipe the perspiration from his head'. But he spoke with clarity and courage. He admitted that he had a considerable reputation as a doctor and that, having been a soldier himself in the Zulu army, he knew very well the difference between the ritual he had organised and a ritual for war.

> He did not know how to doctor for war. They could hang him if he was telling a lie saying so . . . He doctored at the Nkanini at the request of Ntshingumuzi, who said he wanted witness 'to turn out this blackness' . . . in order to benefit the family of the late chief . . . The witnesses for the Crown had been giving evidence for the Government because they wanted to ingratiate themselves after stabbing the Government in the back.[16]

The defence based its case on the argument that after Mbombo had discovered that the late inkosi's *inkatha* had been destroyed, leaving his successors vulnerable, the *inyanga* had organised a ritual which would introduce two new and powerful *izinkatha* into the spiritual life of the tribe. To substantiate this, arrangements had been made to produce the *izinkatha* before the court. For some of those present this was a fearful experience, for they were articles that were 'reverenced very much' and 'not to be played with'. The box was opened and the two circles of bound grass were produced.

What were sacred articles for some were objects of derision for others. The newspaper reported the event under the headlines ' "Crown" Jewels/Amusing Evidence/Native Customs' and suggested that there had been some confusion in the court.

> At this stage the new regalia, called 'Nkata' was produced.
>
> It compromised two rings of plaited rope, being a very poor representation of Crown jewels.
>
> By the Judge President: Mr Foss, we ought to have arranged for some regal ceremony in the production of these 'jewels.'
>
> Mr. Samuelson: Ginger beer would satisfy the occasion.
>
> Mr. Foss: I suggest that the prisoners should be discharged.
>
> The Judge President: Won't the 'jewels' be contaminated by being brought into a common Court?
>
> Mr. Samuelson: It may seem funny, but the evidence is very important.[17]

As indeed it was. But the court did not think so. Mbombo, Ntshingumuzi and Mphobeyana were found guilty on the third count of sedition, doctoring for war in preparation to resist the authority of the king.

Once again, however, it was not the great victory that the Natal authorities had hoped for. Although he kept silent, the Judge President disagreed with his two colleagues and did not think the crown had proved that the accused had been doctoring for war. The prosecution was unable to demonstrate convincingly that the ill, frail men in the dock were a nefarious war-doctor and his clients who had incited rebellion amongst their people. And the links between their war-doctoring and Dinuzulu, for which the Attorney-General had hoped so much, were never established. In fact the political aspects of the trial were eclipsed from the day it opened because on 3 December the Natal government declared martial law in the Province of Zululand in preparation for the arrest of Dinuzulu a week later. The three old men were sentenced to a fine of £100 or eighteen months hard labour, and released on £100 bail, pending an appeal to the Privy Council.

In the event the appeal was not pursued and, unable to pay their fines, Ntshingumuzi and Mphobeyana served their sentences. They were released in December 1909 and made their way to the Governor for an interview. He refused to see them and sent them on to the office of the under-Secretary for Native Affairs who told them 'to return to their homes, but that they must pay respect and give allegiance to the Chief appointed over them, and if they give any further trouble they will be removed from the division'.[18] Mbombo Nxumalo, the *inyanga* who had made the new *izinkatha* for Ntshingumuzi and Mphobeyana, was saved such humiliation. He had died a fortnight after the trial had ended. In the opinion of his attorney this was 'an instance of murder at the door of the Government'.[19]

After the court trial and the sentencing of the three men, the Qwabe *izinkatha* were left behind at the Native High Court. The Registrar Walter Acutt, however, didn't dismiss them as easily as the judges had. He packed up the exhibits, went up the hill to Loop Street and deposited them in the Natal Museum – where the *izinkatha* of Mamfongonyana's section of the great Qwabe clan, made by Mbombo kaSibindi Nxumalo, the famous *inyanga* from Osuthu, to lift the darkness – the *mnyama* – and *ukumisa* – to make the lineage firm and give it strength and power over the forces ranged against it, can be found today.

Notes

1. PAR: SNA I/1/351, 3222/06 Shuter to Commandant of Militia, 22 September 1906.
2. PAR: SNA I/1/351, 3222/06, Shuter to u-SNA 12 October 1906.
3. PAR: AGO I/9/33, Shuter to Attorney-General, 9 July 1907.
4. PAR: AGO I/1/114, Labistour to Shuter, 29 July 1907.
5. Not in this case, the 'jackal skin hat and baboon skin cape', but in the dialogue 'Do you want war? Yes we want war. We will not run away' repeated by crown witnesses.
6. These shifts can be traced in the 1906 statements in PAR: SNA I/1/351, 3222/06 and the 1907 statements in AGO I/1/114 and in differences in statements taken before the completion of Mbombo's preliminary investigation on 22 July 1907 and those subsequent to it.
7. This is perhaps the reason why it is so difficult to establish the date of the ritual at eNkanini. The crown had at one time gathered evidence to fix it at the beginning of the rebellion – 9 February 1906 – but in the formal indictment refused to be more precise than February to July of that year. Harriette Colenso believed that it had taken place in the winter, and Samuelson in the spring, of 1905. Following Samuelson and references to the development of growing crops at the time my guess is October 1905.
8. PAR: Colenso collection, Box 44, Agnes Colenso to H.E. Colenso, 18 November 1907.
9. PAR: Colenso collection, Box 44, Agnes Colenso to H.E. Colenso, 24 November 1907.
10. Belebana, who had given evidence as a crown witness in a number of cases before being released in July 1907, and Mapakhete, admitted that he had been released because he agreed to give evidence against Ntshingumuzi. In a previous case Mapakhete had been accused by a (white) defence witness of using his position as crown witness to settle a personal dispute.
11. PAR: CSO 2599, Friend Addison to Commandant, Natal Militia, 5 December 1906, 4.
12. *The Natal Witness*, 6 December 1907, Evidence of 'Uidubele' (?Zidebele).
13. *The Natal Witness*, 12 December 1907, Evidence of Nozimbaga, a patient of Mbombo.
14. *The Natal Witness*, 10 December 1907, Evidence of a doctor.
15. *The Natal Witness*, 13 December 1907.
16. *The Natal Witness*, 12 December 1907.
17. *The Natal Witness*, 10 December 1907.
18. PAR: SNA 1/1/351, 3222/06, Note, 9 December 1909.
19. PAR: Colenso Collection, Box 44, R.C.A. Samuelson to H.E. Colenso, 29 December 1907.

Select bibliography

I have used primary source material housed in the Pietermaritzburg and Durban Archives Repositories of the KwaZulu-Natal Archives, the Campbell Collections of the University of KwaZulu-Natal, Rhodes House, Oxford, the Public Record Office, Kew, the Natal Society Library, Pietermaritzburg and the Don Africana Library, Durban. Specific citations can be found in the notes on the text. A detailed narrative of the official interpretation of events can be found in the British Parliamentary Papers (BPP). The selection made by the Colonial Office from the correspondence was very comprehensive – a fact that makes the material that was omitted particularly significant. The most usual reason for excluding a document, or portions of a document, was to keep from the parliament and public the provocatively violent comments of Natal's military. I have made use of:

C.2905, Natal. *Correspondence relating to native disturbances in Natal*. May 1906.

C.3027, Natal. *Further correspondence relating to native disturbances in Natal*. July 1906.

C.3247, Natal. *Further correspondence relating to native disturbances in Natal*. December 1906.

C.3563. Natal. *Removal of certain native prisoners from Natal*. December 1907.

C.3888. Natal. *Further correspondence relating to native affairs in Natal*. January 1908.

C.1441, *Langalibalele and the Amahlubi Tribe . . . By the Bishop of Natal*. London 1875.

With five volumes now published, the *James Stuart Archive* has become an indispensable source. James Stuart was also the author of the most important and detailed contemporary account, but A *History of The Zulu Rebellion of 1906* was sponsored by, and reflects the attitudes of, the men who put down the rebellion. The book has nonetheless retained a certain authority, particularly insofar as military matters are concerned. It is time that authority was challenged.

In 1970 Shula Marks published her doctoral thesis as *Reluctant Rebellion: The 1906–8 Disturbances in Natal*, Oxford: Clarendon Press, 1970, and she later revisited the topic in 'Class, ideology and the Bambata rebellion', in *Banditry, Rebellion and Social Protest in Africa* edited by Donald Crumney, London: James Currey, 1986. Although now only a part of an increasing literature on the rebellion or aspects of it (amongst them John Lambert, *Betrayed Trust*, Pietermaritzburg: University of Natal Press, 1995; Paul la Hausse, *Restless Identities*, Pietermaritzburg: University of Natal Press, 2000; and Benedict Carton, *Blood from Your Children*, Pietermaritzburg: University of Natal Press, 2000), Marks's re-creation and analysis of these events laid down the foundations for all subsequent historical work on the topic. This present book could not have been written without it. Confident that the factual, historiographical and analytical parameters are sound I have been able, nearly forty years later in a very different historical context, to go into the minutiae of events and to dig deeper into the local records. This book reflects this process of increasingly specialised research.

Books and articles

Angus, G.I., *The Kaffirs Illustrated . . .* London, 1849.

Binns C.T., *Dinuzulu: The Death of the House of Shaka*, Longman: London, 1968.

Bryant, A.T., *A Zulu-English Dictionary*, Pinetown: Mariannhill Mission Press, 1905.

——. *The Zulu People*, Pietermaritzburg: Shuter & Shooter, 1967.

——. *Zulu Medicine and Medicine-Men*, Cape Town: C. Struik, 1970.

Bosman, W., *The Natal Rebellion of 1906*, London, 1907.

Callaway, H., *The Religious System of the AmaZulu*, Cape Town: Struik, reprint 1971.

Carton, B., *Blood from Your Children*, Pietermaritzburg: University of Natal Press, 2000.

Colenso, J.W., *Zulu-English Dictionary*, fourth edition, 1905, edited by H.E. Colenso.

Doke, C.M. and B.W. Vilakazi, *Zulu-English Dictionary*, Johannesburg, University of the Witwatersrand Press, 1972.

Girvin, S.D., 'An evaluation of the Judge Presidency of John Dove Wilson of Natal (1910–1930)', M. Laws, University of Natal, 1987.

Guy, J., *The Destruction of the Zulu Kingdom: The Civil War in Zululand, 1879–1884*, London: Longman, 1979.

——. 'The destruction and reconstruction of Zulu society', in *Industrialisation and Social Change in South Africa* (eds. Shula Marks and Richard Rathbone), London: Longman, 1982.

——. 'Gender oppression in southern Africa's precapitalist societies', in *Women and Gender in Southern Africa to 1945* (ed. Cheryl Walker), Cape Town: David Philip, 1990.

——. 'Non-combatants and war: the unexplored factor in the conquest of the Zulu kingdom', (forthcoming).

Hobsbawm, E.J., *Nations and Nationalism since 1780: Programme, Myth, Reality*, Cambridge: Cambridge University Press, 1990.

Hyam, R., *Elgin and Churchill at the Colonial Office 1905–1908*, London: Macmillan, 1968.

Keith, A.B., *Responsible Government in the Dominions*, second edition rewritten and revised to 1927, two volumes, Oxford: Clarendon Press.

Kipling, R., 'M.I. (Mounted Infantry of the Line)', in *Rudyard Kipling's Verse: Inclusive Edition, 1855–1926*, London: Hodder and Stoughton, 1927.

Krige, E.J., *The Social System of the Zulus*, Pietermaritzburg: Shuter & Shooter, 1957.

La Hausse de Lalouvière, P., *Restless Identities*, Pietermaritzburg: University of Natal Press, 2000.

Lambert, J., *Betrayed Trust*, Pietermaritzburg: University of Natal Press, 1995.

Lugg, H.C., *Historic Natal and Zululand*, Pietermaritzburg: Shuter & Shooter, 1949.

Marks, S., *Reluctant Rebellion: The 1906–8 Disturbances in Natal*. Oxford: Clarendon Press, 1970.

——. 'Class, ideology and the Bambata rebellion', in *Banditry, Rebellion and Social Protest in Africa* (ed. Donald Crumney), London: James Currey, 1986.

Mahoney, M., 'Between the Zulu king and the great white chief: political culture in a Natal chiefdom, 1879–1906', PhD, UCLA, 1998.

Marx, Karl, *Karl Marx: Pre-Capitalist Economic Formations* (translated by Jack Cohen and edited by E.J. Hobsbawm), New York: International Publishers, 1965.

The Mosquito.

The Natal Mercury.

The Natal Mercury Pictorial.

The Natal Who's Who 1906.

The Natal Witness.

The Native Affairs Commission 1906-7, Evidence, Pietermaritzburg: P. Davis & Sons, 1907.

Ngubane, H., 'The predicament of the sinister healer: some observations on the "ritual murder" and the professional role of the inyanga'. In *The Professionalisation of African Medicine* (eds. Murray Last and C.L. Chavanduka), Manchester: Manchester University Press, 1986.

Nyembezi, C.L. Sibusiso, *Zulu Proverbs*, Johannesburg: Witwatersrand University Press, 1963.

Powell, W.J., *The Zulu Rebellion of 1906: A Souvenir of the Transvaal Mounted Rifles*, Johannesburg, 1906.

The Reader's Digest Illustrated History of South Africa, third edition, 1995.

Samuelson L.H., *Zululand: Its Traditions, Legends, Customs and Folk-lore*, Natal: Mariannhill Mission Press, n.d.

Samuelson, R.C.A., *Long, Long Ago*, Durban: Knox, 1929.

Sedley, S., review of John Langbein, *The Origins of Adversary Criminal Trial* in the *London Review of Books*, 25, 18, 2003.

Stuart, J., *A History of the Zulu Rebellion 1906 and of Dinizulu's Arrest, Trial and Expatriation*, London: Macmillan, 1913.

——. *The James Stuart Archive of Recorded Oral Evidence Relating to the History of the Zulu and Neighbouring Peoples*, edited and translated by C. de B. Webb and J.B. Wright, Pietermaritzburg and Durban: University of Natal and Killie Campbell Africana Library, Vols 3, 4, 5, 1982, 1986 and 2001.

Sundkler, B., *Bantu Prophets in South Africa*, London: Oxford University Press, 1961.

Thompson, E.P., *Whigs and Hunters: The Origin of the Black Act*, New York: Pantheon, 1975.

Thompson, P.S., *An Historical Atlas of the Zulu Rebellion of 1906*, Pietermaritzburg, 2001.

Van Onselen, C., *New Nineveh*, Johannesburg: Ravan Press, 1982.

Index